U.S.
COMMERCIAL
AIRCRAFT

Kenneth Munson

JANE'S

Copyright © Kenneth Munson 1982

First published in the United Kingdom in 1982 by
Jane's Publishing Company Limited
238 City Road
London EC1V 2PU

ISBN 0 7106 0120 4

Designed by Keith Anderson

Printed in the United Kingdom by
Biddles Limited, Guildford, Surrey

Introduction

The date December 17 stands out at least three times, for quite separate but equally valid reasons, not only in the aviation history of the United States but in that of the world as a whole. In 1903 that day saw the first successful true flight ever made by a heavier-than-air flying machine. Exactly ten years later was signed the contract between Thomas Benoist and Paul Fansler for the world's first regular service by passenger-carrying aeroplane, inaugurated 15 days later between the Florida townships of St Petersburg and Tampa. In 1935 it was the occasion of the first flight of the Douglas DC-3, indisputably the most famous, widespread and long-lived transport aeroplane ever built. It does not matter that the Wright Flyer's first aerial journey lasted only twelve seconds and covered a distance not much longer than that of a football pitch; that operations by the Airboat Line lasted only a few months; or that most of the ten thousand-odd DC-3s were built for military rather than commercial reasons. What does matter is that each event, in its own way, marked the beginning of an era in aviation progress.

The course of commercial aircraft development and operation in the United States followed a somewhat different path from that in Europe, for a variety of reasons. The warring nations of Europe were left after 1918 with huge quantities of surplus aircraft, and commercial or other civilian operation was the obvious way to make use of the machines that were suitable. The USA, which had not mass-produced aircraft on anywhere near the same scale, therefore did not have the same incentive to explore the potential of the aeroplane for carrying passengers and cargo instead of bombs and guns. And, as a single nation of continental dimensions with well-established intrastate and interstate road and rail networks, it saw no immediate need, as Europe did, for the aeroplane as a means of internal or international communication.

The spur for the development of air transport in the USA therefore came in the one area where it was obvious that the aeroplane could score over the road and rail systems: by speeding up delivery of the mails. This had actually begun while the European war was still going on, starting with an experimental service between Washington DC and New York City which was inaugurated on May 15, 1918, and flown by US Army Curtiss JN-4s. Three months later, on August 12, the US Post Office Department began operating this route as the first regular airmail service, at first using Standard biplanes and subsequently DH-4Ms and other types as the routes were gradually extended westward.

On March 3, 1919, Hubbard Air Service flew the first US international airmail – from Seattle to Victoria, British Columbia – using a Boeing Type C floatplane. Coast-to-coast airmail in the USA began with an experimental flight on February 22, 1921 (between San Francisco and Mineola, Long Island), and became a regular Post Office night mail operation on July 1, 1924. However, in February 1925 the so-called "Kelly Act" gave Congressional approval for airmail operations to be transferred to private enterprise, and the last flight under the aegis of the Post Office was made on September 1, 1927.

The list of the first dozen contract mail carriers, a roll-call of the founder members of the US airline industry, includes such famous names as Ford, Stout, Varney, Western Air Express (today, as Western Air Lines, the oldest surviving US commercial operator, having begun scheduled services on April 17, 1926), Northwest, and Pacific Air Transport. All were given local routes, feeding into a transcontinental route that was divided into two segments: from Chicago westward to San Francisco, awarded to Boeing Air Transport in January 1927, and eastward to New York, for which National Air Transport won the contract two months later.

In parallel with these developments, the requirements of route patterns were now beginning to prompt and influence the appearance of genuine purpose-designed transport aircraft such as the Boeing 40, Ford Tri-Motor and Fokker Universal, a trend that was given added impetus by the young Charles Lindbergh's epic trans-Atlantic solo flight from New York to Paris in May 1927. Just as Blériot's flight across the English Channel 18 years earlier had awakened Europe to the aeroplane's military possibilities, so Lindbergh's flight made people all over the world aware of its equal potential for more peaceful purposes.

By the end of 1930 no fewer than 43 registered airlines existed in the USA, by no means all of which had the financial benefit of an airmail subsidy. By then, too, the process of streamlining and merging had given birth to three of the "Big Five" in American airline history: Eastern (July 1929), American (January 1930) and TWA (July 1930); United was to follow in July 1931. The fifth, a new-born giant incorporated on March 14, 1927, came into being originally to compete for the modest route between Key West, Florida, and Havana, Cuba, which it began to serve on October 19 of the same year with a borrowed Fairchild floatplane. Impressive financial resources, the dynamic leadership of Juan T. Trippe, and a government decision to provide blanket air transport coverage of Latin America in the form of a subsidised monopoly, led to the selection of Pan American Airways in 1928 as the chosen instrument of this national policy. As R. E. G. Davies has recorded in his indispensable *A History of the World's Airlines*: "PAA's influence was incalculable. . . . In its own sphere of operations, it performed an imperialist duty of much the same kind as Imperial Airways, KLM, Air France and Deutsche Luft Hansa did for their countries. With massive government support, PAA went from strength to strength and was eventually to demonstrate that it had the power to dictate airline matters not only in Latin America but in any part of the world where it was authorised to operate."

The rapid growth of Pan Am gave further impetus to commercial transport aircraft development in the USA. This was a process in which Lindbergh again played a part, for he was engaged at an early stage as the airline's technical adviser. Long overwater routes to the Caribbean, Central and South America led Pan Am to base its immediate and future operations, from then until the Second World War, on a succession of flying boats and amphibians: the Sikorsky S-38, S-40, S-42 and S-43, Martin M-130 and Boeing 314. All of these were designed specifically to meet Pan American route requirements. (In later years Pan Am can claim to have sponsored directly, or been otherwise largely responsible for, the development of such other major airliners as the Stratoliner, Stratocruiser, DC-6B, 707 and 747.)

Forming an unhappy background to this early reshaping of the US airline industry were the Depression years of the early 1930s. But even though these were lean years for those in the business of building and selling aeroplanes, America's aircraft designers were not idle. The US passenger air transport industry may have got off to a slow start by comparison with that in Europe, but it reached the modern era of design far more quickly. Metal monoplanes such as the Boeing 247, DC-1/2/3 and Lockheed Electra followed swiftly upon the heels of such innovative creations as the Boeing Monomail, and by the end of the decade European and other world airlines were queueing up alongside those of the USA to buy these fast, comfortable, sophisticated and – in the full sense of the word – *commercial* transport aircraft.

It can fairly be said that US transport aircraft manufacturers have never looked back since. Entry into the Second World War brought a tacit understanding that the air transport needs of the Allies would be met largely by the American industry, leaving those of the smaller nations free to concentrate primarily on the production of combat types. In turn, this created a huge surplus of ready-made transports in the post-war rundown, and these were snapped up eagerly by airlines the world over, old and new, to form the basis of their fleets in the early years of peace.

It thus came as something of a surprise to find the USA coming third, after Britain and the Soviet Union, in the race to put a jet airliner into regular commercial operation. (Not that being a late starter did Boeing much harm: it delivered its 4,000th jetliner in July 1981, a record unlikely ever to be approached by any other manufacturer.) Curiously, too, America failed to make the grade with a large turboprop airliner. Given the worldwide success of the British Viscount, including its popularity in service with a major US operator (Capital), Lockheed must have felt that its L-188 Electra had every chance of doing very well. But somehow the large market just was not there, though the continuing success of the Electra's naval counterpart, the P-3 Orion, is clear enough evidence that the aeroplane itself was not to blame.

However, there can be no doubt whatever that America regained its pre-eminent position in the commercial transport aircraft world with its dramatic jump into the era of the wide-bodied "Jumbo" jet. In the Boeing 747, Lockheed TriStar and McDonnell Douglas DC-10 the US has produced a unique trio that have brought a whole new dimension to mass air travel. That it failed to enter the supersonic airliner stakes in 1971 was due to a narrow decision by politicians, not airline operators. SST technology in the USA is however still very much alive, should future circumstances ever again make it a viable proposition. Meanwhile, the current trend in design is dictated by considerations of environmental acceptability and the evolution of either alternative fuel systems or powerplants that can make the most efficient use of the world's remaining stocks of petroleum fuels. Fittingly, therefore, this book ends with two new US commercial aircraft designed specifically with this last requirement in mind.

Historical A–Z of US airlines

This is a large and complex subject, and the following list makes no claim to be exhaustive. Its main purpose is to help fill in the background to the aircraft described in the following pages.

Aeromarine Airways Formed in 1919; joined later that year with West Indies Airways to form Aeromarine West Indies Airways. Ceased operating in May 1924.

Airlift International Name adopted in 1964 by Riddle Airlines. Acquired Slick Airways in July 1968.

Air West Formed in April 1968 by merger of Bonanza Air Lines, Pacific Air Lines and West Coast Airlines. Renamed Hughes Airwest in April 1970; acquired by Republic Airlines in October 1980.

Alaskan Airways Formed in 1930 as subsidiary of Aviation Corpn of Delaware. Sold to Pan American in 1932 and renamed Pacific-Alaska Airways.

All-American Airways Formed (as All-American Aviation) in March 1937; renamed in March 1949. Renamed Allegheny Airlines in 1953.

Allegheny Airlines Name adopted from 1953 by All-American Airways. Acquired Lake Central Airlines in July 1968 and Mohawk Airlines in April 1972. Renamed US Air in October 1979.

Aloha Airlines Formed (as Trans-Pacific Airlines) in June 1946; renamed in February 1959. Still operating in 1982.

American Airlines Formed in 1934 as successor to American Airways. Still operating in 1982.

American Airways Formed in January 1930 by merger of Universal Aviation Corpn, Colonial Airways, Southern Air Transport, Embry-Riddle, and Interstate Airlines. Succeeded by American Airlines in 1934.

American Export Airlines Formed in 1936 as subsidiary of American Export Lines shipping company. Acquired as a subsidiary by American Airlines in 1945 and renamed American Overseas Airlines.

American Overseas Airlines Name adopted from 1945 by American Export Airlines after becoming a subsidiary of American Airlines. Acquired by Pan Am in September 1950.

Boeing Air Transport Formed in 1927; acquired Pacific Air Transport in January 1928. Joined with Pratt & Whitney in December 1928 to form United Aircraft and Transport Corpn. This merged with National Air Transport in July 1931 to form United Air Lines.

Bonanza Air Lines Local service operator formed (originally for charter) in December 1945. Merged with Pacific Air Lines and West Coast Airlines in April 1968 to form Air West.

Boston-Maine Airways Formed in July 1931; acquired (and adopted name of) National Airways in March 1937. Renamed Northeast Airlines in November 1940.

Bowen Air Lines Formed in 1930; acquired by Braniff Airways in 1935.

Braniff Airways Formed (as Braniff Airlines) in 1928; became part of Universal Aviation Corpn in March 1929. Re-formed as Braniff Airways in November 1930. Acquired Pan American-Grace Airways (Panagra) in 1967. Ceased operating in 1982.

California Eastern Airlines Formed as freight operator in May 1946; acquired by Slick Airways in May 1948.

Canadian Colonial Airway Formed in 1928 as subsidiary of Colonial Air Transport; became part of Colonial Airways Corpn in 1929.

Capital Airlines Name adopted from April 1948 by Pennsylvania-Central Airlines; acquired by United Air Lines in June 1961.

Capitol Air Formed (as supplemental carrier) in 1946 as Capitol International Airways; began scheduled services in May 1979 and adopted present name in December 1981.

Central Airline Formed in 1928/29; became part of Universal Aviation Corpn in March 1929.

Central Airlines (1) Formed in 1934; merged with Pennsylvania Airlines in November 1936 to form Pennsylvania-Central Airlines.

Central Airlines (2) Local service operator formed in March 1944; acquired by Frontier Airlines in October 1967.

Challenger Airlines Formed (as Summit Airways) in early 1946; renamed in January 1947. Acquired by Monarch Airlines in December 1949.

Chicago Helicopter Airways Formed (as Helicopter Air Services) in August 1949; renamed in August 1956. Ceased operating in 1978.

Chicago & Southern Air Lines Formed (as Pacific Seaboard Airlines) in 1933; renamed in 1934. Merged with Delta Air Lines in May 1953.

Clifford Ball Formed 1927; acquired by Pennsylvania Airlines in November 1930.

Colonial Airlines Formed (as Colonial Airways Corpn) in 1929 by merger of Colonial Air Transport, Colonial Western Airways and Canadian Colonial Airways; renamed in May 1942. Acquired by Eastern Air Lines in June 1956.

Colonial Air Transport Formed in 1925; became part of Colonial Airways Corporation in 1929.

Colonial Western Airways Formed in 1927; became part of Colonial Airways Corporation in 1929.

Colorado Airways Formed in 1926; acquired by Western Air Express in 1927.

Continental Air Lines (1) Formed in 1928; became part of Universal Aviation Corpn in March 1929.

Continental Air Lines (2) Name adopted from July 1937 by Varney Air Transport. Still operating in 1982.

Delta Air Lines Formed (as Delta Air Service) in 1929; renamed Delta Air Corpn in 1934, and Delta Air Lines later. Merged with Chicago & Southern Air Lines in May 1953, retaining former title. Acquired Northeast Airlines in 1972. Still operating in 1982.

Eastern Air Lines Formed (as Eastern Air Lines division of North American Aviation) in July 1929. Renamed Eastern Air Transport in 1930, and Eastern Air Lines in April 1934. Still operating in 1982.

Embry-Riddle Corporation Formed in 1927; became part of American Airways in January 1930.

Empire Air Lines Formed (as Zimmerly Air Lines) in April 1944; became Empire Air Lines in March 1946. Acquired by West Coast Airlines in August 1952.

Florida Airways (1) Formed in 1926; became part of Pan American Airways in March 1927.

Florida Airways (2) Formed (as Orlando Airlines) in early

1943; ceased operating in March 1949.

Flying Tiger Line   Formed (as National Skyway Freight Corpn) in June 1945; renamed in early 1946. Merged with Seaboard World Airlines in October 1980, retaining former title. Still operating in 1982.

Ford Motor Company   Formed 1925; merged with Stout Air Services in 1928. Became part of United Aircraft and Transport Corpn in 1929.

Frontier Airlines   Name adopted from June 1950 by Monarch Airlines. Acquired Central Airlines in October 1967; still operating in 1982.

General Air Lines   Operating name used briefly in 1934 by Western Air Express following formation of Transcontinental & Western Air.

Gulf Air Lines   Formed in early 1928; merged with Texas Air Transport later that year to form Southern Air Transport.

Hanford Airlines   Formed (as Tri-State Airlines) in 1931; renamed Hanford Tri-State Airlines in 1934, and Mid-Continent Airlines in August 1938.

Hawaiian Airlines   Name adopted from October 1941 by Inter-Island Airways. Still operating in 1982.

Inland Air Lines   Name adopted from April 1938 by Wyoming Air Service. Acquired by Western Air Lines in October 1943.

Inter-Island Airways   Formed in January 1929; renamed Hawaiian Airlines in October 1941.

Interstate Airlines   Formed in 1928; became part of American Airways in January 1930.

Kohler Aviation Corporation   Formed in 1933; acquired by Pennsylvania Airlines in 1934.

Los Angeles Airways   Formed (as helicopter operator) in May 1944. Ceased operating in 1978.

Los Angeles–San Diego Air Line (Ryan Air Lines)   Formed in March 1925; ceased operating in autumn 1926.

Ludington Air Lines   Name adopted from September 1930 by New York, Philadelphia & Washington Airway Corpn. Acquired by Eastern Air Transport in February 1933.

Maddux Air Lines   Formed in early 1928; acquired by Transcontinental Air Transport in late 1929.

Mid-Continent Airlines   Name adopted from August 1938 by Hanford Airlines; acquired by Braniff Airways in August 1952.

Monarch Airlines   Formed in November 1946; acquired Challenger Airlines in December 1949. Merged with Arizona Airways in April 1950 and renamed Frontier Airlines in June 1950.

National Airlines   Formed (as National Airline System) in October 1934; renamed in July 1937. Acquired by Pan American in 1979.

National Air Transport   Formed in early 1926; became part of United Aircraft and Transport Corpn in 1929. Merged with Boeing Air Transport in July 1931 to form United Air Lines.

National Airways   Formed in July 1931; acquired by Boston–Maine Airways in March 1937. Renamed Northeast Airlines in November 1940.

National Parks Airways   Formed in 1928; acquired by Western Air Express in 1937.

New York Airways (1)   Acquired by Aviation Corpn of Delaware in June 1928, and by Eastern Air Transport in July 1931.

New York Airways (2)   Formed (as helicopter operator) in August 1949; ceased operating in May 1979.

New York, Philadelphia & Washington Airway Corporation   Original name, before September 1930, of Ludington Airlines.

New York, Rio & Buenos Aires Line   Formed in October 1929; acquired by Pan American in August 1930. (Concurrently, its subsidiary, NYRBA do Brasil, became Panair do Brasil.)

North Central Airlines   Name adopted from December 1952 by Wisconsin Central Airlines. Merged with Southern Airways in June 1979 to form Republic Airlines.

Northeast Airlines   Name adopted from November 1940 by National Airways. Acquired by Delta Air Lines in 1972.

Northern Airlines   Formed in 1928; became part of Universal Aviation Corpn in March 1929.

Northwest Airlines   Formed (as Northwest Airways) in August 1926; renamed in April 1934. Still operating in 1982, including Far East services under name of Northwest Orient Airlines.

Ohio Transport   Joined with Pittsburgh Airways and United States Airways in August 1930 to form United Avigation Co.

Ozark Air Lines   Local service operator formed in September 1943. Still operating in 1982.

Pacific Air Lines   Name adopted from March 1958 by Southwest Airways. Merged with Bonanza Air Lines and West Coast Airlines in April 1968 to form Air West.

Pacific Air Transport   Formed in 1926; acquired by Boeing Air Transport in January 1928. Became part of United Aircraft and Transport Corpn in December 1928.

Pacific-Alaska Airways   Name adopted from 1932 by Alaskan Airways following acquisition by Pan American.

Pacific Marine Airways   Formed in 1922; acquired by Western Air Express in 1928.

Pacific Seaboard Airlines   Formed in 1933; renamed Chicago & Southern Air Lines in 1934.

Pacific Southwest Airlines   Local service operator formed in May 1949. Still operating in 1982.

Panair do Brasil   Formed (as NYRBA do Brasil) in September 1930; acquired by Pan American and renamed in October 1930.

Pan American Airways   Formed in March 1927 as subsidiary of Aviation Corpn of America. Acquired Florida Airways (March 1927); Atlantic, Gulf & Caribbean Airways (June 1928); West Indian Air Express (July 1928); Compania Mexicana de Aviacion (January 1929); NYRBA (August 1930); UMCA (75% holding in 1931); SCADTA (80% holding in 1931); Compania Cubana de Aviacion Curtiss (March 1932); Compania Aero de Transportes (1932, renamed Aerovias Centrales); Alaskan Airways (1932, renamed Pacific-Alaska Airways); China National Aviation Corpn (45% holding in March 1933); and many others subsequently. Still operating in 1982.

Pan American – Grace Airways (Panagra)   Formed in February 1929 by acquisition of Chilean Airways and Peruvian Airways; acquired Huff-Daland in 1930. Acquired by Braniff Airways in 1967.

Pennsylvania Airlines   Formed in 1930 as subsidiary of Pittsburgh Aviation Industries Corpn; acquired Clifford Ball in November 1930 and Kohler Aviation Corpn in 1934. Merged with Central Airlines in November 1936 to form Pennsylvania-Central Airlines.

Pennsylvania-Central Airlines   Formed in November 1936 by merger of Pennsylvania Airlines and Central Airlines. Renamed Capital Airlines in April 1948.

Piedmont Airlines   Local service operator formed (as division of Piedmont Aviation) in January 1948. Still operating in 1982.

Pioneer Air Lines   Formed (as Essair) in January 1939 for local service operation; renamed in November 1943. Acquired by Continental Air Lines in December 1954.

Pitcairn Aviation   Formed in September 1927; became part of Eastern Air Lines in July 1929.

Pittsburgh Airways   Merged with Ohio Transport and United States Airways in August 1930 to form United Avigation Co.

Pittsburgh Aviation Industries Corporation (PAIC)   Merged with Transcontinental Air Transport and Western Air Express in July 1930 to form Transcontinental & Western Air (TWA).

Republic Airlines   Formed in June 1979 by merger of North Central Airlines and Southern Airways. Acquired Hughes Airwest in October 1980; still operating in 1982.

Riddle Airlines   Formed (as Riddle Aviation) in 1945 for non-scheduled operations (scheduled from January 1956); acquired United States Airlines in July 1951. Renamed Riddle Airlines in 1952, and Airlift International in 1964.

Robertson Aircraft Corporation   Formed in 1925 but sold out soon afterwards. Re-formed in 1929, then becoming part of Universal Aviation Corpn.

Robertson Airplane Service Company   Formed in early 1930; ceased operating in 1934.

St Petersburg and Tampa Airboat Line   Formed in December 1913; ceased operating at end of summer 1914.

Seaboard World Airlines   Formed (as Seaboard & Western Airlines) in September 1946 for freight operation; renamed in April 1961. Merged with Flying Tiger Line in October 1980.

Slick Airways   Formed for freight operation in March 1946; acquired California Eastern Airlines in May 1948. Acquired by Airlift International in July 1968.

Southern Air Transport   Formed in 1928 by merger of Gulf Air Lines and Texas Air Transport; became part of American Airways in January 1930.

Southern Airways   Local service operator formed in July 1943. Merged with North Central Airlines in 1979 to form Republic Airlines.

Southwest Air Fast Express (SAFEway)   Formed in early 1929 but ceased operating after less than a year. Southern Air Fast Express, a subsidiary, was in operation 1930–31.

Southwest Airlines   Formed (as Air Southwest) in March 1967; renamed in March 1971. Still operating in 1982.

Southwest Airways   Local service operator formed in early 1941. Renamed Pacific Air Lines in March 1958.

Standard Air Lines   Formed in 1927. Acquired by Western Air Express in early 1930 and sold to American Airways later that year.

Stout Air Services   Formed in mid–1926. Merged with Ford Motor Co in 1928; became part of United Aircraft and Transport Corpn in 1929.

Texas Air Transport   Formed in early 1928; merged with Gulf Air Lines in late 1928 to form Southern Air Transport.

Texas International Airlines   Name adopted from 1968 by Trans-Texas Airways; still operating in 1982.

Transcontinental Air Transport   Formed in May 1928; acquired Maddux Air Lines in late 1929. Merged with Western Air Express and Pittsburgh Aviation Industries Corpn in July 1930 to form Transcontinental & Western Air.

Transcontinental & Western Air (TWA)   Formed in July 1930 by merger of Transcontinental Air Transport, PAIC, and Western Air Express. Renamed Trans World Airlines (so keeping TWA initials) in May 1950.

Trans Ocean Air Lines   Freight operator formed in March 1946; ceased operating in April 1960.

Trans-Texas Airways   Local service operator, formed (as Aviation Enterprises) in November 1944; renamed in July 1947. Renamed Texas International Airlines in 1968.

Trans World Airlines (TWA)   Name adopted from May 1950 by Transcontinental & Western Air (TWA). Still operating in 1982.

United Aircraft and Transport Corporation   Formed in December 1928 by merger of Boeing Air Transport and Pacific Air Transport; joined in 1929 by Ford/Stout, Varney and National Air Transport. Became United Air Lines in July 1931.

United Air Lines   Formed in July 1931, initially as holding company for members of United Aircraft and Transport Corpn. Acquired Capital Airlines in June 1961. Still operating in 1982.

United Avigation Company   Formed in August 1930 by merger of Ohio Transport, Pittsburgh Airways and United States Airways, but failed to gain operating licence.

United States Airlines   Freight operator formed in January 1946; acquired by Riddle Airlines in July 1951.

United States Airways   Formed in 1928; merged with Ohio Transport and Pittsburgh Airways in August 1930 to form United Avigation Co.

Universal Aviation Corporation   Formed in March 1929 by merger of Robertson Aircraft Corpn, Braniff Airlines, Continental Air Lines, Northern Air Lines and Central Airlines. Became part of American Airways in January 1930.

US Air   Name adopted from October 1979 by Allegheny Airlines.

Varney Air Transport   Formed (as Varney Speed Lines) in 1925; became part of United Aircraft and Transport Corpn in June 1930. Varney Air Transport, an offshoot of the original company, was formed in December 1934 and was renamed Continental Air Lines in July 1937.

Wedell-Williams Air Service Corporation   Acquired by Eastern Air Lines in 1937.

West Coast Airlines   Local service operator formed in March 1941; acquired Empire Air Lines in August 1952. Merged with Bonanza Air Lines and Pacific Air Lines in April 1968 to form Air West.

West Coast Air Transport   Formed in late 1927; acquired by Western Air Express in late 1929.

Western Air Express   Formed in July 1925. Became part of Transcontinental & Western Air in July 1930 but continued separate existence, operating briefly in 1934 as General Air Lines before reverting to original name. Renamed Western Air Lines in March 1941.

Western Air Lines   Name adopted from March 1941 by Western Air Express. Still operating in 1982.

West Indian Air Express   Acquired by Pan American in July 1928.

Wisconsin Central Airlines   Local service operator formed in May 1944; renamed North Central Airlines in December 1952.

Wyoming Air Service   Formed in 1932 (?); renamed Inland Air Lines in April 1938. Acquired by Western Air Lines in October 1943.

Benoist flying boat *The Lark of Duluth*. **The Airboat Line's Benoist had an extra wing bay and modified tip floats**

Benoist flying boat

The name of P. E. Fansler would not be instantly recognisable to most students of aviation history, yet it was the enterprise of this Florida businessman which gave America its first commercial air transport service. Plying across Tampa Bay between St Petersburg and Tampa, it covered the 22-mile journey in 20min and ran for nearly four months, making two or more round trips per day. The fare was five dollars per passenger, up to a maximum weight of 200lb (including baggage): fat passengers were charged extra.

The aircraft used by the St Petersburg and Tampa Airboat Line was a Benoist flying boat, a small three-bay biplane seating only a pilot and one passenger, which had flown for the first time in 1913. The bay-crossing service opened on January 1, 1914, with Benoist test pilot Tony Jannus and Mayor Pheil of St Petersburg as his passenger, taking the honours for the first trip, which was watched by hundreds of local sightseers. During its brief existence the Airboat Line carried 1,205 passengers and flew some 11,000 miles; only 22 flights were cancelled, 18 of them as a result of bad weather.

Aeromarine 75

Established before the First World War at Keyport, New Jersey, the Aeromarine Plane and Motor Co Inc became well known during the next few years as a manufacturer of flying boats and other naval aircraft. After the war it engaged in the conversion of surplus DH-4s and other military aircraft for civil uses. Among these was the Aeromarine 75, one of several "civilianised" versions of the Curtiss F-5L flying boat. Two or three of these, adapted to seat 12 people (though they often carried more), were employed from November 1, 1919, on passenger/mail/freight services from Key West to Havana by Aeromarine West Indian Airways, the only airline to operate significant services in and out of the USA for the next seven years. After a short-lived New York—Atlantic City service in May 1921, AWIA operated seasonal services in the north (Detroit—Cleveland, across Lake Erie) during the summer months, returning south to maintain a Miami—Nassau schedule during the Florida winter holiday period. Following the withdrawal of airmail subsidies by the USA and Cuba, the Aeromarine 75 made its last flight on May 1, 1924.

Aeromarine Airways' Model 75 *Columbus*

Dayton-Wright KT Cabin Cruiser

Large-scale production of the British de Havilland D.H.4 day bomber was undertaken in the United States in 1918, after the aircraft had been redesigned to accept the American Liberty engine. In the years immediately after the war many hundreds were modernised or modified by a number of US companies. Boeing, for example, modernised nearly 300 for the Army Air Service, while LWF (Lowe, Willard and Fowler) converted many others as airmail transports.

Among those to make passenger-carrying conversions was the Dayton-Wright company, whose D.4K "Honeymoon Express" had a glazed, framed canopy over two passenger seats aft of the pilot's open cockpit. A deeper fuselage, with a longer, "greenhouse" canopy, characterised the KT Cabin Cruiser of 1920, a three-seat tourer powered by a 300 hp Wright-Hispano or 420 hp Liberty 12 engine.

Dayton-Wright KT Cabin Cruiser, a converted DH-4 bomber

Curtiss Eagle

Curtiss, like many another US manufacturer, anticipated a post-war growth in civil air transport and produced new designs to cater for it. The company's expectations were premature, however, and it failed to foresee that the immediate need would be met by converted wartime types. As a result the Eagle, like many of its domestic and foreign contemporaries, was produced in small numbers only. Curtiss built a few examples of the three-engined Eagle I, which was designed by William Gilmore and appeared in 1919 as an elegant three-bay biplane with a well streamlined fuselage, a roomy, fully enclosed six-passenger cabin, and fairings over the tandem-wheel main landing gear units.

A single Eagle II, powered by two 400 hp Curtiss C-12 engines, proved to have too much power and was nearly lost on its first take-off when one engine failed. The Eagle III, with a single nose-mounted Liberty 12 engine of 400 hp and larger fin, was the final version. The three examples built were all purchased by the US Army Air Service in 1920 as personnel transports; one was subsequently evaluated as a four-stretcher air ambulance.

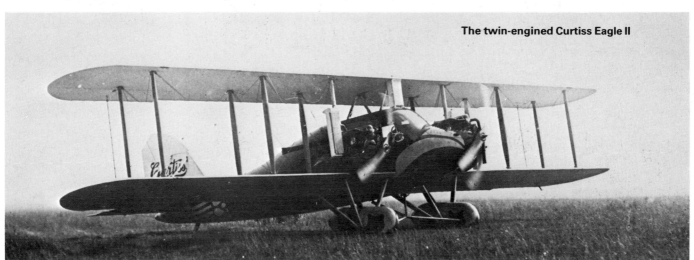

The twin-engined Curtiss Eagle II

The Martin Mail Plane served only briefly with the US Post Office in 1919

Martin GMP/Mail Plane

The aircraft nowadays known by the collective designation MB-1 was Martin's first bomber design after the First World War, and the US Army Air Service and US Navy each ordered ten. Contemporary designations of the Army aircraft were GMB (Glenn Martin Bomber), GMT (Transatlantic), GMC (Cannon) and GMP (Passenger). Seven GMBs were completed, the first of which was flown in August 1918, plus one each of the other three variants. In the summer of 1919 the US Air Mail Service of the Post Office Department ordered six aircraft which were generally similar to the GMB except for a blunt, faired nose replacing the bomber's forward gun position. There was also a "Martin Express" freight-carrying version of the Navy MBT/MT torpedo-bomber, and this differed from the Army Martins in having the Liberty engines mounted directly on to the lower wings. Both types could carry a 1,500lb payload of mail or freight.

The Post Office aircraft were introduced on airmail services in the early autumn of 1919, but their take-off and landing runs were too long to allow satis-factory operations from the small airfields used by the Post Office. Coupled with a poor single-engine performance, this led to their early withdrawal from service.

Davis-Douglas/Ryan Cloudster

The first aircraft designed by Donald W. Douglas after leaving Martin, the original Cloudster was built in collaboration with David R. Davis, a wealthy sportsman later to become known as designer of the Davis wing fitted to the B-24 Liberator bomber of the Second World War. A big, single-bay, two-seat biplane, it flew for the first time on February 24, 1921, and was intended for a coast-to-coast flight across the United States. This was attempted on June 27 that year but was curtailed when the Liberty engine failed over El Paso, Texas.

The Cloudster was sold in 1923 and converted to a six/ten-seater (three rows of open cockpits with two/two/two or four/four/two on benches) before being sold again in 1925 to T. Claude Ryan for his Los Angeles–San Diego Air Line. Ryan had it further modified, moving the pilots' two-seat open cockpit from the rear to the front position, and enclosing the passengers in a comfortable cabin with five-a-side soft seats, carpeted floor, overhead lighting, large windows and other improvements. For a year and a half it served as the flagship of the Ryan fleet, flying both regular schedules and charters. It ended its days on a "beer run" to Tijuana, Mexico, during the Prohibition era, eventually being wrecked in 1927 while making a beach landing at Ensenada.

Cloudster after being modified by Ryan for the Los Angeles–San Diego Air Line in 1925

The elegant but ill-fated Jacuzzi monoplane of 1920–21

Jacuzzi Monoplane

In 1920 Jacuzzi Brothers Inc, a wartime manufacturer of aircraft propellers for the US Government, designed and built a small single-seat monoplane powered by a modified Model T Ford motor-car engine. Its purpose was to prove the concept of a larger aircraft, claimed to be the first high-wing monoplane with a totally enclosed cabin to be designed and built in the United States. With this the brothers intended to operate a passenger service between San Francisco, Oakland, Richmond and Sacramento.

The scaled-up aircraft made its first flight during the first half of April 1921, but its cross-country speed of 90 mph was below expectations, and attempts were made to lighten the structure by such means as hollowing out the bolts securing the wing struts to the main landing gear. Although this produced an improvement of some 15 mph, it was a course of action that led to the undoing of both the aircraft and its manufacturer. During a test flight on July 14, 1921, while the aircraft was flying at 2,000ft over Modesto, California, the port wing strut parted company with the undercarriage, its hollowed-out bolt having sheared off. The aircraft plunged to the ground, killing the company president and the other three men on board.

Friesley Falcon

Friesley Aircraft Corporation was formed in 1921 at Gridley, California, by a group of local wealthy ranchers headed by Harold Friselben. Moral and other support was lent by Captain Eddie Rickenbacker, who was instrumental in obtaining the services of an ex-Army aircraft designer, Bond Spencer, for the company. Bond designed, and was pilot for the first flight of, the Friesley Falcon, a big three-bay biplane with a twin tail unit and a passenger cabin reminiscent of that of Sikorsky's *Bolshoi* of the early war years.

Following the maiden flight on April 17, 1921, the Falcon made its first revenue flight on May 15, to San Francisco; seats were sold by auction to the highest bidders. A few more commercial flights were made during the summer of 1921, including the transportation of an entire local baseball team to and from an away match. However, the expected boom in post-war air transport failed to materialise, and the company was soon in financial trouble, being declared bankrupt in February 1922. The Falcon, its only product, was sold to China; its ultimate fate is not known.

Friesley Falcon 12-passenger biplane, designed by Bond Spencer

Burnelli's RB-1: tremendous lift from the aerofoil-shaped fuselage, but the engines were badly located

Remington-Burnelli RB-1 and RB-2

One of aviation's more imaginative and innovative designers, Vincent J. Burnelli devoted a large part of his life to the development of the lifting-body, or lifting-fuselage, type of aircraft, in which the fuselage was designed in the form of an aerofoil to reduce parasite drag and, simultaneously, provide a substantial component of lift. In 1920 he teamed with T. T. Remington in the Remington-Burnelli Aircraft Corporation at Amityville, Long Island, to produce the first aeroplane designed to incorporate this concept. Its deep, 14ft-wide fuselage made possible a roomy cabin for 25 passengers, with two pilots seated over the nose in open cockpits and flanked by the two partly buried Liberty engines. The airframe was of wooden construction, the wings and twin tail surfaces being fabric-covered, the fuselage skinned with corrugated aluminium.

The 1922 *Jane's All the World's Aircraft* remarked: "Granting the advantages claimed for this machine, it would seem that they are largely neutralised by the close position of the propellers to one another, which may considerably reduce their efficiency through 'blanketing'. The thick section aerofoil must also interfere, to a large extent, with the undisturbed flow-off of the slipstream, which should result in a diminished effectiveness of the tail surfaces." This is exactly what did happen in the summer of the following year.

Burnelli designed an improved version, for cargo work, as the RB-2 Freighter, but the Remington-Burnelli company ceased operation while it was still under construction. It was taken over by a new firm, the Garvan-Burnelli Aircraft Corporation of Hartford, Connecticut, and made its first flight in 1924 at Curtiss Field,

Long Island. With an all-metal fuselage, duralumin wings and a fabric-covered metal tail, it was somewhat larger than the RB-1 and was powered by two 500 hp Galloway Atlantic engines. The rear fuselage was redesigned to prevent the blanketing characteristics shown by the RB-1. For a time the RB-2 was used as a flying automobile showroom, touring various cities to demonstrate not only the cargo-carrying abilities of the aircraft but also to exhibit the virtues of the Hudson Essex two-door sedan installed inside the fuselage.

Dayton-Wright FP2 (Forest Patrol No 2), photographed in August 1921 not long before its first flight

Dayton-Wright FP2

Also known as the Forest Patrol aeroplane, this twin-float, twin-engined biplane was developed to meet the requirements of the Canadian Forest Service, and was equipped extensively for aerial photography, mapping, survey, inspection and timber patrol over otherwise almost inaccessible territory. The four occupants, who were fully enclosed within glazed areas in the nose, sides and bottom of the fuselage, had an excellent view forward and downward. Four bunks could be provided in the rear fuselage, which also housed equipment, baggage, canoes and other gear necessary for its role. Design of the wings, floats and triple vertical tail surfaces was somewhat reminiscent of Curtiss designs of the period.

The FP2 made its first flight, from the shores of Lake Erie, in the summer of 1921. Only one example was completed.

Barnhart Model 15 Wampus Kat

History does not seem to have recorded what, if any, were the previous 14 designs of G. Edward Barnhart, but his Model 15 was, for its time, an ambitious project. A large, three-bay, equal-span biplane, it utilised a British RAF 6A aerofoil section and had a fully enclosed, roomy cabin for its four passengers, with an open cockpit above for the pilot.

The Wampus Kat was built for Barnhart by the C.R. Little Aircraft Works in Pasadena, California, the two combining to form a new company known as Barnhart Aircraft Inc. Design and construction of the aircraft were conventional for their time: according to the 1922 edition of *Jane's All the World's Aircraft*, "its chief point of note is that it embodies folding wings".

G. Edward Barnhart's quaintly named Wampus Kat, which spanned only 22ft with wings folded

Stout Air Pullman

The Air Pullman occupies, to say the least, a controversial position in the history of US commercial aviation. The prototype was forced to land almost immediately after the start of its first flight in early 1924 with a shattered windscreen; pilots did not like the sluggish take-off afforded by its low-lift wings; fatigue cracks were a perennial problem; and one engineer associated with the aircraft has recorded that the structural design was "perfectly awful, and positively dangerous . . . structural members which were supposed to meet at a point, might be several inches apart. It all depended upon whether it was convenient to attach them together . . . I couldn't understand why [they] didn't collapse in the air . . . nobody knew where the [structural] loads went, or what they were, or how strong the structure was."

Yet the Air Pullmans kept flying for nearly three years. One took part in the 1925 Ford Reliability Air Tour and scored full marks. Henry Ford's own Ford Freight Line operated five between Dearborn and Chicago for two and a half years, and others served successfully with Florida Airways (four) and Stout Air Service. However, following the introduction of the ATC (Approved Type Certificate) licensing system, they failed to meet the structural requirements laid down and had been withdrawn by the end of 1927.

Design of the Air Pullman, which was certainly a good-looking aeroplane, was largely the work of George Prudden, assisted in the later stages by Thomas Towle, who subsequently played one of the key roles in developing the Ford Tri-Motor. Instigator of the programme was William Bushnell Stout, head of the 1922 Stout Metal Airplane Co until it became a division of the Ford Motor Co in 1925. It is probably fair to say that the latter event, and the belief that motor-car design and production techniques could be applied to aircraft, was the major cause of the Air Pullman's chequered career. About 11 were built, of which one was later fitted with three engines as the first step towards the highly successful Ford Tri-Motor.

The second Stout Air Pullman, *Maid in Detroit*, **photographed at Selfridge Field**

Douglas M series

Just as its military predecessor, the O-2, replaced the DH-4 as the US Army Air Service's standard post-war observation biplane, so the M series took over from the DH-4 the carriage of the US mails in the mid-1920s. The first civil version, which made its initial flight on July 6, 1925, was the DAM-1 (Douglas Air Mail 1), essentially a modified O-2 capable of carrying two and a half times the modest 400lb payload of the DH-4. Western Air Express ordered five examples of the similar M-2, in which the two forward mail compartments could be converted quickly to carry two passengers, and put the first into service on its Salt Lake City to Los Angeles route on April 17, 1926. Western later ordered a sixth M-2, and also operated the original DAM-1 after it had been brought up to M-2 standard and redesignated M-1.

In March 1926 the Post Office Department placed an order for ten examples of the improved M-3, followed later that year by a contract for 40 M-4s, which had increased-span wings and, in many cases, night-flying equipment and radio. The M-3 and M-4 had provision for one passenger in place of a mail payload. Easily the most numerous version, the M-4 continued in service until the end of the 1920s. When the Post Office handed over its airmail routes to commercial operators in late 1927, National Air Transport, with a fleet of 18, became the largest user of the M-4. Production of the M series was brought to a total of 60 with the completion of two M-4As for Western Air Express and a single three-seat Wasp-engined M-4S for NAT.

Douglas M-2 in the insignia of Western Air Express, which had six for mail and passenger services

Fokker Universal

Appearing in late 1925, the four-passenger Model 4 Universal was designed by Robert Noorduyn and was the first model built by Fokker Aircraft Corporation, the US offspring of the celebrated Dutch manufacturer. Except for the strut-braced wings, construction was generally similar to that of contemporary Dutch-built Fokkers.

Production, which continued until the spring of 1931, totalled 45, the first Universal being delivered in May 1926 to Colonial Air Transport. Other operators included California Airways, Continental Air Express, Dominion Airways, Northwest Air Service, Northwest Airways, Reynolds Airways, St Tammany Gulf

Coast Airways, Standard Air Lines, and Western Canada Airways. Capt Hubert Wilkins acquired one for his polar operations, and one was flown as an executive aircraft by Continental Motors.

About half of the Universals were powered by 200 hp Wright

The improved M-4 appeared in the summer of 1926

J4 radial engines. Most of the remainder (from about 1928) were fitted with 200 hp J5s, and some later production examples with the 330 hp J6. The standard wheel undercarriage could be interchanged with twin floats or skis for water or snow operations.

Typical Fokker Universal production aircraft, for Aero Corporation of California (Standard Air Lines)

Boeing 40B-4 (NC843M) of Western Air Express

Boeing Model 40

After seven years of using converted military DH-4s on its airmail routes, the US Post Office Department held a competition for a replacement in 1925. Boeing's Model 40, which first flew on July 7, 1925, was an elegant biplane with a wood-veneer fuselage and a neatly installed 400 hp Liberty V-12 engine. The Post Office bought the prototype, but no production followed and there was no other customer immediately in prospect. However, later that year Boeing revived and modified the design as the Model 40A with an uncowled 420 hp Wasp radial engine and fabric-covered fuselage, which combined to give it a more utilitarian appearance. Forward of the pilot's rear-mounted open cockpit were two mail compartments separated by a small enclosed cabin between the wings for two passengers.

A Post Office contract for a mail service between San Francisco and Chicago enabled Boeing to launch production of 25 Model 40As; the first of these was flown on May 20, 1927. A new company, Boeing Air Transport Inc, was formed to operate the service, which opened on July 1, 1927. In 1928, after refitting with 525 hp Hornet engines, the existing 40As were redesignated Model 40B. Eventually they became 40B-2s to distinguish them from the four-passenger final production version, the 40B-4 (first flown on October 5, 1928), of which 39 were built. Operators included Boeing Air Transport, United, Western, and Western Canada Airways.

In all, 82 Model 40s were produced, including ten Model 40Cs with 450 hp Wasp engines and four-passenger cabins; nine (some later converted to B-4s) were operated by Pacific Air Transport, a constituent of BAT. The one-off 40X and 40Y were 40Cs converted for use by US oil companies. The four 40H-4s were B-4s built by Boeing Canada.

CA-5 version of the Buhl Airsedan

Buhl Airsedan

The members of this series of small sesquiplane transports were all broadly similar in overall appearance, their main differences lying in size, accommodation and power-plant. All were designed by Etienne Dormoy, the first to appear being the five-seat CA-5 (220 hp Wright J5 engine), which was certificated in September 1927. About a dozen were built, including a few de luxe CA-5As, and most were put to competitive or corporate transport use. After the smaller three-seat CA-3C/3D Sport

Airsedan came the eight-place CA-8A/8B Senior Airsedan (certificated January 1929), the largest of the range and first flown in late 1928. Powered by either a Cyclone (CA-8A) or Hornet (CA-8B) engine of 525 hp, it was also available in six-seat form with a 450 hp Wasp. Only a few were built, however, despite a competitive price.

The most successful model (about 15 were completed) was the CA-6 Airsedan, slimmer

than the CA-5 but carrying one more passenger and having a more powerful engine. On wheel or twin-float gear, it was used mostly as a passenger or cargo carrier in Canada; operators included Cherry Red Airline Ltd. A particularly famous CA-6 was *Spokane Sun God,* which in the late summer of 1929 made a non-stop 7,200-mile round trip from Spokane to New York and back, making 11 in-flight refuellings en route.

Fairchild FC-2W2 (NC8004) used on the New York–Montreal passenger/mail service by Canadian Colonial Airways

Fairchild FC-2

Sherman Fairchild's long tradi-tion of small, rugged utility aircraft began with the little four-seat FC-1 (Fairchild Cabin, design number 1), powered by a 90 hp Curtiss OX-5 engine, which flew for the first time on June 14, 1926. The five-seat FC-2 was its production counter-part, the initial version having a 220 hp Wright J5 engine and 44ft-span wings. The three-longeron fuselage had a "razor-back" top line to enable the wings to be folded back for transportation and storage; a squarer, four-longeron body appeared on later aircraft. About 160 civil FC-2s were built, including 12 in Canada, and a small number of FC-2Cs were produced with 160 hp Curtiss C-6 engines for the Curtiss Flying Service.

The improved FC-2W, flown in the autumn of 1927, had a 6ft-

longer wing and nearly twice the power. Nominally a five-seater, it often carried seven (or equivalent extra cargo), as did the FC-2W2, which featured a 2ft extension to the rear fuselage. Fifty of the -2W series were built. Many FC-2 models operated in the Arctic and Antarctic, frequently with twin

floats or skis replacing the con-ventional wheeled landing gear. Perhaps the best known example was *Stars and Stripes,* used in the Byrd Antarctic expedition. Cy Caldwell flew the first private-enterprise inter-national US airmail, from Key West to Havana, in an FC-2 on behalf of Pan American, and

Panagra employed one across the Andes between Buenos Aires and Santiago. With engine changes, Frise-type ailerons and other modifica-tions, a few Fairchild FC-2s later received Model 51 designations under a different type certificate.

Stinson Detroiter

The original SB-1 Detroiter, flown on January 25, 1926, attracted so much customer interest that the Stinson Airplane Corporation was founded some four months later. Just over 20 of these four-seat biplanes were built, serving as passenger and/or mail transports with Florida Airways, Northwest Airways, Wien Airlines and Patricia Airways.

In November 1927, five months after ending SB-1 production, Stinson received certification of the five-passenger SM-1, a high-wing monoplane version which eventually ran to 74 examples. Among the operators of the SM-1 Detroiter was Paul R. Braniff Inc, which flew its first-ever scheduled service (on June 20, 1928, between Oklahoma City and Tulsa) with one of these aircraft. There were several sub-variants of the monoplane Detroiter, mostly with minor modifications to cabin interiors, landing gear or powerplant. Of these the most significant was the SM-1F, with a 300 hp Wright J6 Whirlwind engine. Production totalled about 26, including four which, in 1928, were used for the first regular airmail services in China. Largest Detroiter version was the SM-6B, carrying seven/eight passengers or 954lb of mail or freight; about a dozen of these, powered by 450 hp Wasp engines, were produced. From 1928 Stinson also built a scaled-down three/four-seat Detroiter Junior for the general-aviation market.

Ryan Brougham

Stable companion of Lindbergh's famous *Spirit of St Louis,* the Brougham began life as a modified Ryan M-2 Bluebird powered by a 220 hp Wright J5 Whirlwind engine. Two hundred and twelve Broughams were built during 1927-31, most of these being B-1s (150) or B-5s (48). Lindbergh's New York–Paris flight, coupled with the successes by B-1 Broughams in the Ford Air Tour and National Air Races, sparked off demand from airlines and private or charter operators, and

SM-1 Detroiter *Pride of Detroit*, **which flew across the Atlantic, Europe and Asia to Tokyo in August/September 1927, a flight of nearly 16,000 miles**

Broughams eventually saw service in Alaska, China, Guatemala, Mexico and Salvador as well as the USA.

The B-5 differed from the B-1 in having a more powerful (300 hp J6) Whirlwind engine and seating five passengers instead of four. Other production models were the B-3 (eight built), a four-seater with a wider cabin, extra baggage space, enlarged tail surfaces and other detail improvements, and the five-passenger B-7 (six built), with a 420 hp Pratt & Whitney Wasp engine, lengthened fuselage, and baggage capacity increased to 100lb. The numerous US domestic operators of the Brougham included Bowman Airways, Embry-Riddle (for airmail transport), Pike's Peak Air Lines and Ryan Airlines.

Ryan B-1 Brougham (NC4559) of Bowman Airways, with ski landing gear

Early Vega (NC624E) of Transcontinental and Western Air Inc

Lockheed Vega

Co-designed by Allan Loughead (Lockheed) and John K. Northrop, the Vega was the aeroplane which, in 1926, relaunched the Lockheed brothers in the aircraft manufacturing business. Not only was it successful in itself (128 were built over the next eight years), but it provided the blueprint for an entire family of high-speed transports and racers: "Lockheed's plywood bullets".

First flown on July 4, 1927, the original Vega (as *Golden Eagle*) was entered in the Dole race from Oakland (California) to Hawaii in August, but was lost en route. Despite this, orders flooded in and, although individual purchases were small, airline use was widespread in the USA, Argentina, Australia, Canada, Costa Rica, Mexico, Nicaragua, Norway, Panama and the UK. Braniff, Varney and Wedell-Williams were among some three dozen US domestic operators of

scheduled Vega services.

Principal variants, in order of appearance, were the Model 1 (28 built), Model 5 (42, including conversions), Model 2 (five, plus one conversion), Model 5B (34, including conversions), and the Detroit-built DL-1 (10). Passenger seating was for four (Vega 1 and 5), five (Vega 2) or six persons (Vega 5B and DL-1); powerplants included the 220 hp Wright J5 (Vega 1), 450 hp Wasp B (Vega 5), 300 hp Wright J6 (Vega 2) and 450 hp Wasp C (Vega 5B and DL-1). There were so many detail variations of landing gear and other features that it is virtually impossible to define a "standard" Vega. Many were converted (often more than once) to other models, and several were custom-built "specials". The famous *Winnie Mae,* in which Wiley Post and Harold Gatty did so much remarkable flying in the early and middle 1930s, began life as a Model 5B.

NC14236, a Model 5C, was the last Vega built by Lockheed at Burbank

Originally called "Universal Special," 3318 was the prototype Super Universal

Fokker Super Universal

Known originally as the Universal Special, the Fokker Model 8 Super Universal, which appeared in late 1927, was essentially an enlarged and improved version of the Universal, with enclosed flight deck, cabin seating for six passengers, a more powerful engine, better performance, and – on the production version – straight-tapered cantilever wings.

The first of 80 production Super Universals was delivered to the Byrd Antarctic Expedition, which named it *Virginia*; others went to operators in Argentina, Australia, Canada, Colombia, Mexico, South Africa, the UK and the USA. Principal North American operators were National Parks Airways, St Tammany, Standard, Universal, Western Air Express, and Western Canada Airways.

Canadian Vickers built 14 under licence, and Nakajima in Japan a further 47 between 1931–36 for both military and civil customers. Three similar F.XIs were produced by Fokker in Holland.

NC8010, the fourth production Fokker F-10, was later sold to the Shell Oil Co

Close-up of Goodyear's Super Universal, showing the beautifully hammered nose panels; low-pressure tyres were favoured by some operators, such as WAE

Fokker F-10/F-10A

Essentially an enlarged Super Universal fuselage mated to an F.VIIb/3m wing, the F-10 was developed originally to meet the requirements of Western Air Express. In addition to the prototype, which flew at the beginning of 1928, a total of 65 were built, including two military examples. Only seven of the initial F-10 version were completed; the wings were Dutch-built while the remainder of the airframe was produced in the USA at Teterboro, NJ. The remaining aircraft were F-10As, with longer-span, tapered, American-built wings and other detail improvements; two of the F-10s were also brought up to F-10A standard. Production ended in October 1929. Balanced ailerons were retrofitted to all F-10s in service after one of them crashed in March 1931.

First operator of the F-10/10A was Western Air Express, which introduced the type on its Los Angeles–San Francisco service on May 26, 1928. WAE eventually acquired a total of 13. Other major commercial operators included Pan American (12), Standard, and Universal Airlines (15). American Airlines later bought 16 from other users to acquire the largest single fleet. Corporate users included the Richfield and Shell oil companies.

Sikorsky S-38

First flown on June 25, 1928, the S-38 was the first big commercial success for Igor Sikorsky in the United States: a total of only ten examples of his eight previous designs had been built, but the S-38 achieved a production run of 114. After the S-36 it was the company's second amphibian, developed for use by Pan American and NYRBA on Caribbean and South American routes. Carrying eight passengers and a crew of two, the initial S-38A could cruise at 100 mph on its two 410 hp Wasp engines and had a range of 600 miles.

The major version, with more powerful Wasps, was the S-38B, over 75 of which were built. This carried ten passengers, had increased fuel capacity, and was used extensively by Pan American, in particular, to expand its route network in the Caribbean.

Final production version was the S-38C, with the same power-

plant but two extra passengers and less fuel. Four of the eight or more S-38Cs completed were operated by Inter-Island Airways of Hawaii, one remaining in service until as late as 1946. Other operators of the various S-38 models included American Airways, Canadian Airways, Colonial-Western Airways, Northwest Airways and Western Air Express; examples went also to the US Navy and to private or corporate owners. Throughout their service they built up an enviable reputation for ruggedness and versatility.

In July/August 1930 an S-38BH, one of two converted to the 575 hp Hornet B power-plant, set three height-with-payload world records for seaplanes, having had its wheel gear removed in order to qualify for this class. This performance directly encouraged development of the larger S-41 of 1932.

Simple but strong: the steel-tube fuselage and wooden wing framework of the Cessna AW

Cessna AW

Clyde V. Cessna survived 15 crashes in the first aeroplane of his own design before, in 1911, he finally persuaded it to fly. Thereafter, he established a reputation as an exhibition pilot and designed several more aircraft, all monoplanes, before parting from Walter Beech at the Travel Air Company to produce his first high-wing cabin monoplane in 1926. The Cessna Aircraft Company was incorporated on the last day of 1927, and in the following summer there appeared the Model AA,

forerunner of Cessna's first production-status design. The year saw the production of 21 examples of the Models AA, AC, AF and AS, all four-seaters differing only in the power-plants fitted (120 hp Anzani, 130 hp Comet, 150 hp Axelson Floco, and 125 hp Siemens-Halske respectively, all air-cooled uncowled radials).

Major model was the AW, the first example of which won the New York–Los Angeles Air Derby in 1928 and was certificated on September 7 that year.

By July 1929 Cessna had built 47, adding one more in 1930. The cantilever wooden wings of the A series were stress-tested in a 350 mph power dive. The fuselage was of welded steel tube and the overall covering of fabric. Following its Air Derby success, the original AW made a remarkable flight in April/May 1929 from Wichita to Detroit, Nome (Alaska) and East Cape (Siberia), returning via Detroit to New York. Flown by Parker D. Cramer, it completed the 13,000-miles-plus journey in

only 127 flying hours, the only maintenance required being the adjustment of two valves and the cleaning of a spark plug.

Cessna was able to sell these aircraft on their economy as well as their reliability. Delivery flights to New York (1,325 miles from Wichita) were regularly made in 11–12hr at a cost below 25 dollars, compared with the fastest available rail service of over 40hr and a fare of more than 55 dollars.

NC6448, a standard production Cessna AW

Wilbur Wright, **an early "air yacht" of 1921, was a five-seat flying boat with a Liberty engine**

Loening Air Yacht

Grover Loening built an experimental "air yacht," a monoplane flying boat, in the early 1920s. It was followed in April 1928 by his first certificated commercial amphibian, a four/six-passenger development of the US Navy's OL-8, which was designed in collaboration with

Hornet-powered Loening C2H Air Yacht, operated on the Catalina Island service by WAE

Leroy Grumman and flown for the first time in late 1927. Powered by a 410 hp Wasp engine and known simply as the Wasp Amphibian or Cabin Amphibian, it featured Loening's characteristic "flying shoe" configuration, having a central float/hull and large

biplane wings with outboard stabilising floats. From this was developed the first "official" Air Yacht, a larger aircraft with a 500 hp Hornet engine and more spacious accommodation for its six passengers. As in the earlier aircraft, the pilot occupied an open cockpit above and forward of the fully enclosed passenger cabin. Flight testing took place in spring and summer 1928, with type certification following in August of that year. Sales were made to both airlines and private owners, to whom the 500 hp Wright Cyclone was offered as an optional (and actually more popular) powerplant.

Three months after certification of these two models, ATCs were issued for the further developed C2C (Cyclone) and C2H (Hornet) Air Yachts, with numerous detail improvements and both engines uprated to 525 hp. Interiors ranged from de luxe four-place executive cabins to eight-passenger commuter layouts.

The ultimate Air Yacht was the C4C, developed by Loening and built by Keystone-Loening, following a merger in late 1928, under the new designation K-85. This retained the basic C2 wings but introduced a true flying-boat hull/fuselage in which the pilot, as well as his seven passengers, had enclosed accommodation. The 525 hp R-1750-E Cyclone was relocated on the centre-section of the upper wing. The K-85, which ran to just two examples, was certificated in January 1931.

Hamilton Metalplane

Designed in 1926 by James S. McDonnell and built by the Hamilton Aero Manufacturing Co, the original Metalplane, designated H-43, was a rugged all-metal monoplane with a thick (modified Clark Y section) cantilever wing and corrugated duralumin skin. With its original 220 hp J4 Whirlwind engine replaced by a J5 Whirlwind, a Metalplane came second in the 1927 Ford Air Tour.

Production aircraft, re-designed by Prof John Ackerman, had high-mounted wings, causing them to resemble more closely the Ford and Fokker transports of the period, and were built by the Hamilton Metalplane Co of Milwaukee, Wisconsin. Designated H-45 (with a 410/450 hp Wasp engine) or H-47 (with a 500/525 hp Pratt & Whitney Hornet), they were certificated in November and December 1928 respectively, although deliveries (to Northwest Airways) actually began in September of that year. Northwest eventually operated eight Metalplanes, initially on its St Paul–Chicago route and later extending as far west as Seattle. Other operators included Isthmian Airways and Universal.

Both the H-45 and H-47 were available with twin Hamilton metal floats instead of the standard wheeled landing gear, and both were re-certificated in the spring of 1929 following an increase in the span and area of the wing.

Wasp-engined Hamilton H-45, noted for its skin of Alclad corrugated dural

Ford 4-AT-B (NC7863) in corporate ownership with Monarch Foods

Typical interior of a Ford Tri-Motor

Ford Models 4-AT and 5-AT Tri-Motor

In the course of a career that began in the mid-1920s and which, many would claim, had hardly ended 50 years later, there can be few tasks that the Ford Tri-Motor has not attempted, including such unlikely activities as serving as a flying grocer's shop and performing snap-rolls at an air display. But it is as a go-anywhere, carry-anything passenger and utility transport that the ''Tin Goose'' is remembered with affection and respect by pilots and passengers alike.

The Tri-Motor's genesis, as a development of William B. Stout's Model 2-AT, was not a happy one. There is controversy still over who really did design it, and certainly no designer could have felt proud of the awkward, ugly Model 3-AT, the first attempt to turn the 2-AT into a three-engined aeroplane. However, when a hangar fire conveniently destroyed this monstrosity, Harold Hicks and Thomas Towle led a drastic redesign which resulted in 1926 (first flight June 11) in the prototype Model 4-AT, powered by three 200 hp Wright J4 Whirlwind seven-cylinder radial engines. Seventy-eight production 4-ATs followed, of which

the first 14 were Model 4-AT-As, similar to the prototype, with a two-seat open cockpit and cabin accommodation for eight passengers. The Model 4-AT-B, certificated in November 1928, seated 12 passengers, was powered by 220 hp Wright J5s, and had increased wing span. Some 35 of this version were built, followed by one 4-AT-C (with a 400 hp Wasp in the nose), three 4-AT-Ds (all with different powerplants), 24 Model 4-AT-Es (three 300 hp J6s), and a single 4-AT-F.

The improved Model 5-AT of 1928 featured a further increase in wing span, higher power and cabin seating for 13–15 passengers according to version. The 117 production total was made up of three 5-AT-As, 42 5-AT-Bs (certificated in June 1929), 48 5-AT-Cs and 24 5-AT-Ds. Re-engined or otherwise converted 4-AT/5-AT Tri-Motors appeared from 1929–31, leading to the designations 6-AT, 7-AT, 8-AT, 9-AT, 11-AT and 13-A. (The Ford 12-A was an unbuilt project; the Model 10-AT, unbuilt as such, was revamped as the Model 14-A and was an unrelated design.)

Production of the Tri-Motor ended in September 1932. Its career traverses virtually the whole pre-war period of airline development in the United States, and in all it served with more than 100 scheduled air transport operators in Australia, Canada, China, Mexico, the USA, and Central and South America, on floats or skis as well as the more usual wheeled landing gear. Others served with polar expeditions, as oil company executive transports, and as barnstormers or fire-fighters. Countless individual modifications were made to cabin layouts, door shapes and sizes, internal equipment and other aspects of the aircraft. Although it was the only significant aeroplane ever produced by the Ford company, the Tri-Motor is one of the immortals of aviation history.

X8499 was the Ford Model 8-AT, a single-engined freighter development of the 5-AT-C. It was used briefly by Pacific Alaska Airways

Fairchild Model 71

The Model 71, of which some 142 examples were built from 1928–34 (121 in the USA and 21 in Canada), was essentially a "cosmetic" development of the earlier FC-2W2 and was used widely as a feederliner and bush transport in the late 1920s and early 1930s. Several survived in operation into the mid-1950s. Principal original operators included Pan American and Universal in the USA, Canadian Airways, Canadian Colonial Airway, and CMA of Mexico. Nearly 20 served with the RCAF, and a further 18 with the US Army Air Corps, chiefly on aerial photography duties.

The 145 cu ft cabin had standard accommodation for a pilot and six passengers or equivalent cargo, typical payload being about 1,500lb on the landplane models, rather less for the twin-float or twin-ski versions. There were several sub-variants, including the five-seat Model 71A, built with 5° of wing sweep for experimental work by Bell Telephone Laboratories and certificated in January 1930; the lighter Canadian Model 71B and slightly heavier 71C; and the Model 71CM, a Canadian prototype with a metal-skinned fuselage. The Models 71D and 71E were, respectively, a projected mail-carrying version and the USAAC XF-1 photographic version.

Fairchild Canada built a Super 71 and two Super 71P prototypes. The former, first flown on October 31, 1934, was a nine-place development of the 71C with a metal fuselage and 520 hp Wasp engine. The Super 71P was a photo-survey version of this, intended for the RCAF.

Meanwhile, Fairchild in the USA had built three examples of the Model 72 (first flight July 31, 1929), a modified 71 with an elevated flight deck to improve the pilot's field of view. This did not go into production, and further development led instead to the Fairchild (later Pilgrim) 100.

The seven-place Fairchild 71 (420 hp Wasp engine)

Prototype Commercial Aircraft C-1 Sunbeam

Commercial Aircraft C-1 Sunbeam

First flown in the late 1920s, the Sunbeam was an equal-span, single-bay biplane built by Commercial Aircraft Corporation of Pasadena in its factory at Los Angeles Municipal Airport. The structure was of fabric-covered welded steel tube except for the wing spars, which were of wood. The fully enclosed passenger cabin had four removable wicker chairs, and the two-place open cockpit to the rear of the cabin had side-by-side seats and was equipped with dual controls. Only one example is thought to have been completed.

Air Express NR3057 was sold to the Gilmore Oil & General Tire Company

Lockheed Air Express

Designed by John K. Northrop and utilising the same basic fuselage as the already celebrated Vega, the Lockheed Model 3 Air Express was, as its name indicated, developed to meet the high-speed airmail transport requirements of Western Air Express. A fully cantilevered wooden wing was mounted parasol-fashion above the wooden monocoque fuselage on short, sturdy struts. A four-seat cabin below the wing was convertible for passenger, mail or mixed payload, with the pilot occupying an open cockpit well to the rear. In the event, WAE ordered only the first aircraft (in October 1927), received it in 1928 and sold it back to Lockheed in 1929. This aircraft was completed on April 12, 1928, made its first flight shortly afterwards and received ATC No 102 on January 11, 1929. Seven other Air Expresses were built, original customers being Texaco, NYRBA (two), the General Tire and Rubber Co, Texas Air Transport, Reginald L. Brooks and the Atlantic Exhibition Co. Standard power-plant was the Wasp radial, although a Hornet engine was fitted in one or two cases. The WAE aircraft entered service in June 1928, those of NYRBA in February 1930.

Most famous of these "barrel-nosed cigars" was the Texaco Air Express, in which three solo, non-stop coast-to-coast records were set in 1929 by Frank M. Hawks. The first of these, on February 3/4, was a flight from Los Angeles to New York in 18hr 21min 59sec. On June 27/28 Hawks made the same journey in the east-west direction in 19hr 10min 32.6sec, returning to New York on June 28/29 to better his February record by completing the trip in 17hr 38min 16.6sec.

Bach Aircraft Company 3-CT-4 Air Yacht (one Wasp and two Ryan-Siemens engines)

Prototype Lockheed Air Express in the markings of the airline which instigated its design

Bach Model 3-CT Air Yacht

Design of the Air Yacht by L. Morton Bach began in 1927 at Santa Monica, California, and the prototype flew for the first time on August 17 of that year. A tri-motor, it was powered by a nose-mounted 250 hp Waterman engine and a 100 hp Kinner under each wing. Uncommon for its time, this system of unmatched power-plants persisted throughout the Air Yacht's development, as did the equally unusual adherence to a wooden airframe with a fabric-covered plywood skin. The 3-CT-2 and 3-CT-4 models had a Wright J5 Whirlwind and Pratt & Whitney Wasp respectively in the nose, the underwing units being in each case a pair of Ryan-Siemens. First type-certificated model was the eight-passenger 3-CT-6 of 1929, of which about half a dozen were built for West Coast Air Transport and Pickwick Airways. The latter was also the chief purchaser of the more powerful Model 3-CT-8 (two 165 hp Wright J5s underwing), which was certificated in July 1929, five months after the 3-CT-6.

Fitted with a 450 hp Wasp in the nose and 225 hp J6 Whirlwinds under the wings, the Models 3-CT-9 and 3-CT-9S (certificated in November 1929 and March 1930 respectively) enjoyed a more proportionate distribution of the steadily increasing power available, improving still further the Air Yacht's excellent top speed and airfield performance. The one and only 3-CT-9S was completed with a four-place executive cabin interior, with veneered walls and ceiling, comfortable armchairs, electric cigar lighters, card tables, a concealed iced-water tank and several other amenities. Final model was the 3-CT-9K (210 hp Kinner C-5s underwing, plus a nose-mounted Wasp).

Useful load of the Pacemaker freighter (2,310lb) was greater than its empty weight of 2,290lb

Bellanca Pacemaker

Derived from the earlier Wright-Bellanca monoplanes, the Pacemaker's immediate ancestor was the CH-200, designed by Giuseppe M. Bellanca after parting from the Wright company in 1927. The CH-200, certificated in June 1928, was a six-place high-wing cabin monoplane with a 220 hp J5 Whirlwind engine and typical Bellanca "bow-legged" main landing gear. From it was developed the CH-300 (300 hp J6 Whirlwind), which first flew in late 1928 or early 1929 and was the most numerous model, some three dozen being built for regional airlines, charter operators and utility use.

First of the line to bear the name Pacemaker was the PM-300 freighter, essentially a modified CH-300 with "straightened-out" main gear legs (for wheels, skis, or twin floats). The PM-300 could carry four persons and still offer 34 cu ft of cabin space for 850lb of freight. It was followed by the 300-W, certificated in June 1930, with a 300 hp Wasp Junior engine.

The Depression meant that only about half a dozen of this variant were built, but Bellanca survived the economic troubles better than many and in 1932 introduced the Pacemaker Model E with increased wing area, wheel spats and a Townend-ringed 420 hp Wright R-975-E2, which greatly improved performance. Again, however, only a handful were completed, and the same fate attended the ultimate Senior Pacemaker version, which received type approval in July 1935 as the Model 31-40 (R-975-E2) and 31-42 (R-975-E3).

Larger and faster than its predecessors, seating up to eight people, and with a NACA-cowled engine, the Senior still had a competitive performance, but by then later Bellanca designs were winning the orders. A rugged, go-anywhere aeroplane that could carry "anything that would go through the door," the Pacemaker was especially popular in areas with cold climates, notably Canada, Alaska and Norway.

K-5 version of the Kreutzer Air Coach (NC983H), certificated on September 6, 1929

Cowling, low-pressure tyres and tailwheel identify this Cunningham-Hall as a PT-6F

Kreutzer Air Coach

Designed by A. K. Peterson and test-flown by Henry H. Ogden, the Air Coach was intended to appeal to the feederline and corporate transport markets. The K-1 prototype of this small tri-motor, which appeared from the Joseph Kreutzer Corporation of Venice, California, in the second half of 1928, was a four-place aircraft with three 55 hp Velie engines. The 13 production aircraft which followed were all built as six-seaters. Four of these were K-2s, with a 90 hp LeBlond radial in the nose and a 65 hp LeBlond under each wing. With 85 US gal of fuel, this version had a payload capacity of 1,000lb and was certificated in July 1929.

The K-3, which gained its ATC a month earlier, had a greater reserve of power (all three engines being 90 hp LeBlonds), but only three, including one converted from a K-2, were completed. This converted aircraft subsequently became the first of eight K-5s, the principal and most powerful model, and received its type certificate in September 1929. The Air Coach was well built, well appointed and reliable, but production in Depression-hit America ended in 1930 or 1931. An unsuccessful attempt was made to revive it in 1935 as the Air Transport Manufacturing Company T-6.

Second production Flamingo, the six-seat G-2 (NC588)

Cunningham-Hall PT-6

First flown on April 3, 1929, the PT-6 (Personal Transport, six-place) was a tubby, orthodox biplane designed by Randolph F. Hall of the Cunningham-Hall Aircraft Corporation of Rochester, New York. One passenger sat beside the pilot, the other four in the roomy and comfortable enclosed cabin to the rear; powerplant was an uncowled Wright J6 Whirlwind radial engine. The PT-6 was certificated in July 1929 but only one other example was built. A further six, with 365 hp Wright engines in NACA cowlings, were completed in the late 1930s as PT-6F freighters, with payload and maximum take-off weight increased by about 200lb.

Metal Aircraft G-2 Flamingo

The Flamingo was designed by Ralph R. Graichen of the Halpin Development Co, the prototype G-MT-6 (Graichen Metal Transport, six-place) appearing in 1928. Powered by a 420 hp Wasp engine, it showed such promise that the Metal Aircraft Corporation was formed later that year in Cincinnati to undertake series production. At least 21 Flamingos were built, the first two aircraft being designated G-1 (a five-seater) and G-2 (six seats). Each was powered by a 450 hp Wasp, and most other Flamingos (designated G-2-W) were eight-seaters with the same powerplant. There were three examples (a six-seater and two eight-seaters) of the G-2-H, which had a 525 hp Hornet engine, higher operating weights and improved performance. Dual controls and night flying equipment were standard.

Original purchasers included two local operators, Embry-Riddle (later to become part of American Airways) and Mason & Dixon Air Lines, and United States Airways of Kansas City. The Flamingo entered service in the autumn of 1928. Its reliability quickly enabled the manufacturer to offer a six-year constructional warranty, and the type continued in airline use until the mid-1930s, when it began a new career as a bush transport.

Cessna DC-6

In late 1928, following the AW and its higher-powered BW derivative, Clyde Cessna produced the six-seat CW-6. In 1929 he and his handful of workers moved into a new 55,000 sq ft factory in Wichita, where they built a new four-seat cabin monoplane known as the DC-6. Powered at first by a 170 hp Curtiss Challenger engine, it flew on April 3, 1929, and took Cessna's cantilevering philosophy a stage further by dispensing with the tailplane bracing struts that had characterised his earlier designs.

Certification of the DC-6 was received in August 1929. Five examples were completed, of which four were later re-engined with 225 hp Wright J6 Whirlwinds. Take-off and landing characteristics of the DC-6 were demonstrably better than those of any other participant in the National Air Tour of 1929. Follow-on models were the DC-6A and DC-6B, differing in their powerplants and performance. About two dozen of each were built over the period 1929–35, and production would doubtless have been greater but for the fact that for three of those years the factory was closed because of the Depression. Four DC-6As and four DC-6Bs survived to be impressed for military service with the USAAF in 1942, when they were designated UC-77 and UC-77A respectively.

Clyde Cessna resumed the presidency of the company in early 1934 and appointed as plant manager his nephew Dwane Wallace, an engineer formerly employed by Beech Aircraft Corporation. Together with Eldon Cessna, Clyde's son, they combined the best features of the AW and DC-6 to produce the C-3, which in turn was developed into the highly successful C-34.

DC-6B (C631K), a typical Clyde Cessna design of the late 1920s

Boeing Model 80

The Model 80, first flown in August 1928, was designed as a 12-seat luxury passenger transport. Its roomy cabin was equipped with leather-upholstered seats, individual reading lamps, hot and cold running water, and forced-air ventilation; a 39 cu ft baggage hold was located beneath the crew cabin. A full-time cabin attendant (male) was carried on early flights, but before long Boeing Air Transport introduced

on its daily Golden Gate–Lake Michigan service the world's first airline stewardesses, all of them trained nurses. The enclosed crew cabin itself was an airline novelty: veteran pilots, used to feeling the wind in their faces, persuaded Boeing to convert one Model 80A into an open-cockpit 80B, but it was soon restored to Model 80A standard.

The 18-passenger 80A, of which ten were built, differed

C226M, the fourth Boeing 80A, had enlarged overwing fuel tanks and a modified vertical tail

from the original Model 80 (four built, 410 hp Wasp engines) in having more powerful engines (525 hp Hornet Bs), increased fuel capacity and a modified fin and rudder, as well as more seats. In its turn the 80A was updated as the 80A-1 with reduced fuel load and auxiliary fins and rudders. The 80A-1 was a mixed-traffic version (12 passengers plus 1,145lb of mail or cargo), although it was used by BAT, with the passenger

seats removed, as an airborne post office/sorting office for a scheduled night mail service between Salt Lake City and Oakland, California. Appearance of the Boeing 247 led to the withdrawal of the Model 80 from regular service in 1933. One other example, designated Model 226, was completed as a six-seat executive transport for the Standard Oil Company of California.

Typical of the Boeing 80A after entry into service, this United Air Lines aircraft (NC224M) was operated with engine cowlings removed and small auxiliary fins and rudders added. In this form it was designated Model 80A-1

Keystone K-78D Patrician (NC10N) in the insignia of
Transcontinental Air Transport Inc

Keystone K-78D Patrician

A descendant of the Huff-Daland Airplane Co, builder of America's first cropdusting biplane, Keystone Aircraft Corporation was formed in March 1927 and is best remembered for the biplane bombers that it built for the US Army Air Corps. The company's first venture in the commercial transport aircraft market was the K-78 Patrician, a large-capacity tri-motor which was built in late 1928, in anticipation of the expected boom in air transport. It received Group 2 approval in June 1929 and a full ATC four months later, but was yet another victim of the Depression. Only three examples are known to have been built, although govern-

ment approval was given for an initial batch of ten.

After completing flight tests the prototype Patrician carried out charter work with Colonial Air Transport between New York and Boston. The first K-78D production example was sold to Wright Aeronautical Corporation (as a Cyclone engine testbed and corporate transport) and the second was delivered to Transcontinental Air Transport (TAT), though its career was short-lived. The Patrician was the largest and fastest tri-motor commercial transport of its day, with a 20ft-long cabin accommodating 18 passengers, 600lb of baggage and a toilet compartment.

**Consolidated Model 16
Commodore**

Forerunner of the Pan American flying-boat "Clipper" fleets of the later 1930s, the Commodore was built initially to an order for 14 from the New York, Rio and Buenos Aires Line (NYRBA), set up in 1929 to link the major cities of North, Central and South America. The design (by I. M. Laddon) was based on that of his earlier XPY-1 long-range patrol flying boat for the US Navy, and the prototype (X-855M) was completed in the early part of 1929. A large twin-engined, twin-tailed flying boat, the original Model 16 had seating for 18 passengers in addition to the crew of three. Only the first three Commodores were built to this configuration: the Model 16-1 (nine built) seated 22 passengers, and the Model 16-2 (two completed) had maximum accommodation for 30 passengers. The prototype was later modified to Model 16-1 standard. The cabin of the Model 16-1 was divided into two eight-seat forward compartments, with a six-seat lounge to the rear. On the Model 16-2 the lounge was at the front, followed by three eight-seat compartments. Other features included a toilet, radio compartment and a 200 cu ft cargo/baggage hold.

NYRBA made its first route-proving flight with the Commodore (flagship *Buenos Aires*) in July 1929. Certification was received in November 1929 and the first scheduled services (Miami–Buenos Aires) began in the following February. In August 1930 NYRBA and the ten Commodores then in service were acquired by Pan American, which bought the outstanding four aircraft from Consolidated in October and opened a service from Kingston (Jamaica) to Panama in early December. Commodores continued to operate with Pan Am for many years, some still flying on local-service routes in the Bahamas in the mid-1940s.

NYRBA's *Havana* **(NC659M) was an 18-passenger Model 16 Commodore. Later versions accommodated 22–30 people**

The twin-tailed F-32 prototype (X124M) in Universal Air Lines
markings

Western Air Express Fokker F-32 (NC334N)

Fokker F-32

A 1920s equivalent of the latter-day "Jumbo," the F-32 (so designated on account of the number of passengers it could accommodate) was a design ahead of its time. It was also ill timed, however, for it was undoubtedly a victim of the Depression years. The prototype, originally twin-tailed, flew for the first time on September 13, 1929, but was destroyed in a take-off crash just over two months later, causing Universal to withdraw its order for five. The other launch customer, Western Air Express (which had also ordered five), in the end accepted only two; one F-32 underwent US Army evaluation as the YC-20 troop transport; the fifth and sixth aircraft were retained as Fokker demonstrators; and the seventh and last was fitted out as a personal "air yacht" for Anthony Fokker.

The two airline Fokkers, which began operating on the Los Angeles–San Francisco route on April 1, 1930, maintained an unblemished safety record with Western (and, after the WAE/TAT merger, with TWA) until their retirement in June of the following year. Their cabins were divided into eight compartments, each containing four armchairs and a folding table (or two sleeping berths for night operation). But Western found difficulty in filling all the seats and for a time operated its F-32s as 28-passenger aircraft. The aircraft was tail-heavy, not easy to fly, and was said to suffer problems with the cooling of the rear elements of its back-to-back paired engines. Its CAA licence was revoked in December 1931, ending the career of the first Fokker airliner to have four engines and the last to be designed in the United States.

Consolidated Fleetster

The Fleetster's *raison d'être* was the need for back-up local feederline services at the South American end of the routes flown by NYRBA (New York, Rio and Buenos Aires Line). Reuben H. Fleet, president and general manager of Consolidated Aircraft Corporation, inspired the type's creation and gave it his name. Designed by I. M. Laddon, the first (Model 17) Fleetster flew in October 1929. Three were delivered to NYRBA three months later, flying services from Rio and Buenos Aires into Bolivia, Chile, Paraguay and Uruguay. The five passenger seats in the cabin could be removed for cargo-carrying, and the Fleetsters operated with either wheel or twin-float landing gear. A fourth Model 17 was used by the Assistant Secretary for War as a personal transport; one Model 17-2C was operated by Pacific International Airlines in Alaska; and three nine-passenger Model 17-AFs were used by Ludington Air Lines for a New York–Washington shuttle service.

The parasol-winged Model 20 Fleetster, also developed originally for NYRBA, was a passenger/cargo or all-cargo version which appeared in 1930. Four Model 20s were produced, followed in 1932 by the final version, the Model 20-A, which combined the parasol layout with the longer-span wings, modified landing gear and other features of the 17-AF. Seven were built for TWA (Transcontinental and Western Air), three later gravitating to Spain for use by the Republican forces during the Civil War.

The Fleetster was designed for the internal South American services of NYRBA. This Model 17 (NC657M) also operated on twin-float landing gear

Bellanca Skyrocket D (NC35N) of Pacific Seaboard Air Lines, which operated in the Los Angeles—San Francisco area in 1933

Model 31-55 Senior Skyrocket (NC15953) operated by the *Des Moines Register and Tribune*

Bellanca Skyrocket

The Skyrocket, a single-engined six-seater with an appropriate name (it had an initial climb rate of 1,250ft/min), came into being to meet demands for a livelier version of the popular CH-300 Pacemaker, and production totalled about 50. The first and most numerous version, of which 32 were built, was designated CH-400 and was powered by a 420 hp Wasp engine as standard, with a 450 hp supercharged version available optionally. Certification for this model was issued on April 30, 1930. It was followed two years later by approval for the Skyrocket Model D, a slightly heavier version with a 14in increase in wing span, new main landing gear, and the supercharged Wasp engine as standard. About six or seven Model Ds were built.

In April 1935 Bellanca received certification for the Senior Skyrocket 31-50 (525 hp Wasp S1D1) and 31-55 (550 hp Wasp S3H1), of which about a dozen were built. The Model D performed much better at altitude than the CH-400, and the significant power increase in the Senior Skyrocket produced a performance, in the 31-55 de luxe version, that included a top speed of 190 mph at 5,000ft and a cruising speed of 180 mph at 12,000ft. Other changes in the Senior included a wider fuselage, a long-chord NACA engine cowling, and an 8ft 6in increase in wing span.

Most Skyrockets were custom-built for business corporations or wealthy private owners (Hollywood actor Wallace Beery was one), but airline operators included Colorado-Utah Airways, which found the CH-400 ideal for its routes over mountainous areas. At least one CH-400 was still active at the end of the 1950s.

Boeing Model 200 Monomail (X725W) in 1930 demonstration scheme of green, grey and orange

Boeing Monomail

It took great courage for Boeing, in Depression-hit America, to break away from the safe tradition of wood-and-fabric, fixed-undercarriage biplanes and build this streamlined, cantilever-wing, all-metal monoplane with a semi-retractable landing gear. The original Monomail (Model 200), which first flew on May 6, 1930, in fact proved too far ahead of its time for its own good. Lacking a variable-pitch propeller (not yet developed), it could not fully benefit from the performance inherent in its 575 hp Hornet B engine. As the name implied, it was designed for mail or cargo transportation, with a 220 cu ft payload compartment in the fuselage; a curious anachronism was the retention of an open cockpit for the pilot.

On August 18, 1930, Boeing flew a second aircraft (Model 221), which had an 8in-longer fuselage with a six-passenger cabin between the engine bay and a smaller mail compartment. This aircraft was operated by Boeing Air Transport, and subsequently both Monomails were modified to Model 221As, characterised by a further 2ft 3in fuselage stretch permitting the carriage of eight passengers plus 750lb of freight. Both served with BAT in this form, and the original aircraft continued for some time afterwards with United Air Lines.

Monomail prototype after conversion to Model 221A standard. Used commercially for brief periods by Boeing Air Transport and United Air Lines, it is shown here with an experimental fixed landing gear

Ogden Osprey

X150W was an Ogden Osprey PB, with three Menasco B-4 engines. This version received type approval on October 30, 1930

Founded in May 1929 at Inglewood, California, by Henry H. Ogden, formerly of the Joseph Kreutzer Corporation (and test pilot of that company's Air Coach), the Ogden Aeronautical Corporation's first product was the Osprey, a neat little tri-motor aimed at the feeder airline and business transport markets. Designed by Frederick G. Thearle, the Osprey made its first flight in summer/autumn 1929, reportedly powered by three 90/100 hp Kinner radial engines. These were soon replaced by Cirrus inverted in-lines, the smaller frontal area of which created less drag, and the Osprey was type-certificated in June 1930 as the Model PC (though frequently referred to also as the Model C).

Timing – it was the height of the Depression – was against commercial success, and only about six Ospreys were completed, some fitted or refitted with the 100 hp Cirrus, others as the Model PB with 95 or 125 hp Menasco B-4 in-lines. One is known to have been equipped with banners and loudspeakers for aerial advertising. In January 1933 Ogden was obliged to offer four Ospreys, one of them unused, for a knockdown price of $10,000 including spares; this compared with the 1931 fly-away factory price of $16,000 per aircraft.

Stinson SM-6000

Nearly 60 of these sturdy, reliable tri-motors were produced by the Stinson Aircraft Corporation of Wayne, Michigan, primarily for short-haul feeder services with the New York, Philadelphia & Washington Line (their first operator), American Airways (which eventually had about 24), Boston-Maine, Century Airlines, Chicago & Southern, Eastern, Delta, Pennsylvania Airlines and Transamerican. About half of these aircraft were still active at the end of the 1930s, and at least one still survived in 1982. Ten of the 14 initial-production SM-6000s went to NYP&WL, which also operated some of the upgraded SM-6000-B.

The SM-6000, certificated on July 10, 1930, was developed by Stinson from the smaller (seven-place) Models 3000 and 6000 tri-motors designed by the Corman Aircraft Corporation of Dayton, Ohio, and all or most were upgraded to the more versatile SM-6000-A standard, which gained certification in September 1930. This offered a standard ten-passenger version, one for eight/nine passengers plus 350lb of mail or cargo, an all-cargo model, and a six/eight-passenger club version. Wheel spats and Townend cowling rings were optional. The SM-6000-B, also known as the Stinson Model T, was the production version of the SM-6000-A. Further development, via the Model U, led to the Stinson Model A, described separately on page 69.

Forerunner of Northeast Airlines, Boston–Maine/Central Vermont was one of several Stinson SM-6000 operators in the early 1930s

Prototype Solar MS-1 (X258W) during an early test flight. A Group 2 type approval was granted on August 8, 1930

Solar MS-1

Well known today as a manufacturer of gas-turbine aero-engines and accessories, Solar had its origins in the Prudden-San Diego Airplane Co of the mid/late 1920s, run by the former chief engineer of the Stout Metal Airplane Co and producer of an all-metal eight-seat tri-motor monoplane designated XM-1. (According to one report, this aircraft "took off at 80, cruised at 80, and landed at 80"!) The company was joined in 1928 by Edmund T. Price, and became the Solar Aircraft Co in April 1929. By this time the TM-1 (a modified XM-1) had appeared, and had been further redesigned (as the SE-1) to single-engined configuration by fitting it with a Pratt & Whitney Wasp radial engine.

The MS-1, the company's third design, differed in having a sesquiplane configuration and made its first flight on January 21, 1930. Designed by William L. Lewis, it was described by test pilot Doug Kelley as "one of the finest closed planes I have ever flown". Comparable praise was soon forthcoming from no less an authority than Charles Lindbergh, who flew with Kelley in the MS-1 a few days later. Unfortunately, the Depression meant that no orders materialised, though there was almost a sale of 10 to Northwest Airways in the autumn of 1931. The prototype barely earned its keep with occasional charter flights, and it was eventually sold to a Mexican operator, who used it for transporting coffee beans.

Southern Air Transport's C8880 was an S-6000-B, a predecessor of
the Sedan 6-B built in 1929 by Travel Air before the Curtiss takeover

Curtiss-Wright Travel Air Sedan 6-B

A fattened-up version of the
Travel Air 6000 – the only Travel
Air design to continue in production after its acquisition (and
closure of its Wichita factory) by
Curtiss in the late 1920s – the
six-place Sedan 6-B was aimed
primarily at the business transport market, offering somewhat
better payload and performance. It first flew in mid-1930
and was certificated on August
13 of that year, but Curtiss-
Wright's Travel Air division at
St Louis, Missouri, built only a
handful. These were sold
initially to corporate owners but
were later resold as bush
transports, a role to which they
were perhaps more suited.

Bellanca P-100 in its original form, with Curtiss Conqueror engine

Bellanca Airbus

Giuseppe M. Bellanca's "lifting strut" philosophy reached its evolutionary zenith in the Airbus, a unique design perhaps best described as a cross between strut-braced biplane and sesquiplane. Derived from a 1928 design (the Model K), it flew for the first time in May 1930 and was certificated only three months later. In its original P-100 form the Airbus could accommodate 11–13 passengers in addition to the pilot, and with 65 per cent full fuel could carry a 3,000lb payload – almost one-third of its maximum take-off gross weight – on the power of only a single 600 hp Curtiss GV-1570 Conqueror V-12 engine. The P-100 successfully demonstrated direct operating costs of only eight cents per mile, but its price of $38,500 was too high to attract buyers, who were also not over-keen on the choice of powerplant.

The P-100 was accordingly converted to the much more acceptable (and suitable) Cyclone radial, and in this form, designated P-200, it gained certification as a 12-passenger transport on January 26, 1931; a 15-passenger P-300 model was available optionally. However, only three more civil examples were built, including one twin-float P-200-A which was operated for a short time by New York & Suburban Air-lines. More powerful versions (650 hp Cyclone or Hornet) were offered during 1932–34, and 14 Airbus with 550 hp Hornets were built as C-27 transports for the US Army Air Corps. In 1935 the Airbus was superseded by the larger Aircruiser, described separately on page 71.

Northrop Alpha 3 (NC942Y) of Transcontinental and Western Air

Northrop Alpha

A contemporary of the Boeing Monomail, the Alpha lacked a retractable undercarriage but was otherwise almost as advanced a design for its time. It was designed by John K. Northrop and made its maiden flight in the spring of 1930. Like the Monomail, it had an aft-of-the-wing open cockpit for the pilot. Six passengers could be accommodated in the fully enclosed cabin of the original Alpha 2, or three plus 465lb of mail/cargo in the mixed-traffic Alpha 3. TWA, with three Alpha 2s, six Alpha 3s and four mail-only Alpha 4s (payload 1,060lb), was the principal commercial operator. In four years of operation (1931–35) TWA's Alpha fleet flew nearly 5½ million miles. National Air Transport acquired one Alpha, the US Assistant Secretary of Commerce for Aeronautics had one as a personal transport, and three others were evaluated (unsuccessfully, so far as a production contract was concerned) as military transports by the Army Air Corps.

The Alpha 4 differed from earlier models in having trousered main-wheel leg fairings and a single cabin window on each side. TWA eventually brought all of its Alphas up to Alpha 4 (or similar Alpha 4A) standard, except for one Alpha 2 which was converted into an Alpha 3.

Sikorsky S-41

Although begun later than the bigger S-40 amphibian, the S-41 was completed more quickly. Making its first flight some months earlier, in the autumn of 1930, it was certificated as the S-41A in April 1931. The S-41 was essentially a scaled-up development of the earlier S-38 with more powerful engines (Hornet Bs instead of Wasps), the lower half-wing deleted, and the upper one increased in span. The hull was of new design and all-metal construction. Seven S-41As were built by Sikorsky Aviation Corporation. Three or four were operated by Pan American, chiefly in the Caribbean but also on its Boston-Halifax route and in South America.

Sikorsky S-41, a monoplane development of the S-38

Lockheed Orion

Last in the family of small monoplanes descended from the original Vega, the Orion was the most numerous of the four low-wing derivatives of this famous design. (The others were the Explorer single-seat racer, the two-seat Sirius and the Altair.) Forty Orions were built, including five by the conversion of other models. Principal versions were the Model 9 (18 built) and Model 9D (13 built). Both had accommodation for six passengers but the 9D differed in having flaps and a 550 hp (instead of 450 hp) Wasp engine. The Orion served with a number of US airlines, the largest domestic fleets being those of American Airways and Varney (six each); three others (Northwest, TWA and Wyoming Air Service) each had three. Ten Orions served in Mexico – five with Trasportes Aéreos de Chiapas, three with Aerovias Centrales and two with Mexicana – and two others were operated by Swissair.

Various other Orion variants included the Models 9B, 9F and 9F-1 (with 575, 645 and 650 hp Cyclone engines respectively); the Model 9E was powered by a 450 hp Wasp radial.

TWA's red-and-silver livery looked particularly effective on its Orions; NC12277 is illustrated

Pilgrim Model 100-A

The high-wing Fairchild 100 and low-wing Fairchild 150, both ten-place all-metal transports, eventually developed into the Pilgrim 100-A and General Aviation GA-43 (see page 63). Both were designed by Virginius E. Clark, and their common ancestry is immediately apparent. Rugged, reliable and easy to fly and maintain, the Pilgrim 100-A was deservedly popular, both in its initial incarnation with American Airways and in later service as a versatile bush aircraft. It was certificated in August 1931 and all 16 built remained with American until 1934, when some were acquired by Alaskan Airways and others by Pan American's Pacific-Alaska division. Another Pilgrim served with Byrd's second Antarctic expedition.

Able to operate as a nine-passenger transport or as a pilot-only all-cargo aircraft, the Pilgrim 100-A had underfloor belly compartments for baggage or freight which gave it a distinctly tubby outline. It could also combine a payload capacity of more than a ton with excellent STOL characteristics. The Model 100-B (certificated in March 1932), of which American Airways had six, was powered by a 575 hp R-1820-E Cyclone engine instead of the A model's Hornet, but otherwise differed only in detail. Production, by the American Airplane & Engine Corporation at Farmingdale, Long Island, was brought to an overall total of 26 by four Y1C-24 prototypes for the United States Army Air Corps. This variant was based on the Pilgrim 100-B but had a slimmer fuselage without the belly compartments.

Pilgrim 100-A of American Airways, which received all 16 of this version and six of the later 100-B

American Clipper **(NC80V), flagship of Pan Am's fleet of three Sikorsky S-40s**

Sikorsky S-40

One of Igor Sikorsky's prized possessions was a cheque for 5 cents, received in payment of a bet that the S-40 would not fly. This 17-ton amphibian was certainly a giant of its time, but it took to the air successfully in early 1931 and in the following year became the first Pan American "Clipper" type to enter service. Designed for an overwater range of 950 miles with 24 passengers, or to carry 40 people plus a ton of baggage or freight over 500 miles, it was at the time of its construction the largest aeroplane ever built in the USA.

Three S-40s were built, all for Pan Am, which used them extensively for a decade after their October 1931 certification, mostly in the Caribbean. They were generally operated as flying boats and in the mid-1930s were converted by Pan Am to S-40A standard, with 660 hp Hornet T2D1 engines. After Pearl Harbor, the S-40As were requisitioned by the US Navy for transport and training before being retired in 1943.

The second of Pan Am's S-40s, NC81V *Caribbean Clipper***; the third was NC752V** *Southern Clipper*

Ford Model 14-A

The Model 14-A was the last fling of the Ford Motor Company before it pulled out of the manufacture of aeroplanes in January 1933. The 14-A was actually a redesign of an earlier project, the Model 10-A, which was to have had four Pratt & Whitney Hornet engines but which was never built. Instead, the design was reworked as the three-engined Model 14-A with a 1,100 hp Hispano-Suiza above the fuselage and two 715 hp Hispanos buried in the wings. Span and length were 110ft and 81ft respectively. Completed in February 1932, the 40-passenger 14-A was ground-tested but never flown.

X9660, the one-off Ford Model 14-A. It never flew

Beechcraft Model 17

It took a lot of courage, and a lot of his own money, for Walter H. Beech to form Beech Aircraft in April 1932 after selling off Travel Air to the Curtiss-Wright Corporation. Yet, with the Depression at its worst, he set out to build a fast and luxurious four/five-seat cabin biplane capable of a 200 mph top speed and 1,000 miles range at a price of $19,000. His faith was rewarded, for his Model 17 became one of the most popular civil aircraft ever built, the surviving examples of which are prized possessions whose value continues to increase as the years go by.

The Model 17 began as a development of the Travel Air "Mystery" racing monoplane, to which was added an upper wing with backward stagger, hence the type's popular sobriquet of "Staggerwing". The first four aircraft, all with fixed undercarriage, comprised two 17Rs (with 420 hp Wright Whirlwind) and two A17Fs (700 hp Cyclone). First flight, by one of the 17Rs, was made on November 4, 1932, and certification was received on December 20 of the same year. First production model, introducing retractable main gear, was the B17L of 1934 with a 225 hp Jacobs L4 engine. Successive airframe improvements were marked by prefix letters C to G, and engine changes by suffix letters A (350 hp Whirlwind), B and D (Jacobs L5 and L6), S (450 hp Wasp Junior) and W (600 hp Cyclone). Most popular model was the D17S, certificated under ATC No 649 on July 16, 1937, which accounted for 300 or more of the 781 Staggerwings built before production ended in 1948. Included in this total were 207 wartime UC-43s and 63 GB-1/2s for the US Army and Navy, many of which came on to the civil market after the war. Final model was the post-war G17S, of which 87 were completed.

About 200 Staggerwings are still flying today in many parts of the world. Their pilots are true aficionados who don't worry about their age, their thirsty engines or the fact that, on the ground, there is virtually no forward and downward view from the cockpit. They find them a delight to fly and still as reliable as ever, and know that they own examples of one of the civil-aviation immortals.

Second production Beechcraft B17L (NC12584), in the insignia of Aero Mobiloil

This view of a Boeing 247 (NC13315) shows well the "undercut" windscreen of the initial version, some of which were operated by Western Air Express after their withdrawal by United

Before joining United Air Lines this Boeing 247D (NR257Y) was a successful competitor in the 1934 MacRobertson air race from England to Australia

Boeing Model 247

When it appeared in 1933 the Boeing 247 was at least 50 mph faster than the standard airliners then in service. That alone would have been enough to attract the attention of potential operators; added to individual armchair seating (at a generous 40in pitch) for its ten passengers, a galley and toilet facilities, large compartments for up to 400lb of baggage, and a stewardess, it represented a most attractive improvement over the standards of the day. The first 247, a production aircraft, made its initial flight on February 8, 1933, by which time Boeing already had orders for nearly 60. Most of these were from BAT, Pacific Air Transport, National Air Transport and Varney Air Lines, which all operated from 1934 as United Air Lines; two others went to DLH in Germany.

United also received ten of the 13 later Model 247Ds. These had geared engines, long-chord NACA cowlings, variable-pitch propellers and a conventional windscreen instead of the cut-back screen of the original model. The 247/247Ds continued to be operated by United until early 1942, when all but one of the fleet were impressed into USAAF service as C-73s. By then, however, the United fleet was of modest size, having shrunk to 24 by January 1938 after the sale of 36 of the 60 originally acquired to other airlines in the USA and elsewhere.

Eastern Air Transport Curtiss T-32 Condor (NC12353)

Curtiss Condor

Thirty-four civil and 11 military examples of this portly biplane, comprising 21 of the initial T-32 model and 13 of the later AT-32 with supercharged engines and increased fuel tankage, had been manufactured by September 1934. First flight by a T-32 was made on January 30, 1933; the name Condor perpetuated that of the earlier (1929) Curtiss Model 18. Curtiss built nine T-32s for Eastern Air Transport, nine for American Airways, two (as YC-30s) for evaluation by the US Army Air Corps, and one (with extra tankage and non-retractable wheel/float/ski gear) for Richard E. Byrd's 1933 Antarctic expedition.

Superchargers and variable-pitch propellers significantly improved the performance of the AT-32. Two AT-32-E 12-seat transports went (as R4C-1s) to the US Navy, and in 1934 one 15-seat AT-32-C served briefly with Swissair before being lost in a crash. The other ten, consisting of three AT-32-As (12 seats, 710 hp SGR-1820-F3 engines), three AT-32-Bs (12 seats, 720 hp SGR-1820-F2 engines), and four AT-32-Ds (-F2 engines and 15 seats), all went to American Airlines/ Airways. The A and B models were dual-role daytime or sleeper transports. The Condor had a long and active life, the civil examples later serving with operators in Alaska, Burma, Canada, Central and South America, China, Europe and Mexico. Several survived the Second World War, the last example being a Peruvian Air Force Condor which was not scrapped until 1956.

First example (X13149) of the Pitcairn PA-19

Pitcairn PA-19

In spite of its successes with smaller, private-owner auto-gyros, the Pitcairn Autogiro Company of Willow Grove, Pennsylvania, tackled an ambitious venture for the early 1930s in the form of the larger PA-19. The design – by R. C. B. Noorduyn – was ahead of its time and incorporated a degree of stability, aerodynamic cleanness, reliability and passenger comfort unprecedented in auto-gyros at that time. It first flew in September 1932 and received certification on June 23, 1933. Unfortunately, the PA-19 could not survive the economic climate of the times, and only four or five had been built when Harold F. Pitcairn's company decided to cut its losses and withdrew from the manufacture of autogyros.

Sperry Gyroscope's Reliant NC17114 was an SR-9D

Stinson Reliant

The Reliant started out in the spring of 1933 as the 215 hp four-seat Model SR and ended its civil production life, eight years and nearly 800 aircraft later, with versions carrying five people in much greater comfort on more than twice the original power. It remained popular, many customers trading in early Stinsons for the newer models as they appeared. After the original SR (88 built) the next large-scale series was the SR-5 of 1934, of which about 150 were built in models up to the SR-5F, mostly with Lycoming R-680 engines of 225 to 260 hp. About 50 SR-6s were produced in 1935, and a similar number of SR-7s in the following year.

Most variations between models concerned powerplant and/or cabin comfort. The only major design change came with the SR-7, which introduced a new, double-tapered wing offering a 21.5 sq ft increase in area despite a 1ft 8in reduction in span. This worked wonders for Reliant performance and sales, and remained standard on the subsequent SR-8 series (over 120 built), SR-9 (175-200) and SR-10 (over 80). More than 100 Reliants were powered by versions of the Wright R-760 seven-cylinder Whirlwind, and the Pratt & Whitney Wasp Junior appeared in the SR-9F and SR-10F of 1937–38. But throughout its career the most

popular engine was the 245 hp Lycoming R-680-6, although ratings went as high as 300 hp in the SR-10J.

A deservedly successful aeroplane, ready to do almost anything asked of it, the Reliant was used most of all by corporate and private owners, though airline operators included Alaskan Airways, Wien Airways, Wyoming Air Service and Northwest Airlines.

Douglas DC-1

In 1932 Jack Frye, vice-president (operations) of TWA, asked five American companies to produce an airliner that would compete with the Boeing 247. Most major US airlines at that time were flying such types as the big Curtiss Condor biplane or the Ford and Fokker tri-motors; Frye's specification also called for three engines, to preserve the existing safety factor if one engine failed. However, Douglas convinced him that its twin-engined DC-1 could meet his safety requirements and delivered the prototype to TWA in September 1933, following a first flight on July 1.

During the first half of 1934 the DC-1 set 11 US and eight international class records for distance and speed, so impressing TWA with its potential that the airline decided *not* to order it. Instead, TWA opted for the slightly larger and more powerful DC-2. The DC-1 was flown originally with 700 hp Pratt & Whitney Hornet engines, but these were replaced after its November 1933 certification by a pair of 710 hp Wright Cyclones. In the latter form it had a much better payload/range performance than the Boeing 247, carried 12 passengers compared with its rival's ten, and had 35 mph more cruising speed.

The Douglas DC-1 (X223Y), photographed on the day of its maiden flight

General Aviation (Clark) GA-43

The GA-43 remains relatively little known among US commercial transport aircraft, yet it was one of the most innovative designs of the early 1930s and worthy of comparison with the Boeing Monomail and Northrop Alpha. A cantilever all-metal monoplane with retractable main landing gear, it could accommodate 10 or 11 passengers seated individually on leather-upholstered seats in a roomy, heated, ventilated and sound-insulated cabin which was also provided with a toilet. There were two fuselage cargo/baggage compartments totalling 87 cu ft, and a further 52 cu ft of space could be found in the wing roots. Its high speed and economical operation should have ensured its success, but only five were completed, of which only three went into airline service.

The GA-43 originated as the Fairchild (later Pilgrim) Model 150, designed in 1931 by Virginius E. Clark, and the fixed-gear prototype (X-775N) flew for the first time on May 22, 1932. This aircraft and the design rights were sold later that year to the General Aviation Manufacturing Corporation of Dundalk, Md, which was responsible for introducing the rearward-retracting main gear and a number of detail improvements. General's first three production GA-43As were to this standard, with 710 or 715 hp Cyclone engines, and the first was delivered to Swiss Air Lines (Swissair) in March 1934. The second was retained as a company demonstrator; the third, after a brief spell with General Air Lines (alias Western Air Express), went to Swissair in March 1935. The fourth and final production aircraft, for SCADTA, Pan American's South American affiliate, was delivered in November 1934 as a GA-43J, powered by a 650/700 hp Hornet T1C engine, and fitted with split flaps, twin Edo floats and an enlarged fin.

By the time that the GA-43A was certificated, in February 1934, General had merged with the Berliner-Joyce company to become a division of the newly formed North American Aviation Inc. Later that year the Fairchild 150/GA-43 prototype was sold to Japan, where Nakajima gleaned much useful structural information before re-selling it to the paramilitary transport fleet of Manchukuo. Swissair's original GA-43A turned up in Spain during the Civil War, flying for the Republican forces; its second aircraft was lost in a crash in April 1936.

Clark GA-43 (NC13903) of Western Air Express at Denver Municipal Airport, Colorado

Two of the four DC-2s operated by General Air Lines (the former Western Air Express, later to become part of Western Airlines)

Douglas DC-2

Carrying 14 passengers – two more than its predecessor – the DC-2 maintained the overall performance of the DC-1 with only a modest initial increase in power and despite being more than 1,000lb heavier at take-off. TWA placed an order with Douglas for 20 DC-2s (later increased to 31), and first put the type into operation on its Columbus–Newark route on May 18, 1934, exactly one week after the aircraft's maiden flight. Other US customers included American (16), Eastern (ten), Pan American (nine), Panagra (five) and General (four). Principal foreign operators of the DC-2 were KLM/KNILM (24), Japan Airlines (six), Swissair (six), CLS of Czechoslovakia (five), LAPE of Spain (five), CNAC/Canton Airlines (four) and LOT of Poland (two). During the Second World War about ten captured examples were included among the Deutsche Lufthansa fleet.

Total DC-2 production, including 63 military examples for the Army Air Corps and US Navy, amounted to 198 aircraft, most of which had a basic powerplant of Cyclone, Hornet (DC-2A) or Bristol Pegasus (DC-2B) engines. A standard KLM DC-2 won the transport section of the 1934 MacRobertson England–Australia race, and in the overall speed section was second only to the D.H.88 Comet racer.

Control tower at Croydon Airport forms the background for three of Swissair's four DC-2s, which began a Switzerland–UK service in the winter of 1935–36

Pan American Airways System S-42. Take-off time was less than 20sec

Sikorsky S-42

Before the huge S 40 had been in service very long, Pan American made known its requirement for an even larger overwater transport with more speed and longer range, including the ability to fly non-stop stages of 2,500 miles with a reduced load of 12 passengers. The S-42, one of two designs produced to meet this requirement (the other was the Martin 130), was a great advance on its predecessor. It was built almost entirely of metal, with a flush-riveted skin and two-step hull; the braced wings had split flaps and outrigger floats instead of the more fashionable fuselage-mounted sponsons. The wing-mounted engines drove three-blade variable-pitch propellers.

First flight was made on March 29, 1934, and by the end of that year the S-42 had set ten world seaplane records: one for height with payload (20,407ft with 11,025lb), one for payload to height (16,610lb to 6,560ft), and eight for speed over a 1,000 or 2,000km closed circuit. Ten aircraft of this type were built altogether: three S-42s (certificated July 1934), four S-42As (December 1935) and three S-42Bs (fitted with additional fuel tanks for route-survey flying across the Atlantic and Pacific).

The S-42 entered Pan Am service in April 1935, operating initially between San Francisco and Hawaii. Later the type also flew on the airline's New York–Bermuda, Miami–South America and Manila–Hong Kong routes. Although capable of seating up to 40 daytime passengers, the S-42s more usually accommodated 32 and the available 14-passenger sleeper layout was seldom if ever used. However, even with only 12 daytime passengers they fell well below the range required of them, and the longer trans-oceanic routes were left to the Martin 130.

A Pan Am Sikorsky S-42B at its moorings

NC13764, the first production V-1A, in American Airlines insignia

Vultee V-1A

A contemporary of the Northrop Delta, Gerard Vultee's V-1A was cast in a similar mould as a high-speed, high-comfort passenger-carrier of modest capacity. Of all-metal construction, with a monocoque fuselage and retractable landing gear, it was flown for the first time in early 1933 and gained its ATC in July of the following year. One V-1 prototype and 25 V-1A production aircraft were completed by the Aircraft Development Corporation of Glendale, California.

The major operator was American Airlines, which used the prototype for early route-proving and then had a fleet of ten on its Fort Worth–St Louis–Chicago service. Bowen Air Lines of Texas had two, and Colonial Airways one; most of the others went to oil and newspaper companies as corporate transports.

High cruising speed was a feature of the V-1A, which set a number of impressive point-to-point records, beginning in January 1935 with a trans-US flight from Burbank to New York by Jimmy Doolittle in one minute under 12hr. A twin-engined development of the V-1A was planned, but in 1936 Vultee decided – with justification, as events were to prove – to concentrate his activities in the more lucrative area of military aircraft design.

British Airways Model 10A Electra (G-AEPN)

Lockheed Model 10 Electra

In June 1932, when Lockheed was re-formed at Burbank under Lloyd C. Stearman as Lockheed Aircraft Corporation, the company's prime objective was still to build fast, economical short-range transports. Now, however, there was a major difference, for the aircraft on which it pinned its post-Depression hopes was twin-engined. The Electra did not let Lockheed down and became the progenitor of a family of company twins that achieved success after success, keeping the production lines busy for a decade.

The Model 10 first flew on February 23, 1934, and 22 had been ordered by mid-year. Production, which extended into 1941, eventually totalled 149, including small numbers for the US Army and Navy and other military customers. The commercial order book was opened by Northeast and Pan American, airline service beginning with the former operator in August 1934, only a few days after certification. Other domestic operators of the Model 10A (the main version, of which more than 100 were completed) included Boston–Maine, Braniff, Mid-Continent and National, while Delta, Eastern and Chicago & Southern preferred the Model 10B with 440 hp Wright R-975-E3 Whirlwinds.

More powerful versions, mainly for use in Alaska,

Ten-passenger interior of a Boston–Maine/Central Vermont Airways Electra. Side by side in the seat pockets are airline and railway timetables: the airline was owned and operated at the time by the Maine Central railroad

Mexico and South America, were the Model 10C (450 hp Wasp SC1) and Model 10E (550 hp Wasp S3H1). Foreign sales of the Electra were made to Australia (Ansett and MacRobertson Miller), Brazil (Panair do Brasil), Canada (TCAL), Guinea (Guinea Airways), Mexico (Mexicana), Netherlands (KLM), New Zealand (Union Airways), Poland (LOT), Romania (LARES), the UK (British Airways), Venezuela (LAV) and Yugoslavia (Aeroput).

It was in a Model 10E Electra that Amelia Earhart disappeared while on a round-the-world flight in July 1937. Happier Electra 10Es included the one which, two months earlier, rushed urgent press photos of the coronation of King George VI across the Atlantic to America, and another which, as the US Army's XC-35, carried out much useful high-altitude research flying which benefited later generations of pressurised commercial transport aircraft.

One of six Electra 10As ordered by Pan American for its Mexico and Central/South American routes

The Richfield Eagle (**NC13777**), a Delta 1D in corporate ownership with a well-known oil company

Northrop Gamma/Delta

Although used less widely for revenue-earning flying than its predecessor, the Alpha, the Northrop Gamma played a useful part in advancing the performance levels of commercial aircraft in the 1930s. Appearing in 1933, it was basically a development of the mail/cargo Alpha 4, and TWA augmented its Alpha fleet by ordering three Gamma 2Ds. Jack Frye, the airline's vice-president, set a new US transcontinental record for transport aircraft in one of these on May 13/14, 1934, by flying with a 440lb payload from Los Angeles to Newark in 11hr 31min. Another TWA Gamma, fitted with a turbocharger, explored icing, turbulence and other high-altitude weather problems at heights of up to 35,000ft. An early Gamma, *Sky Chief*, was flown from San Diego to New York in 13hr 27min, at an average speed of 183 mph, in June 1933.

The Delta, planned originally as an eight-passenger development of the Gamma, saw comparatively little commercial service, though Canadian Vickers produced 20 for the RCAF. Civil Deltas were sold to TWA (one, used as a mail transport), Aerovias Centrales of Mexico and AB Aerotransport of Sweden.

Stinson Model A

Structurally similar to Stinson's 1931 Model 6000, the Model A was – despite an appearance to the contrary – a cantilever monoplane design. The one-piece wing had a single steel-tube truss spar, steel ribs, and a stressed dural skin inboard of the engine nacelles and fabric outboard. The two prominent overwing struts on each side were added not to provide support for the wing but to absorb some of the stress during landings. There were baggage compartments in the rear of each wing-mounted engine nacelle, in addition to the main baggage/freight hold at the back of the passenger cabin. On some Model As the nose engine was fitted with a NACA cowling. The Model A entered service with Delta in mid-1934 and shortly afterwards with Central (later a part of Pennsylvania-Central); the former operator relegated its Stinsons to night duty only a year later. American Airlines also briefly operated the Model A.

In 1936 Airlines of Australia operated three Stinson As between Sydney and Brisbane. These were acquired six years later by Australian National Airways, which converted them after the war by fitting 600 hp Wasps on the wings and deleting the nose-mounted third engine. In this A/2m configuration the aircraft had a gross weight of 11,200lb and could cruise at 166 mph at 7,000ft.

Fine study of a Delta Air Lines Stinson Model A (NC14598)

Burnelli UB-14 prototype (X15320)

Burnelli UB-14

The Remington-Burnelli RB-1/2 biplanes (see page 17) represented Vincent J. Burnelli's first attempts to prove his "lifting fuselage" concept. They were followed in 1928 by a strut-braced monoplane, the CB-16, which flew just before Christmas. Built for Sky Lines Inc by the Aeromarine company of Keyport, New Jersey, the all-metal CB-16 was powered by two 500 hp Curtiss Conqueror engines, carried a crew of two in open cockpits, and could seat up to 20 passengers. The main landing gear was retractable. In 1929 came the UB-20, another 20-passenger aircraft and powered by two 750 hp Packard engines. The "UB" designation reflected the fact that Burnelli had joined forces with I. M.

Uppercu of Aeromarine and become vice-president and chief designer of the newly formed Aeromarine Klemm Corporation.

Further development led to the UB-14 with tapered wings and fully retractable under-carriage. This made its first flight in late 1934 but was lost in a crash in January 1935 (happily non-fatal) following a control system failure. A second aircraft, from which this problem was eliminated, was designated UB-14B and was later re-engined with 750 hp Hornets. Arrangements were made in mid-1936 for a version with Rolls-Royce Kestrels to be built under licence in London by the Scottish Aircraft and Engine Co, but this company went into

liquidation in early 1937. Subsequent plans for a round-the-world record flight by the UB-14B were thwarted by the outbreak of war, during which the aircraft was operated by TACA for three years. Meanwhile, a British version had appeared as the Cunliffe-Owen OA-1, first flown on January 12, 1939, and certificated in November 1940. Similar externally to the UB-14B, it was redesigned structurally and was powered by 710 hp Bristol Perseus XIVC engines. The planned Mk II production version did not materialise, but the OA-1 prototype served first with the RAF and then with the Free French Air Force before ending its days on a VJ-night bonfire.

Wartime Burnelli designs included the XCG-16A experimental heavy-lift glider of 1943, before the return of peace brought the final instalment in the Burnelli story. This was the CBY-3 Loadmaster, based very much on the UB-14B and built by Cancargo, a subsidiary of the Canadian Car & Foundry Ltd. Powered by 1,200 hp R-1830 Twin Wasp engines, the CBY-3 made its first flight in August 1945 and was operated for several years by various US and South American owners before being returned to the USA and refitted with R-2600 Wright Cyclones. The Loadmaster was acquired by the Connecticut Air Museum in the mid-1960s.

Bellanca Aircruiser

Joseph P. Juptner, in Volume 6 of his indispensable *US Civil Aircraft,* describes the Aircruiser (certified on March 16, 1935) as "just an old Airbus with a little more guts and a lot more muscle". Just how much muscle is indicated by the contribution to overall lifting area made by the lower stub wings and aerofoil-shaped outer lifting struts: 198.5 sq ft, to add to the 465.7 sq ft of the main wing. The resulting total of 664.2 sq ft explains the first element in the designations applied to Bellanca aeroplanes at this time. The second element indicated engine power: thus the Aircruiser was offered in 66-67, 66-70, 66-75, 66-76 and 66-85 form, with Cyclone or Hornet engines of 670, 715, 730/750, 760 and 850 hp respectively. This extra "guts and muscle" was best demonstrated by the all-cargo version of the Aircruiser 66-70, which had an empty weight of 5,731lb yet could lift a useful load of 6,100lb, including 150 US gal of fuel.

Ironically, the Aircruiser's very ability was its undoing, for single-engined transports of such size and weight were virtually excluded on safety grounds from US airline operation. Bellanca had always believed that the use of one good, reliable engine was preferable to the additional problems and cost of a multi-engine installation. But no exceptions could be made, and the handful of Aircruisers built all went to delighted owners in Canada, where some were still in operation 30 years later as living proof of their efficiency and reliability.

Bellanca 66-75 Aircruiser bearing Philippine registration NPC41. It was later operated in Canada as CF-BTW

Cessna C-34

Prototype Cessna C-34 (NC12599)

In 1934 Cessna's Pawnee Road (Wichita) factory began to make its mark in general aviation after the rigours of the Depression. The Model 34 (indicating the year of its design) was rolled out on June 1 of the following year and received its CAA type certificate shortly afterwards. A direct descendant of the AW and DC-6 series, it marked the beginning of a new family of four-seat cabin monoplanes, all retrospectively dubbed Airmaster. The prototype was still flying in the 1970s.

One C-34 won the *Detroit News* Trophy race in 1935, and after another example won the same event in 1936 the C-34 was widely publicised as "the world's most efficient airplane". These achievements helped Cessna to reach a C-34 production rate of three per month in 1936, a total of 33 being produced in that year compared with nine in the preceding year. The C-34, the first Cessna type to be fitted with flaps, was exported to Argentina, Australia, Canada, Mexico and Portugal (one each), South Africa (two) and the UK (two). Two US examples were impressed as USAAF UC-77Bs in 1942.

The first Martin M-130 on an early test flight as X14714. It subsequently became Pan American's *Hawaii Clipper*

The third and last M-130 was NC14716 *China Clipper*, a name often used collectively for all three M-130s

Martin M-130

These huge trans-oceanic flying boats, of which only three were built, established a reputation in the 1930s out of all proportion to their number. Like the Sikorsky S-42, the M-130 was developed to meet the requirements of Pan American World Airways, chosen by the US Government as the carrier to set up air routes across the Pacific. While the Sikorskys were used for many of the preliminary survey flights, the larger Martins possessed the greater payload/range performance needed for regular service (though, even by mid-1930s standards, 12 passengers over non-stop stages of 2,500 miles was hardly an economic proposition).

Martin laid the first keel in May 1933 and Pan Am confirmed an order for three M-130s in the following year. A feature of the all-metal design

was the first use on a US flying boat of aerofoil-shaped sponsons, or "sea wings," to stabilise the aircraft on the water, provide additional lift and serve as extra fuel storage. (In fact nearly half of the 3,800 US gal fuel load was carried in the sponsons.) Aft of the flight deck the 45ft cabin was divided into three eight-seat/six-berth passenger compartments and a 16ft, 12-seat lounge, all with large, square windows. As one description put it, the passengers "rattled around in the vast expanse of hull in a degree of comfort never known before".

First to fly, on December 30, 1934, was *China Clipper*, to which fell the distinction of making the inaugural (airmail) trans-Pacific flight, leaving San Francisco on November 22, 1935. Its return on December 6 marked the first-ever commercial double crossing of the

Pacific Ocean, with stops at Honolulu, Midway, Wake Island, Guam and Manila. On the outward journey, after waiting a whole day on Guam because it was ahead of schedule, *China Clipper* arrived at Manila two minutes late at the end of its 8,210-mile trip from the USA. When it arrived back in San Francisco – in 123hr 12min flying time instead of the advertised 130hr – *China Clipper* had set 19 international records en route.

The other two M-130s entered service on December 9, 1935 (*Philippine Clipper*), and May 2, 1936 (*Hawaii Clipper*). It was the latter which, on October 21 that year, flew the first regular passenger-carrying service. Unfortunately it was also the first to be lost, disappearing without trace on July 28, 1938, while on the Guam–Manila sector of the route. The two

survivors had by 1940 flown about 10,000hr each (equivalent to about 5½hr per day), representing more than 12½ million passenger-miles in addition to their mail and express flights. In 1942 the US Navy took them over as war transports, still flown by Pan Am crews, and *Philippine Clipper* was lost in the following January. *China Clipper*, restored to Pan Am in October 1943 and used across the South Atlantic (Miami–Leopoldville), survived until January 8, 1945, when she struck an unlit boat during a night landing at Port of Spain, Trinidad, and sank with the loss of 23 of the 30 people on board. Like Britain's Handley Pages in Europe, the Martin boats did a tremendous job for many years and laid the foundations for some of the later route networks of one of the world's greatest airlines.

Pan Am Sikorsky S-43 (NC15063), with single vertical tail

Sikorsky S-43

With graceful lines that belied its size, the S-43 was perhaps the most elegant of all the Sikorsky amphibians. It was also the world's largest at the time of its first flight in 1935. Certificated on December 24 that year, it was contemporary and competitive with the Boeing 247 and Douglas DC-2, in which context its production total of 54 can be accounted a respectable success.

There were four basic versions: the single-tailed S-43 and S-43W with Hornet and Wright Cyclone engines respectively, and their twin-tailed counterparts the S-43B and S-43WB. However, only about five Wright-powered examples were built. Apart from 11 US Navy JRS-1s and six US Army OA-8/OA-11s, all S-43s went to civilian owners, airline operators including Pan American and affiliates (12 or more), Air France (four), Inter-Island Airways of Hawaii (two), and KNILM (two). Two S-43s went to wealthy private owners Howard Hughes and W. K. Vanderbilt, and others to operators in China, Chile, North Africa, Norway and the USSR.

Twin fins and rudders identify this Pan Am Sikorsky as an S-43B

Twin-Wasp-engined DST-A (NC18101) in joint United/Western Air Express markings

Douglas DC-3

There cannot have been many occasions when airlines already employing a type of aircraft with entirely acceptable direct operating costs were offered a new model one-third cheaper to operate yet capable of seating 50 per cent more passengers. It is thus hardly surprising that Douglas had sold about 450 DC-3s before America's entry into the Second World War. Production for military requirements then boosted output to such an extent that 10,654 aircraft of the DC-3 type were produced, not including licence manufacture in Japan and the USSR. Had Douglas known then how much time and effort would be expended in a vain attempt to find a DC-3 replacement in the 1960s and 1970s, the company would no doubt have built several thousand more. Even so, nearly half a century after the prototype's first flight, the number of civil and military DC-3s giving yeoman service all over the globe still runs well into four figures.

It was C. R. Smith, president of American Airlines, who started the DC-3 ball rolling. His company, which flew a large number of night sleeper services using obsolescent Curtiss Condors or Fokker tri-motors, needed a modern replacement

DC-3 *Flagship Arkansas* (NC17331) of American Airlines

which could accommodate as many passengers (14) in sleeping berths as the DC-2 carried in daytime seats. By making the basic DC-2 fuselage fatter and slightly longer Douglas was able to offer the DST (Douglas Sleeper Transport), which flew for the first time on December 17, 1935. It had a greater wing span than the DC-2 and a larger, broader vertical tail, and could accommodate 14 sleeping berths plus a luxurious "honeymoon suite".

Production of the DST, powered by either Wright Cyclone or Pratt & Whitney Twin Wasp engines, totalled 40. Some 380 more were built pre-war as DC-3 or DC-3A day transports, for with the sleeping berths removed the fuselage was large enough for an extra row of seats, permitting carriage of 21 passengers compared with 14 in the DC-2. Ten others, as convertible day/sleeper transports for TWA, were designated DC-3B. The

DSTs were themselves later converted to DC-3 standard Substantial pre-war DC-3 fleets (20 or more aircraft) were operated in the USA by American, Braniff, Eastern, Northwest, Panagra, Pan American, Pennsylvania-Central, TWA and United. Major foreign operators included Aeroflot (USSR) and KLM (Netherlands). Foreign licence manufacture began in Japan in 1938 (485 Nakajima/Showa L2Ds) and in the Soviet Union in 1940 (about 2,000 Lisunov Li-2s).

Of just over 10,000 built under wartime military contracts, nearly 85 per cent were C-47As or C-47Bs, and these flooded both the civil and foreign military markets after the war ended. Production continued only briefly thereafter, with the completion of 28 DC-3Ds (the DC-3C designation applying to refurbished C-47A/Bs). Delivery of the last DC-3, a DC-3C for Sabena (Belgium), was made on March 21, 1947.

One of the most familiar shapes in the sky: a DC-3 (NC28340) of Delta Air Lines

Early post-war BEA DC-3 at Hamburg Airport

DC-3s have seen worldwide post-war service in Canada (CF-IQR of Borek) . . .

. . . the United States (Trans Texas Airways' N17336) . . .

. . . **Great Britain (Gibair's G-AMFV at Gibraltar)** . . .

. . . **Europe (LN-IKI** *Einar Viking* **of Scandinavian Airlines System at Gothenburg)** . . .

. . . Pakistan (AP-AAH of Pakistan International) . . .

. . . Australia (VH-MMA *Ashburton* of MacRobertson Miller Airlines) . . .

Lockheed Model 12A Electra (NC17309)

Lockheed Model 12 Electra

Having captured a healthy slice of the short-haul, medium-capacity airline market of the mid-1930s with its Model 10, Lockheed decided to produce an "Electra Junior" aimed at the feederline and business aircraft markets. The Model 12 was therefore essentially a scaled-down Model 10 seating a maximum of six passengers instead of ten. But, by virtue of retaining its predecessor's powerplant, the new type possessed an even more lively performance. It flew for the first time on June 27, 1936, and the Model 12A was certificated four months later.

Sixty-three civil and 66 military examples were built, the latter comprising 14 for the USAAC, seven for the US Navy, eight for Brazil and 37 for the Dutch East Indies. Two others, designated Model 12B and having 450 hp Wright Whirlwind engines instead of the standard Wasp Juniors, were supplied to the Argentinian Army. Most of the civil Model 12As went to corporate owners (notably in the oil industry) and government agencies, but commercial operators included Santa Maria Air Lines, Varney/Continental, Byrd-Frost Air Transport, Western Air Express, Associated Airlines (Australia) and British Airways.

Cessna C-37 and C-38 Airmaster

A wider cabin with more head-room, electrically operated flaps, improved shock-absorption and a new engine cowling were the chief points of difference between the C-37 and its predecessor, the C-34. Power-plant and performance remained unchanged, although range could be extended by using a 52.5 US gal optional fuel tank instead of the standard 35 US gal unit. The C-37 appeared at the end of 1936 and production totalled 46, including exports to Australia (one), Canada (two), Finland (one), Norway (one), the Philippines (two) and West Africa (one). Several of these were fitted with floats or skis instead of wheels on the main undercarriage legs. One C-37, equipped for aerial photo-graphy, had an extra window in each side of the forward fuselage and one in the cabin floor. This aircraft, and two standard C-37s, were impressed in 1942 as UC-77Ds for the USAAF; the Finnish C-37 was impressed into that country's air force.

The name Airmaster, later applied to the whole series from the C-34 to the C-165, was first used officially for the C-38, the prototype of which was com-pleted on October 11, 1937. Six of the 16 built were completed as photographic aircraft in similar fashion to the C-37 conversion, but the standard C-38 generally had the same configuration as the standard C-37. The principal differences were a hydraulically actuated underfuselage flap (instead of electrically operated wing flaps), a larger fin, and a bow-legged main landing gear offering a 10½in-wider wheel track. The C-38 gave way on the production line to the C-145 in August 1938, and two C-38s later had the underbelly flap deleted and C-145 wings fitted.

The Cessna C-37 was a handsome four-seater

Model D18S, although of post-war manufacture, typified the general appearance of the Beechcraft 18

Beechcraft Model 18

Record-holder among pre-war designs for the longest unbroken period of production — 32 years — the Beech 18 was designed in 1936, first flown on January 15, 1937, and type-certificated on June 15, 1938. When production ended in early 1969 a total of 9,388 aircraft in the series had been completed: over 1,800 before the Second World War, nearly as many after the war, and more than 5,700 during the period of hostilities. Pre-war models included the 18 (300 hp Jacobs L6 engines), A18 and B18 (350 hp Wright R-760-E Whirlwinds), and C18S (450 hp Pratt & Whitney R-985 Wasp Juniors). Wartime production covered the UC-45/JRB Expeditor, AT-7 Navigator, AT-11/SNB Kansan and the F-2 photographic version.

Post-war civil production resumed with the C18S, soon replaced by the D18S (certificated on April 26, 1946) and the Continental-engined D18C of 1947; a total of 1,030 C and D models were completed. Major changes appeared with the E18S, which first flew on December 10, 1953. This introduced redesigned wings, more

efficient R-985 engines and a greater degree of passenger cabin comfort. Next production model was the G18S of 1959. On July 11, 1962, the FAA awarded a type certificate to the final version, the H18S, many examples of which were built by Beech to incorporate an optional tricycle landing gear developed by Volpar. Combined production of the E/G/H models totalled 756.

The great majority of Beechcraft 18s built, including many wartime versions released on to the civil market, were operated as executive transports, air taxis or third-level airliners, or with more than 30 air forces in all parts of the world, though at the time production ended some 150 were in service with nearly 100 scheduled carriers. Several modified versions have appeared, including the Dumodliner, Hamilton Westwind (see page 166) and Volpar Turboliner. Others included the Pacific Airmotive Tradewind of 1963, a remanufactured UC-45/D18S with tricycle landing gear and a single sweptback vertical tail.

ZK-AHO of New Zealand Aerial Mapping Ltd, photographed at Wellington Airport in 1973. Built as a wartime F-2 in 1943, it was bought by the New Zealand government that year for urgent aerial mapping work — and was still doing similar work 30 years later

Alcor C-6-1

In 1929, after the firm which they founded had been taken over by Detroit Aircraft Corporation, Allan and Malcolm Lockheed left to pursue a separate career and in 1930 formed Lockheed Brothers Aircraft Corporation at Glendale, California. Its principal product was the Olympic, a twin-engined high-wing monoplane in which the in-line engines were laid on their sides on each side of the nose in a faired horizontal structure, with the object of reducing drag by keeping the propellers as close together as possible. Later, as president of the Alhambra Airport and Air Transport Company (Alcor), Allan Lockheed continued to develop this idea with the high-wing, fixed-gear Duo-6, seating a crew of two and four passengers. Powered by two 210 hp Menasco Buccaneer engines, this was first flown in 1933 but work on it was suspended in the following year.

Lockheed formed the renamed Alcor Aircraft Corporation in February 1937 to continue developing the concept. This took the form of the larger, low-wing, retractable-gear Alcor C-6-1, an eight-passenger aeroplane with clean and pleasing lines and more powerful Super Buccaneer engines. At the same time Menasco was working with

Vega, formed in 1937 as a subsidiary of Lockheed Aircraft Corporation, on a powerplant called the Unitwin, in which two Super Buccaneers were coupled side by side to drive a single propeller. This unit was flight-tested in a Lockheed Altair in 1938 and subsequently powered the Vega Starliner five/six-seat cabin monoplane. The Alcor C-6-1 did not enter production.

NX15544, the prototype Alcor C-6-1

Ex-US Navy JRF Goose in post-war civil livery

Grumman G-21 Goose

Designed as an eight-place commercial amphibian, the G-21 prototype Goose flew for the first time on May 30, 1937, and was certificated on September 29 of the same year. Before America's entry into the Second World War Grumman sold 42 civil G-21As, with improved R-985 engines and higher all-up weight. Production during the war comprised OA-9s for the USAAF and JRFs for the US Navy and Coast Guard, plus 12 G-21Bs (an armed, non-amphibious model) for the Portuguese Navy, taking the overall total to 334, including the prototype.

Small numbers of commercial G-21As were impressed for military service during 1941–45. After the war this process was reversed when many ex-Navy aircraft were released on to the civil market, serving as business, third-level airline and bush aircraft with a large number of operators, chiefly in the USA, Alaska and Canada. Beginning in 1958, with the first flight on January 25 of the G-21C, McKinnon Enterprises offered a series of improved Goose conversions. The G-21C

Partially modified Goose with retractable wingtip floats

was a four-engined G-21A with 340 hp Lycoming GSO-480s, up to 11 passenger seats, increased fuel capacity, retractable wingtip floats and other refinements. The G-21D was similar but had a lengthened bow and could seat up to 16 passengers. First Turbo-Goose conversion was the G-21E of 1966 (certificated in February 1967), based on the D but with two 579 ehp PT6A-20 turboprop engines, and similar Turbo versions of the C and D were offered subsequently. Final McKinnon version (the proposed G-21F with Garrett TPE331 turboprops having failed to materialise) was the G-21G Turbo-Goose, certificated in August 1969 with 715 ehp PT6A-27s. Volpar has produced a "Packaged Power" conversion kit for the installation of TPE331 turboprops in the Goose airframe, among others.

Barkley-Grow T8P-1

So similar outwardly to the Lockheed 10 Electra (except for its fixed landing gear) that its career probably suffered as a result, the T8P-1 was however much different in design and construction. Its chief feature was a multi-cellular wing, without ribs or bulkheads, that could accept very high bending and torsional loads. This was the inspiration of Archibald Barkley, who joined forces in early 1936 with Harold B. Grow, a former US Navy officer then running an aircraft brokerage company. Barkley, a pioneer aircraft engineer, had assisted in the construction of early Wright brothers gliders and had worked with Curtiss, Verville and other US designers before building the little Barkley-Warwick monoplane incorporating his patented wing construction in 1931.

The T8P-1 was first flown in the spring of 1937 and certificated six months later, but despite extensive demonstration tours only 11 examples were sold. One of these went to the Peruvian Air Force, no doubt through the influence of Cdr Grow, who earlier had been on the staff of a US Naval mission to that country. In October 1939 this aircraft was used for a record flight from New York to Peru. Another T8P-1 gave good service to Admiral Byrd during his South Polar expedition of 1939–41. Most examples of the type were sold to customers in South America or Canada, however, and operators in the latter country included Mackenzie Air Services in the North-Western Territories and Maritime Central Airways. On wheels, skis or twin floats the T8P-1 thus proved its value in both the Arctic and the Antarctic, and a few were still serving in parts of Canada as recently as the late 1970s – proof enough of their reliability and the ruggedness of their construction.

YR-AHA *Traiasca Regele*, the Barkley-Grow T8P-1 in which Captain Alex Papana twice attempted, unsuccessfully, to fly from New York to Bucharest. It was later sold to the Peruvian Air Force

Lockheed Model 14 Super Electra

The Model 14 was not just a scaled-up Model 10, as its name might suggest, although the cabin could accommodate two more people. Whereas the original Electra had been designed essentially as a passenger transport, the Super was intended for airlines which wanted a little more flexibility, enabling them to operate with mixed passenger/cargo or all-cargo payloads when required. Hence the tubbier fuselage of the Model 14, to which was allied a redesigned wing by Clarence L. "Kelly" Johnson that incorporated large-area Fowler flaps and introduced "letterbox" slots near the outer leading edges.

Lockheed flew the Model 14 prototype for the first time on July 29, 1937, and there were 24 orders in the book by the end of August. It looked as though the company had got the formula about right, and they had: subsequent development of the

Model 14 led to the wartime Hudson/Ventura bomber series, and to the Model 18 Lodestar civil/military transport.

Deliveries of the initial Model 14-H, with 850 hp Hornet S1E-G engines, began on September 12, 1937, some two months ahead of certification. The more powerful 14-H2 with 875 hp Hornet S1E2-Gs was also available, and a total of 53 Hornet-powered Super Electras were built, the largest fleets being those of Trans Canada Air Lines (16), LOT of Poland (ten) and Northwest Airlines (nine). In the following February Lockheed began delivering the Model 14-WF62, of which it built 21, all for export: 11 to KLM/KNILM, eight to BOAC and two to the Italian operator Teoranta. The third version, also sold exclusively overseas, was the Model 14-WG3B with 900 hp GR-1820-G3B Cyclones. Four of these went to LARES of Romania and 30 to Japan,

where in 1940–42 Tachikawa and Kawasaki built 119 more, with 900 hp Mitsubishi Ha-26-I engines, as Type LO military transports. In addition, Kawasaki produced 121 of a developed version as the Ki-56 for the Japanese Army Air Force. Lockheed production was brought to a total of 112 by four Model 14-Ns with 1,100 hp Cyclones for private owners. One of these was Howard Hughes, who with a crew of four flew his Super Electra on a round-the-world record flight in July 1938, covering approximately 14,800 miles in only three days 19hr 8min.

Foreign Super Electra operators, in addition to those already mentioned, included Aer Lingus, DNL (Norway), Flugfelag (Iceland), Greater Japan Air Lines, Guinea Airways, LAV (Venezuela), Sabena (Belgium) and Widerøe (Canada).

Super Electra PJ-AIT *Troepiaal*, **operated in the Dutch East Indies by KNILM**

Lockheed Model 14 in post-war service with DETA of Mozambique

Model of the Kinner Invader seven-passenger transport

Kinner Invader

Formed in September 1919 and
known chiefly for its radial air-
cooled engines, the Kinner Airplane and Motor Corporation of
Glendale, California, produced
a range of small, two/four-seat
lightplanes during the 1930s
before going into receivership
in 1938. Its last venture was the
twin-engined, seven-passenger
Invader, described in contemporary accounts as "being
worked on" in 1937. It is
uncertain whether the
prototype was completed, and
the accompanying photograph,
a montage based on a picture of
a model, seems to be the only
surviving illustration.

Cessna C-145 Airmaster (NC19484)

Cessna C-145 and C-165 Airmaster

Identical except for their power-plants (the horsepower of which now determined the designation, instead of the year of production), the C-145 and C-165 were derived from the C-38 Airmaster, from which they differed in having electrically operated split flaps at mid-span (the underfuselage flaps having been deleted) and, for the first time on a Cessna product, hydraulic wheel brakes. Production, during the period 1938–42, totalled 42 C-145s (prototype completed September 10, 1938) and 38 C-165s, the two types being manufactured simultaneously for most of that time.

Several C-145s were com-pleted as photographic aircraft or with twin-float landing gear, and single examples were sold to customers in Brazil, Finland and Puerto Rico. One C-165 was completed in 1940 as a flying testbed (first flight September 27) for the unorthodox 175 hp General Motors X-250 eight-cylinder liquid-cooled engine. Test pilot for these trials was Tony LeVier, later to achieve renown with Lockheed and in air racing. Four others, fitted with a more powerful Super Scarab of 175 hp, were re-designated C-165D, and in 1942 three C-165s were impressed into military service by the USAAF and allocated the designation UC-94.

Kellett KD-1

The Kellett Autogiro Corporation, formed in 1929, held a manufacturing licence for early models of the Cierva Autogiro, its first product being a two-seat rotorcraft built in 1931 and known as the K-2. Towards the end of 1934 it produced the first example of the KD-1, the D in the designation indicating direct control. This went into production as the KD-1A, powered by a 225 hp Jacobs engine and having tandem open cockpits for the pilot and passenger. The three blades of the main rotor could be folded rearwards over the top decking of the fuselage. One KD-1A, converted to a single-seater, demonstrated the carriage of mail between the centre of Washington and the city's Hoover Airport on May 19, 1939, and on July 6 that year a similar aircraft, with an enclosed cockpit, inaugurated the first-ever scheduled airmail service by a rotary-wing aircraft. Bearing the colours of Eastern Air Lines, it was known as the KD-1B and operated on that service for about a year.

After evaluating a KD-1A in 1935 the US Army Air Corps acquired another 15 similar aircraft for test purposes; military development of the type ended in 1943. Meanwhile Japan, which had evaluated a KD-1A in 1939, put the type into production (with a German 240 hp Argus As 10C engine) as the Kayaba Ka-1. A total of 240 were built for use by the Army and Navy during the Second World War for artillery observation/co-operation and anti-submarine patrol duties.

Kellett KD-1B (NC15069) in Eastern Air Lines markings, 1939

NX18601, the single-finned Boeing 314 prototype, nearing
completion at Seattle in 1938

Dixie Clipper (NC18605) of the Pan Am Boeing 314 fleet at Lisbon
after its first trans-Atlantic flight on June 28/29, 1939

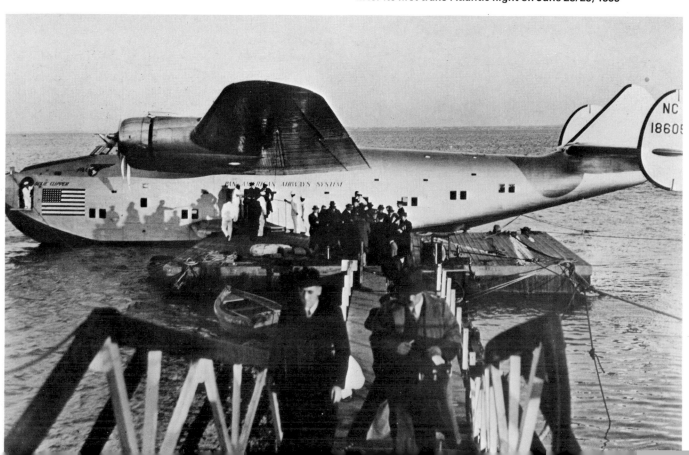

Boeing Model 314

The Boeing 314 was designed to make use of the wings and horizontal tail of Boeing's XB-15 experimental heavy bomber, its engines also being installed in nacelles similar to those of the XB-15. Pan Am accepted the proposed design in 1936, ordering six in July of that year. Up to 74 passengers could be accommodated on daytime services or 40 in sleeping berths.

One of the most stately flying boats ever built, the 314 flew for the first time on June 7, 1938, at that time having a single fin and rudder. To meet the need for more positive directional control it was refitted with twin fins and rudders, to which were later added a large central fin and rudder. The Pan Am 314s were delivered between January and June 1939, flying their first revenue service on May 20. On June 28, 1939, they inaugurated the first-ever regular passenger service across the Atlantic. A second half-dozen, designated Model 314A, had uprated engines and 1,200 US gal more fuel, and could carry three more passengers. After the first Model 314A flew on March 20, 1941, three went to Pan American, which in 1942 had five of its earlier 314s brought up to the same standard. The other trio of 314As was purchased by BOAC, with which they served throughout the war; they were sold to Transocean Airlines in 1948. Meanwhile, in 1942 the USAAF requisitioned four of the Pan Am 314/314As, designating them C-98. The Army Air Force later transferred three of them to the US Navy, which acquired two others directly from Pan Am.

Two of these flying boats were lost during the war, one in a landing accident, the other when struck by a nearby ship. In an unusual tribute to the type's excellent seaworthiness, it took 1,300 rounds of 20mm ammunition to scuttle the latter aircraft. Model 314s carried President Roosevelt and Winston Churchill across the Atlantic for some of their wartime summit conferences. Post-war, Pan Am continued to operate the 314/314A until 1946. Of the survivors, one was sunk in 1947, six went for scrap in 1950 and the last was wrecked in a storm in 1951.

DC-5 prototype (NX21701) on an early flight, testing single-engine performance

Douglas DC-5

With more than a hint in its design of its military contemporary, the DB-7 bomber, the DC-5 was a handsome all-metal twin-engined short-haul transport with a fully retractable tricycle undercarriage. Designed by Leo Devlin and Ed Heinemann, it made its first flight on February 20, 1939, and soon attracted orders from KLM (four), Pennsylvania-Central (six), British Airways (nine), SCADTA of Colombia (two) and the US Navy (seven).

Flight-test problems – cured by the introduction of a dihedral tailplane – delayed progress until after the outbreak of war in Europe, causing British Airways and the two American airlines to cancel their orders. For similar reasons in 1940 KLM diverted two of its DC-5s from Europe to its West Indies division. A year later these aircraft joined the other two in service with KLM's East Indies subsidiary KNILM. One was captured by the Japanese but the other three escaped to operate in Australia and New Guinea until impressed in 1944 to serve as C-110s with the USAAF; one of these was subsequently operated during 1946–47 by Australian National Airways. The US Navy had two R3D-1s (one being lost before delivery), plus one R3D-3 (the DC-5 prototype, re-engined to production standard, sold to William E. Boeing and subsequently impressed). Of the four R3D-2s which went to the US Marine Corps, one was shot down during the war and the other three were retired in late 1946.

Douglas DC-4E

The "E" (for Experimental) suffix was applied retrospectively to this original DC-4 design to distinguish it from the later, less complex aircraft produced as the military C-54 Skymaster and commercial DC-4 airliner. The prototype – the only example built – was initiated in 1936 under the sponsorship of United, American, Eastern, Pan Am and TWA, although the two last-named transferred their affections later that year to the Boeing Stratoliner.

Designed to accommodate 42 daytime passengers (later increased to 52) or 30 by night (including a "honeymoon" berth), the DC-4E first flew on June 7, 1938, and was certificated on May 5, 1939. Internal comforts included electric shavers, toasters and hair curlers, wardrobes, washrooms and toilets, and pressurised accommodation was planned for the production version. However, although the DC-4E handled well, its complex internal systems and disappointing economics led to its abandonment in favour of a new and simplified DC-4 design. In late 1939 the DC-4E was sold to Japan, where it was used by Nakajima as the basis for the G5N1 Shinzan long-range bomber, which itself ultimately failed to achieve production and operational status.

The triple-tailed DC-4 (DC-4E) prototype (NX18100)

Model 18 Lodestar (NC25687) operated by National Airlines in the early 1940s

Lockheed Model 18 Lodestar

Representing the final scaling-up of the Model 10/12/14 Electra/Super Electra series, the Lodestar was produced in greater numbers than all three earlier types put together. The first Model 18 was in fact converted from a Northwest Airlines Model 14, making its initial flight in its new form on September 21, 1939. Two more similar conversions were made before the first true production Lodestar flew on February 2, 1940. A total of 55 Lodestars had been built by the end of that year, and 625 by the time that production ended in 1943. Of these, 325 were C-60A troop transports built on USAAF contracts, and more than 100 civil Lodestars were also impressed for war service under other Air Force and Navy designations.

Lockheed designated seven Lodestar variants according to powerplant. These comprised the Hornet-powered Model 18-07 (730 hp S1E2-Gs); three with Twin Wasps (Models 18-08/900 hp SC3-G, 18-10/900 hp S1C3-G, and 18-14/1,050 hp S4C4-G); and three Cyclone-engined versions (Models 18-40/900 hp GR-1820-G102A, 18-50/1,000 hp -G202A, and 18-56/1,200 hp -G205A). Most numerous of these was the Model 18-56/C-60A.

Early US operators of the Lodestar included Mid-Continent (the first to use it), Continental, National, United and Western Air Express. Overseas the type figured in the fleets of BOAC (for which it flew all wartime services in Africa and the Near East), LAV of Venezuela, Panair do Brasil, Sabena and South African Airways. Most wartime service examples were back in civil operation by the end of 1944, and early post-war users included Linjeflyg (Sweden), East African Airways and Trans-Australia Airlines. In the mid-1960s there were still some 275-300 civil-registered Lodestars worldwide, many of them serving as freighters or corporate transports.

Modified post-war modernisations have included the Super Lodestar executive conversion by Minnesota Airmotive, and two models of William P. Lear's PacAero Learstar, first flown on May 19, 1954. Both Learstar models are powered by 1,425 hp Cyclones and have outer-wing fuel plus optional tip tanks. The Mk I has a reworked airframe and cabin interior; the Mk II retains the existing internal layout.

Stratoliner prototype (NX19901) taking off on a maximum-load test flight

This TWA Stratoliner was registered NC1940 to indicate the year that it entered service

Boeing Model 307 Stratoliner

Conceived originally as a transport counterpart of the Flying Fortress bomber, the Model 307 combined the wings (with "letterbox" slots in the outboard leading edges), power installation and tail unit of the B-17C with a portly, circular-section new fuselage. With orders in 1937 from Pan American (four) and TWA (six, later reduced to five), Boeing laid down a production line of ten Stratoliners. The initial flight, on December 31, 1938, was made by the first aircraft for Pan Am. The second and subsequent aircraft all had a fully pressurised passenger cabin – the first in a four-engined US commercial transport – and an enlarged vertical tail akin to that later fitted to the B-17E. There were minor power-plant and structural differences between the Pan Am and TWA aircraft, which entered service in 1940. One other Stratoliner was built for millionaire Howard Hughes and equipped in mid-

1939 for a proposed attempt on his own 1938 record (in a Lockheed Electra) for a round-the-world flight. This was fore-stalled by the outbreak of war in Europe and Hughes had the air-craft refitted with a luxury interior as his personal trans-port, but made little use of it.

TWA's Stratoliners flew more than 4½ million accident-free miles before America's entry into the war, and Pan Am also achieved a high rate of utilisa-tion with its three 307s. Both fleets then flew extensively on military transport duties with Air Transport Command of the USAAF until late 1944, when they were returned to airline ownership with uprated engines, B-17G wings and other improvements. Subsequent operators, from 1951, included Aigle Azur and Airnautic of France, Air Laos and (as a presidential transport) the air force of Haiti, and a few sur-vivors were still flying in the early to middle 1960s.

Attractively painted Widgeon (ZK-CHG) of New Zealand Tourist Air Travel Ltd

Grumman G-44 Widgeon

Three hundred and eighteen Widgeons were built, the G-44 prototype flying for the first time on June 28, 1940. In effect a scaled-down, four/five-place counterpart to the G-21 Goose, it was powered by a pair of 200 hp Ranger L-440C-5 engines. Some 32 commercial G-44s were sold before the USA became a full-scale participant in the Second World War. Twelve others were built for the Portuguese Navy, 25 for the US Coast Guard as J4F-1s, and 131 to US Navy orders as J4F-2s, including small numbers Lend-Leased to the RAF and RCAF. On August 8, 1944, Grumman flew the first of 76 examples of the Model G-44A, a refined version with a modified hull, deeper at the forward end; some of these aircraft had Continental W-670 or Lycoming O-435-A engines. Though the last US-built G-44A was delivered in January 1949, the French company Société de Constructions Aéronautiques Normande turned out a further 41 under licence. Designated SCAN 30, most of these aircraft were sold in the USA.

As with the Goose, McKinnon Enterprises marketed for many years a Super Widgeon conversion powered by 270 hp Lycoming GO-480 engines and having increased fuel capacity, hull and landing gear improvements, optionally retractable wingtip floats, and other refinements such as "picture" windows in the cabin. More than 70 Widgeons are known to have been converted to Super Widgeon standard.

Consolidated Model 28 Catalina

Produced almost entirely for military purposes, the Catalina first flew in XP3Y-1 prototype form on March 21, 1935. Before the Second World War American Export Airlines used a PBY-2 (Model 28-4) to survey a proposed scheduled service across the Atlantic and applied in May 1939 for an operating certificate, but its plans were thwarted by the outbreak of war in Europe.

During the war BOAC operated a small fleet of seven Catalinas, for which the first British C of A was issued on December 13, 1940. These carried a 1,000lb payload (three passengers plus mail or other freight) and seven tons of fuel. Qantas put the Catalina into service in July 1943 between Perth and Colombo on what was then the world's longest non-stop air route (3,513 miles). The Catalina remained in post-war service with Qantas until the summer of 1958, and with various US, Canadian, South American and other airline operators until the late 1960s. Several have also been used in a water-bombing role or for geophysical survey work.

A Venezuelan-registered civil PBY-5A Catalina (YV-O-CFO-4)

Geophysical survey Catalina operated by Barringer Research Ltd of
Canada and equipped with tail magnetometer, trailing magnetic
probe (under rear fuselage) and loop aerials

Liberator SX-DAA *Maid of Athens*, converted for Hellenic Airlines by Scottish Aviation

Consolidated Model 32 Liberator

Although designed (as the B-24) for the heavy bomber role, the payload/range capability of the Liberator led to its early adaptation for transport duties. As a result, several derivatives designed specifically as military transports appeared later. First to be used in the transport role were the early Liberators ordered by Great Britain, BOAC employing the LB-30/LB-30A Liberator I/II/III on its trans-Atlantic Return Ferry Service from the spring of 1941. The BOAC fleet totalled 27 Liberators, the last of which was not retired until September 1949.

Civil conversions were pioneered by Qantas, which turned the capacious fuselage into a passenger cabin, transferring the auxiliary fuel tanks to the wings and adding a baggage/freight compartment in an extended nose. Square cabin windows were introduced in a Scottish Aviation 30-passenger conversion which was operated after the war (until about 1949–50) by Hellenic Airlines and Flugfelag of Iceland.

Curtiss CW-20 prototype in BOAC wartime finish as G-AGDI *St Louis*

Cargo loading door of a Northeast Airlines C-46F

Curtiss C-46

A contemporary of the Douglas DC-3, the significantly larger C-46 was designed in 1936 to carry 36 passengers and 8,200lb of cargo in a "double-bubble" fuselage, the upper lobe of which was intended to be pressurised (though it never was). The twin-tailed CW-20T prototype made its first flight on March 26, 1940. After refitting with a single fin and rudder it was acquired by the USAAC for evaluation, and the first contract was for a 50-troop/33-stretcher/10,000lb cargo military transport version designated C-46. Over 3,100 were eventually built for the USAAF or as R5Cs for the US Navy. Many of these were supplied to America's wartime allies, and the name Commando was adopted. The CW-20 prototype, sold to BOAC in September 1941 as G-AGDI *St Louis,* served with the British airline for two years as a 24-seat wartime transport.

After the war the proposed civil CW-20E for Eastern Air

Lines did not achieve production status. Instead the market was glutted with several hundred surplus C-46s, and by 1960 — after a slow start resulting from difficulties in meeting FAA conditions regarding maximum operating weights — these aircraft were in service with more than 90 operators under a variety of post-war type certificates. Some were used by US feeder and foreign passenger airlines (seating up to 62 passengers), but their capacious fuselages meant that most C-46s were employed as freighters. The majority were C-46As (single loading door) or C-46Ds/Fs (double doors and modified nose). Operators included Flying Tiger, Airlift International, Riddle and a number of Central and South American carriers. Specially-modified versions included Riddle's C-46R, and the generally similar Super 46C. About 70 C-46s remained in service in early 1982.

VS-44A *Excalibur* **during its first flight on January 18, 1942**

Vought-Sikorsky VS-44A

Largest and last of the Sikorsky flying boats, the VS-44A resulted from a June 1936 US Navy contract for a large, long-range experimental armed patrol aircraft. First flown on August 13, 1937, the XPBS-1 prototype was powered by four 1,050 hp XR-1830-68 Twin Wasp engines and carried a six-man crew. Armament comprised twin-gun nose, tail and dorsal turrets, and an internal weapon load of 4,000lb could be carried over a range of 3,170 miles. Its take-off run was prodigious: nearly six minutes to become airborne at

its maximum gross weight of 47,455lb. Delivered to the Navy in October 1937, the XPBS-1 was used subsequently for "special mission" flights until it capsized in San Francisco Bay in early 1942.

Meanwhile, three commercial VS-44As with uprated engines and higher all-up weight had been ordered in 1940 by American Export Airlines. With the outbreak of war in the Pacific the USN took over these aircraft as well, designating them JR2S-1. The first VS-44A, flagship *Excalibur*, made its

maiden flight on January 18, 1942, and all three had been delivered by June of that year, when they went into service (operated by AEA under US Navy contract) across the North Atlantic to Britain.

Excalibur crashed on take-off in Newfoundland in October 1942, but the other two flying boats survived the war (during which they made over 400 trans-Atlantic crossings) to be sold in 1946 to Tampico Airlines. Later they served in South America, where one was lost in August 1947 while acting as a supply

transport for Paraguayan insurgents. After several ownerships the last survivor was acquired in 1957 by Avalon Air Transport, with which it served for a number of years between Long Beach and Catalina Island. In 1968 it was bought by the Virgin Islands operator Antilles Air Boats. But in the following January it was damaged beyond reasonable repair while taxiing for take-off. After a period as a land-based hot-dog stand, the remains are now at the US Naval Aviation Museum at Pensacola, Florida.

The second VS-44A (N41881) in Avalon's colours in about 1960

Flying Tiger Line's first aircraft, the Budd Conestoga (NC45356 illustrated)

Budd RB-1 Conestoga

One of the first aircraft to be conceived as a DC-3 replacement – though not for the usual reasons – the Conestoga was designed around the time of Pearl Harbor, when it was thought that wartime demands for aluminium alloy might create a shortage of this vital material for types other than first-line combat aircraft. The Budd company, then engaged mainly in manufacturing munitions and railway rolling stock, responded by designing the RB-1 (its US Navy designation) in stainless steel, with the exception of fabric covering for the control surfaces and the rear portion of the wing skin. Budd won the competition and in August 1942 received a Navy contract for 200; a further 600 were ordered by the USAAF as C-93As. In the event, aluminium remained plentiful, assuring large-scale production of the C-47 (military version of the DC-3). As a result, the AAF contract was cancelled entirely and only 17 RB-1s were delivered to the Navy, although nine other Conestogas from the initial production batch were completed by Budd.

First flight of the RB-1 was made on October 31, 1943, and CAB certification (a condition of Navy acceptance) was gained on July 15, 1944. An innovative design for reasons other than the choice of constructional material, it was intended to carry about the same payload as a DC-3 on similar power but with a greater internal volume available for cargo. This was amply provided by its 8ft × 8ft cabin cross-section, larger than the external cross-section of the DC-3 fuselage. Other features novel for their time included the tricycle landing gear, elevated flight deck, clamshell loading doors and a rear-loading ramp under an upswept tail.

The nine surplus Conestogas were bought by Flying Tiger, which operated them successfully for nearly three years. Resale of these aircraft and ex-Navy RB-1s subsequently took them to other US operators and as far afield as Canada, Mexico, Cuba, Brazil and Ecuador. Some remained in service until the middle/late 1960s.

Chicago & Southern L-649A Constellation (N86521 *Ciudad Trujillo*)

Transports old and new: BOAC L-749A Constellations *Banbury* and *Brentford*

Lockheed Constellation

Although its commercial career did not begin until after the Second World War, the Constellation originated in 1939 as a 40-passenger design for TWA, which placed an order for 40. All such plans were interrupted by the war, and the prototype did not fly until January 9, 1943, by which time it was the first aircraft of a USAAF contract for 202 military transports designated C-69. Very few C-69s were delivered before the war ended, and 180 of those on order were cancelled. The other 22, bearing the Lockheed designation L-049, had their interiors converted for commercial operation, with standard accommodation for 43–48 passengers or a high-density maximum of 60. Certificated on December 11, 1945 (deliveries having already started in November), the L-049 entered service on February 3, 1946, with Pan American (to Bermuda) and three days later with TWA to Paris. British Overseas Airways introduced the Constellation on its London–New York service in July 1946.

A further 66 Model L-049s were built post-war but the first true peacetime version was the 48/64-passenger (maximum 81) L-649, powered by 2,500 hp R-3350-C18-BD1 engines and flown for the first time on October 19, 1946. Twenty of this model were completed, entering service with Eastern Air Lines in May 1947. The most numerous "Connie" was the L-749: 113 were produced, including L-749As and 12 military examples, plus some converted from L-649s. Accommodation remained basically unchanged, but the L-749 carried more in-wing fuel and the L-749A had the landing gear strengthened to cater for higher operating weights. In June 1947 Pan American inaugurated the first round-the-world regular air service with an L-749, NC86530 *Clipper America*. Production of the Constellation ended in 1951, when it gave way to a stretched development, the Super Constellation.

Douglas DC-4

The original DC-4 design (known retrospectively as the DC-4E, see page 94) proved too ambitious and uneconomical for its sponsors. As a result, Douglas developed a smaller, simpler, single-finned version to seat up to 42 passengers in an unpressurised fuselage. Orders totalling 61 aircraft were placed by American, Eastern and United, but by the time of the prototype's first flight on February 14, 1942, the USA had been brought into the Second World War and all transport aircraft production had been earmarked for the armed forces. The Douglas output of 1,315 aircraft was thus made up predominantly of Air Force C-54 or Navy R5D Skymasters, and only 79 were actually built as genuine commercial DC-4s.

In the years immediately after the war, until the appearance of such post-war designs as the DC-6 and Super Constellation, DC-4s and demobilised Skymasters were among the principal types used to re-equip the major national and international airlines. Many were still flying more than a quarter of a century later, although by the mid-1970s most of these had been relegated to freight-carrying.

In addition to Douglas production, during 1946–49 Canadair built a total of 23 C-54GM/DC-4M-1 North Stars for the RCAF, 42 pressurised DC-4M-2s (with some features of the DC-6) for Trans-Canada Air Lines (20) and BOAC (22), and four C-4-1s for CPAL. These 40/55-seat aircraft, powered by 1,725 or 1,760 hp Rolls-Royce Merlin 620 V-12 engines instead of the standard Twin Wasp radials, continued in service (though not with their original owners) until the mid-1970s.

A highly specialised version of the DC-4 was the ATL.98, of which 23 were converted by Freddie Laker's Aviation Traders in Britain as Carvair ("car-via-air") vehicle transports. Modifications included a new, longer forward fuselage with a sideways-opening nose door, a new flight deck above the forward hold, and a DC-7C vertical tail. The first Carvair was flown on June 21, 1961 (having already accumulated 37,000hr as a DC-4 before conversion). The type was subsequently operated by British United Air Ferries, Aer Lingus, Aviaco, Cie Air Transport and Ansett/ANA, among others. Most had disappeared by the mid-1970s.

Built post-war as a genuine DC-4, South African Airways' ZS-AUB *Outeniqua* **also served for a short time with the SAAF**

Delta's NC37472 was a demilitarised C-54 Skymaster

The first Aviation Traders ATL.98 Carvair conversion was G-ANYB *Golden Gate Bridge*, originally a C-54 Skymaster modified for airline service with Braniff

Canadair-built DC-4M-2 (G-ALHX *Astraea*) of British Overseas Airways

Early Bell Model 47B-3

Bell Model 47

Five prototypes of the experimental Bell Model 30 were built, the first example making its initial flight in 1943 on the power of a 165 hp Franklin engine. The Model 47 was the 178 hp production version, flown for the first time on December 8, 1945. On March 8 of the following year it became the world's first commercial helicopter to be awarded an official type certificate. The ten Model 47s were followed by 28 similarly powered 47As for evaluation by all three US armed services. Civil equivalent of the 47A was the 47B, and from the B-3 was developed the first mass-production model, the Bell 47D, characterised by its large "goldfish bowl" canopy. This received civil certification in February 1948 and was also built in large numbers for the US Army and Navy as the H-13 and HTL respectively.

Chief D model was the three-seat 47D-1, and this basic airframe, combined with the

200 hp Franklin 6V4-200-C32 engine that powered the Bell 47E, yielded the other major production version, the Model 47G. Type approval of the 47G was granted in June 1953 and it stayed in production, latterly with foreign licensees, until the late 1970s.

Fitted with a Lycoming VO-435 of 200 hp, the 47G-2 could fly at higher operating weights. The same type of engine also powered the G-2A (240 hp), G-3B (280 hp turbocharged TVO-435) and G-5 (265 hp), and other G models included the G-3 (225 hp supercharged Franklin) and G-4 (280 hp Lycoming VO-540). Bell's other main development was the Model 47J Ranger, which first appeared in 1954. Powered by a 220 hp VO-435, it had a fully enclosed fuselage with a car-type cabin and seated four people.

Model 47s were licence-built by Agusta (Italy), Kawasaki (Japan) and Westland (UK), the

Bell Model 47B (G-AKCX) in use as a UK sales demonstrator

Okanagan Bell 47D (CF-GZJ), with "goldfish bowl" canopy

last-named assembling 50 Model 47G-3B-1s from Agusta-built components as Sioux AH.1s for the British Army. Kawasaki built 239 (mostly Gs) plus another 211 of its own Bell 47 derivative, known as the KH-4. Agusta, which also developed a variant or two of its own, kept Bell 47 manufacture (mostly Gs and Js) going from 1954 until the late 1970s, long after all other production lines had been closed down. Other variations on the basic design included the Continental Copters El Tomcat, a single-seat conversion with a much simplified airframe and equipped for agricultural operations. Bell 47 production from all sources totalled well in excess of five thousand.

The first civil Sikorsky S-51 on an early test flight as NX92800

Sikorsky S-51

Certificated very shortly after the Bell 47, Sikorsky's S-51 originated in the VS-372, of which five XR-5 two-seat prototypes were completed for USAAF evaluation, the first of them flying on August 18, 1943. Subsequent production was predominantly military, only about 65 of the 285 or so built by Sikorsky being civilian S-51s. Developed from the R-5D, the S-51 had tricycle landing gear, a slightly larger main rotor and a four-seat cabin.

First flight of an S-51 was made on February 16, 1946, and deliveries began in the following August. Four months later Westland acquired a licence to build the S-51 in Britain, and flew its first WS-51 on October 5, 1948. Again, military production predominated: most of the 139 built were for the RAF (15), Royal Navy (71) or foreign air forces, and fewer than 20 found their way on to the civil market. The WS-51, known as the Dragonfly, was powered by the 520 hp Alvis Leonides. Three were bought by Sabena and others were used for a time by British European Airways, whose Liverpool–Cardiff schedule, inaugurated on June

1, 1950, was the first regular passenger-carrying helicopter service anywhere in the world.

Westland also built small numbers of a variant known as the Widgeon, with an S-55-type rotor head and four-blade main rotor. This flew for the first time on August 23, 1955. Sikorsky production of the R-5/S-51 ended in 1951.

Northrop N-23 Pioneer and YC-125 Raider

High-lift wings, STOL performance, rugged construction and three-engined safety were the chief characteristics of the N-23 Pioneer, which flew for the first time on December 21, 1946. At that time the specified Wright Cyclone engines were not available (they were installed in the following autumn), and early flight testing was carried out using three Pratt & Whitney R-1340-S3H1 Wasps. With the Wrights the aircraft was able to take off in a guaranteed 700ft at an all-up weight of 25,500lb.

The Pioneer was developed with an eye on the Central American route network, and TACA (Transportes Aereos Centro-Americanos) ordered a fleet of 40 but was obliged to cancel when the Civil Aeronautics Board refused the airline permission to operate into the United States. The prototype was lost in a crash in March 1948, but shortly afterwards Northrop received a USAF contract for 13 similar YC-125A Raider assault transports and ten YC-125Bs for Arctic rescue. The first YC-125 was flown on August 1, 1949, and CAB certification (required by the Air Force) was almost completed when, in 1955, the USAF declared the type surplus to its requirements.

Twenty Raiders were then sold on the civil market: one to Planet Airways and 19 to dealer Frank Ambrose. Re-sales by Ambrose included two to Servicios Aereos de Chiapas of Mexico, one to another Mexican airline, one to the Surinam government, and two or more to US operators. The original YC-125 powerplant (three 1,200 hp R-1820-99 Cyclones) was replaced in one Mexican aircraft by 1,350 hp R-1820-56As, and this aircraft was equipped with bucket seats for 30–40 passengers.

Prototype of the Northrop N-23 Pioneer (NX8500H)

Boeing B-17F converted for civil use by Svensk Interkontinental Lufttrafik AB (SILA) and used in 1945 on services between Sweden and Scotland

Flying Fortress US civil conversion (N7227C) operated by Aero Service Corporation of Philadelphia

Boeing Model 299 Flying Fortress

Although less amenable to passenger conversion than its celebrated contemporary, the Liberator, the B-17 Flying Fortress bomber was converted for civil use in significant numbers. Among the first and best known were the seven Fs and Gs modified from the large number of B-17s interned after force-landing in neutral Sweden during the war. Provided with rectangular cabin windows and an elongated baggage nose, they were operated for several post-war years by SILA (internationally) and AB Aerotransport (on Swedish domestic routes). The first trans-Atlantic flight by a SILA B-17 was made on June 27, 1945.

A year or so later a Vega-built B-17G was converted in similar fashion in the USA and was flown by TWA on domestic and foreign route-surveying flights during 1946–47. This aircraft had the Boeing model number 299AB. In the mid-1960s Lloyd Aereo Boliviano was still operating three B-17s in a 20-passenger configuration; several other B-17s continued in service as freighters with other Latin American operators; eight were then on charge to the French Institut Géographique National; and there were more than three dozen B-17s on the US civil register, including nine in use as water-bombers.

Beechcraft Bonanza V35B, the current production model

Beechcraft Models 33 and 35 Bonanza

Few aircraft can have been so appropriately named as this attractive little V-tailed light-plane produced by Beech Aircraft Corporation. The Second World War had been over only a few months when, on December 22, 1945, the four-seat prototype made its first flight. Deliveries of production aircraft started by Beech and by 1982 the Bonanza had entered its 36th year of continuous manufacture. Well over 10,000 had then been built – more than

a quarter of all the aeroplanes produced by Beech since the company was founded in 1932 – in what must be one of the longest production runs in aviation history. The number of seats has now increased to five, and there are also conventionally tailed Model 33 and Model 36 Bonanzas which themselves have a fine manufacturing and service record, running into several thousands since the Model 33 entered production in 1959.

The first V-tailed version was known as the A35, new prefix letters then being introduced to indicate later modifications. The current model, which first appeared in 1966, is the V35. Engine power has risen from 185 hp in the A35 to 285 hp in the V35B; square-cut instead of rounded wingtips were introduced in 1960 with the M35; increased cabin window area, a pointed spinner and other changes came with the S35 in 1964. Variations in seating,

baggage and equipment account for most of the other distinctions between successive models.

The Model 33, known originally as the Debonair, continues in production as the F33A and F33C, while the A36 Bonanza is a full six-seater which can also be used in the cargo/light utility role. Completing the family is the Turbo Bonanza A36TC with six seats and a 300 hp turbocharged Continental TSIO-520 engine.

The present-day Bonanza family: from left to right, Models A36, V35B and F33A

CF-CUO *Empress of Lima*, **a DC-6B of Canadian Pacific Airlines**

Billed as "The Mandarin Flight," this DC-6B (B-1006) and others were operated by Civil Air Transport of Taiwan for several years from 1958

Douglas DC-6

The DC-6 began life in 1944 as a scaled-up C-54 Skymaster, and the prototype (first flown on February 15, 1946) was one of three USAAF XC-112As; the civil prototype made its first flight on July 9, 1946. Utilising the same basic wing as the C-54/DC-4, the new transport was 6ft 8in longer than its predecessor and had a pressurised fuselage that could accommodate a three-man crew plus 68 passengers. Other improvements included more powerful engines, large square cabin windows, and enlarged wing and tail areas. Commercial type approval was gained in March 1947, and United Air Lines (which had ordered 35) put the DC-6 into US domestic operation in April of that year. American Airlines, with an order for 47, was another early customer, as were Sabena, KLM and SAS in Europe.

Production of 175 DC-6s was followed from 1951 by 77 DC-6A freighters (plus 167 C-118/R6D Liftmasters for the US Air Force and Navy) and 286 DC-6Bs. The DC-6A, flown for the first time on September 29, 1949, was 5ft longer than the original DC-6, with a strengthened cabin floor, cargo-loading doors in the fuselage and R-2800-CB17 engines, plus a much increased payload capacity. First operator was Slick Airways, with which it entered service in April 1951. The DC-6B first flew just before this, on February 10, and also entered service in April, with Western Air Lines. Essentially the same airframe as the DC-6A except for a further 1ft 1in increase in length, the DC-6B could carry up to 107 passengers, almost one and a half times the payload of the original DC-6. Production of the DC-6/6A/6B ended in late 1958, and substantial numbers of these aircraft remained in worldwide airline service until well into the mid-1970s. A number of DC-6As were modified as convertible passenger/cargo aircraft with the payload capacity of the DC-6B, and were then redesignated DC-6C.

Martin 2-0-2

First US twin-engined airliner to be both designed and flown after the Second World War, the Martin 2-0-2 failed to achieve the success of its contemporary look-alike, the Convair 240. Flown for the first time on November 22, 1946, and certificated on August 13, 1947, it carried 36–40 passengers in an unpressurised fuselage. Powerplant, as in the Convair, was a pair of Pratt & Whitney Double Wasp piston radials.

Production totalled only 43, of which 31 were divided between LAN-Chile (first operator of the type, with which it entered service in October 1947); LAV of Venezuela, which had two; and Northwest Orient Airlines, easily the major operator with a fleet of 25. The 2-0-2 was grounded for a period in 1948 when a structural weakness was discovered in the wings, and the next dozen aircraft were completed as 2-0-2As with a strengthened airframe, increased gross weight of 43,000lb and -CB16 (instead of -CA18) Double Wasps. The 2-0-2A was produced for TWA as an interim type pending deliveries of the later Martin 4-0-4. The 2-0-2A first flew in July 1950 and entered service on September 1 of that year.

Model 2-0-2 prototype (NC93002) in manufacturer's demonstration livery

Grumman G-73 Mallard

Design of the Mallard as a modernised successor to the Goose began in early 1945 and was in its final stages by VJ-Day. Its graceful lines encompassed a heated, ventilated and well-appointed cabin for 10–12 passengers; design features included a tricycle landing gear and fuel in the wingtip floats. The prototype made its initial flight on April 30, 1946, and deliveries began five months later. Unfortunately, Grumman had much over-estimated the potential market and sold only 59 Mallards instead of the anticipated 250; production ended in May 1951. However, the aircraft was not quite the failure that this record might suggest, for its use was both widespread and long-lived.

Most Mallards were used originally as VIP and executive aircraft (including three by the Dutch and Egyptian royal flights), though a small number were operated on airline services in the 1950s by Air Community Inc, Air Tahiti and Pacific Western. Nitto Airlines of Japan had a fleet of five in the early 1960s, and a decade later fleets of similar size were being operated by Antilles Air Boats (four) and Chalk's International (six). Several others were converted to PT6A-powered Frakes Turbo Mallards following the testing of a turboprop-engined prototype in 1971.

Grumman G-73 Mallard (N3010) of Chalk's International, the Florida-based commuter division of Resorts International, photographed in March 1980

Convair-liner Model 240 (N8410H) operated in the late 1940s and early 1950s by Western Airlines

Convair Model 240

On July 8, 1946, Convair flew the prototype of its 30-passenger Model 110, which had been designed to meet the requirements of American Airlines. Powered by two 2,100 hp Pratt & Whitney R-2800-S1C3-G radial engines, it did not offer sufficiently attractive payload/range characteristics and did not go into production. Instead, Convair developed the design into the Model 240, seating 40 passengers in a slimmer fuselage and powered by 2,400 hp R-2800-CA18 engines. This flew for the first time on March 16, 1947, and an order for 75 was received from American Airlines. Production began in late 1947 and deliveries in February 1948, and the Convair 240 entered service with American on June 1 of that year. Other customers for ten or more included Pan American and Western in the USA, and KLM in the Netherlands.

About 50 airlines operated Convair 240s, including Continental, Ethiopian, FAMA (Argentina), Mohawk, Swissair and TWA; many others became business executive transports. Production ended in 1958 after the completion of 571, of which 179 were for the civil market; the remainder were made up of 365 T-29 aircrew trainers and 26 C-131A transports for the US Air Force.

Development of a turboprop-engined version was initiated by Convair, which had two Allison 501-A2s installed in a modified Convair 240. Known as the Turboliner, it flew for the first time on December 29, 1950. No immediate orders for such a version were forthcoming, but it paved the way for the later Convair 540, 580 and 600/640 (see pages 143, 148 and 168).

Boeing Stratocruiser (N90941) of American Overseas Airlines

Boeing Model 377 Stratocruiser

Production numbers alone are not the only guide to the success or fame of a transport aeroplane. Although only 55 were built, Boeing's big Stratocruiser impressed the travelling public with the spaciousness and comfort of its passenger cabin, and will remain more permanently in the memory than many of the characterless metal tubes which followed it. Yet the capaciousness of that "double-bubble" fuselage, which certainly *looked* as if its upper deck had been fattened out to give travellers more room, was an illusion: for the same floor area, the contemporary DC-4 had a greater cabin volume and seven inches more headroom, even if it could not offer the Stratocruiser's pressurised cabin.

The "Strat" originated in the wartime Boeing 367, a military transport with a new pressurised fuselage mated to the wings, tail, powerplant and landing gear of the Superfortress bomber. The YC-97 prototype of this design flew on October 9, 1945, and was followed by large-scale production of C-97s and KC-97 tankers for the USAAF. One of these, modified as the Model 377, became the prototype Stratocruiser, flying for the first time on July 8, 1947. Planned originally to carry 100 passengers or 35,000lb of cargo, the Stratocruiser in service more typically accommodated 89 on the upper deck in five-abreast seating, and the cabin also incorporated a cocktail bar and lounge on the lower deck.

Largest Stratocruiser fleet was that of Pan American, which ordered 20 in June 1946 and put them into service from September 1948; other US customers were American Overseas Airlines (eight, of which six later went to Pan Am), Northwest (ten) and United (seven). British Overseas Airways, which began services in December 1949 with six aircraft, later also acquired four others ordered originally by SAS, six from United and one from Pan Am. Stratocruisers served for ten years with BOAC but all had disappeared from airline service by the early 1960s (Transocean, with ten, was the last major operator), though some later served as freighters or provided components for the Aero Spacelines "Guppy" conversions.

Night scene at London's Heathrow Airport, with BOAC Stratocruiser G-ALSA *Cathay* **and Pan Am's** *Clipper Yankee*

Martin 4-0-4 (N40419) of Piedmont Airlines

Martin 4-0-4

On June 20, 1947, Martin flew the prototype of its 3-0-3 pressurised development of the Model 2-0-2; a 3-0-4 cargo version was projected at the same time. Neither went into production, being shelved two years later to make way for the Martin 4-0-4, which was essentially a pressurised 2-0-2A with a 3ft 3in-longer fuselage and higher operating weights. The launching orders received from Eastern (35) and TWA (30) were later increased to 60 and 41 respectively, accounting for all except two of the entire 4-0-4 production run. (The other two were built as RM-1s for the US Coast Guard.)

A converted Martin 2-0-2, first flown on October 21, 1950, served as prototype for the 4-0-4. Service entry followed in October 1951 with TWA and in January 1952 with Eastern.

Aircraft from both airlines were subsequently re-sold to other operators and established a sound reputation for safety and reliability. By 1971, when about 40 were still in service, the largest fleets were those of Piedmont and Southern. Three years later the latter still had 14, but by the late 1970s the surviving 4-0-4s had moved on again to work for smaller operators such as Florida Air Lines or in the business world as corporate transports.

CF-TGC, an L-1049C Super Constellation of Trans-Canada Air Lines, photographed over Toronto

N1010C *London Airtrader*, **an L-1049H of Seaboard & Western**

Lockheed Super Constellation

Nine basic versions of the Super Constellation were designated by Lockheed, though there were many more variations on the military L-1049A, B and F, produced for the US Air Force and Navy as the RC-121 and WV/R7V respectively.

The L-1049 represented a massive 18ft 4in stretch of the standard Constellation fuselage, its other features including uprated R-3350-CB1 engines (2,700 hp each), much greater fuel capacity, and larger, rectangular cabin windows. The original Constellation prototype, converted as the first L-1049, made its initial flight on October 13, 1950. But the available power was not enough to offset the increase in size and weight, and only 24 of this model were built. They were produced for Eastern and TWA, entering service with the former in December 1951.

Next civil model (56 built) was the L-1049C, first flown on February 17, 1953. It entered service with KLM that August and TWA in the September; it was powered by the 3,250 hp Turbo Compound version of the R-3350, already introduced on the L-1049B/RC-121C/R7V. The L-1049D, of which four were built (first flight September 1954), was a cargo conversion of the C; the 18 passenger-carrying L-1049Es offered detail improvements.

Payload/range performance was improved again in the L-1049G with uprated (3,400 hp) Turbo Compounds, wingtip fuel tanks and accommodation for up to 95 passengers. The "Super G" made its first flight on December 12, 1954, and went into service with Northwest Airlines in the spring of 1955. It proved the most popular "Super Connie" model, a total of 104 being manufactured. The final model in the L-1049 series was the L-1049H, a mixed-traffic counterpart of the G with a maximum payload of 24,293lb. Production of the L-1049H totalled 53.

Sikorsky S-55 (N414A) of Los Angeles Airways

Sikorsky S-55

Sikorsky's second large-scale production helicopter, the S-55 was also the company's second most successful type in terms of numbers built, surpassed only by the S-58. Total S-55 production over more than a decade amounted to 1,828, including versions built or assembled by foreign licensees Westland (485), Mitsubishi (71) and SNCA du Sud-Est (five). More than a thousand of the 1,200-plus manufactured by the parent company were military or naval models, as were most of the foreign examples. Over 200 were used by civilian operators, however, and many survive today, often in re-engined form with turbine powerplants.

First flight was made on November 10, 1949, by a YH-19A prototype for the USAF; American civil certification was granted on March 25, 1952. There were initially two basic civil models: the S-55A with 600 hp Pratt & Whitney R-1340 engine, and the S-55B with a 700 hp Wright R-1300. The commercial equivalent of the Wright-engined H-19B/D, with downward-angled tailboom, was designated S-55C. Westland-built WS-55s were known as Whirlwinds; the Whirlwind Series 3 (again mostly for military use) was a Westland development with a nose-mounted Rolls-Royce Gnome gas-turbine engine.

In the United States the S-55 was (in 1953) the first helicopter to be certificated for scheduled passenger operations, which were started on July 8 of that year by S-55s of New York Airways between that city's three major airports. Other early commercial operators of the type were Los Angeles Airways and Chicago Helicopter Airways.

North Central Airlines Convair-liner 340 (N90854)

Convair Model 340

A stretched version of the Convair 240, the Model 340 differed in having 13ft 7in more wing span, a 4ft 6in-longer fuselage (seating four extra passengers) and R-2800-CB16 Double Wasp engines; it flew for the first time on October 5, 1951. The first operator was United Air Lines, which began using this version of the Convair-liner on March 28, 1952, and 222 were built, initially for nearly 20 domestic or overseas airlines. Many of these later became corporate transports.

Production also included 108 military examples: 71 C-131B/C/Ds for the US Air Force and 37 R4Y-1s for the US Navy. Of these, the C-131D and R4Y-1 were, like the commercial version, 44-seaters; the C-131B could carry 48 passengers. The two YC-131Cs (first flight June 29, 1954) were powered by Allison T56 turboprops and were later used to obtain civil certification for the Allison-powered Convair 580.

Sunliner Arapahoe **(N73112), a Convair 340 in service with Frontier Airlines**

Douglas DC-7

Developed to combat TWA's introduction of the Super Constellation on domestic trunk routes, the DC-7 represented yet another stretch of the DC-6/6A/6B series. A fuselage 2ft 3in longer than that of the DC-6B enabled it to seat up to 95 passengers. The new Douglas Commercial designation DC-7 was prompted by its introduction of Wright R-3350 Turbo Compound engines, four 3,250 hp examples of which powered the prototype on its first flight on May 18, 1953. Production of the initial model totalled 120, but despite the extra power the DC-7's direct operating costs were disappointing, and engine vibration and noise were greater than on the DC-6B. Nevertheless, Douglas built 96 examples of the basically similar DC-7B, an "overseas" version first flown on April 25, 1955, and put into service by Pan American a month later.

Despite its extra payload/range capability, the DC-7B still fell somewhat short of true intercontinental range, and more extensive design changes were introduced on the DC-7C, which flew for the first time on December 20, 1955. Making a virtue of necessity, an additional 5ft section was inserted in each wing between the fuselage and inboard engine nacelle, simultaneously reducing the cabin noise level and providing space for the carriage of additional fuel. Control-surface area was increased proportionately, and the 3,400 hp version of the Turbo Compound was adopted. Fuselage length was increased yet again, an additional 3ft 4in plug permitting the maximum passenger capacity to be increased to 105. Vertical tail surface areas were increased to offset the longer fuselage.

Thus, with a payload capacity more than 25 per cent better than that of the original DC-7 (25,350lb compared with 20,000lb), and a maximum range in excess of 5,600 miles, the DC-7C at last realised fully the intercontinental potential of the design. With avionics, equipment and airfield performance also improved, it seemed set fair to enjoy a long and profitable career. Unfortunately, the jet age in commercial air transport was about to begin in earnest, and production of the total of 120 DC-7Cs, the last model in the series, ended in late 1958. By the mid-1970s only about 20 DC-7-series aircraft remained in scheduled airline service, though many operators were still using DC-7F freighter conversions.

Panagra DC-7B (N51700 *El Inter Americano*). This DC-7 version still had the old DC-6-size vertical tail

Superb air-to-air study of a DC-7C, Braniff International's N5900

Flight deck of a BOAC DC-7C (G-AOIF)

Historic rollout: the Boeing 367-80 (N70700) emerges from its
hangar on May 14, 1954

Boeing Model 367-80

In March 1981 sales of Boeing
jet transports passed the 4,500
mark, representing an average
of nearly 200 a year since the
first production 707 flew in
1957, almost 24 years earlier.
Most of these were of four basic
types (707/720, 727, 737 and
747), which between them had
flown 96 million revenue hours,
nearly 43,000 million miles, and
carried almost 3,500 million
passengers. Major US
customers over the years, each
buying 50 or more aircraft, have
been American (299), Braniff
(120), Continental (72), Delta
(118), Eastern (170), Northwest
(165), Pan American (200), TWA
(233), United (352) and Western
(105); these operators account
for more than two-thirds of the

2,556 Boeings sold by that date
to 55 domestic customers. Of
the 157 overseas customers,
only Lufthansa (137) tops the
100 mark, though Air France
(94), All Nippon (69), British
Airways (77) and Qantas (56)
have each bought more than 50.

It is a success story that is
unlikely ever to be rivalled in
the history of air transport. The
aeroplane that began it all,
N70700, was rolled out of its
hangar at Renton, Washington,
on May 14, 1954, and made its
first flight two months later, on
July 15. It had begun life in 1950
as the Model 367-64, a paper
design for a Stratocruiser
development with underwing
pairs of J57 jet engines. A
modified design with singly

podded engines and a new
fuselage was frozen in 1952 as
the Model 367-80, and this
designation was retained until
the prototype was completed.
After 707 production was well
established the "Dash Eighty"
reverted to that designation and
served for many years as a
flying testbed for new engines,
high-lift devices and other aerodynamic improvements,
landing gears, avionics, in-flight
refuelling tanker equipment,
and many other features. In so
doing it acquired a "modification record" that has probably
never been surpassed in commercial aviation history.

Convair 440 Metropolitan of Swissair (HB-IMC)

Convair Model 440

Also known – mostly in Europe – as the Metropolitan, the Convair 440 was an improved Model 340 with increased payload capacity (maximum 52 passengers), higher gross weight, uprated R-2800-CB17 engines in redesigned nacelles, better cabin soundproofing and (on most aircraft) nose-mounted weather radar. The prototype, converted from a Convair 340, made its first flight on October 6, 1955, and was quickly followed on December 15 by the first production Model 440.

Apart from 15 TC-131Es for the US Air Force, all of the 179 examples built were for civil operators, the major US airline customers being Allegheny, Eastern, Mackey and North Central. In Europe the type was operated by Iberia, SAS and Swissair. Several Convair 340s were also eventually modified to Model 440 standard.

Scandinavian Airlines System Convair 440 (SE-BSR *Bjarne Viking*)

Sabena Sikorsky S-58 (OO-SHI) at Rotterdam heliport

Sikorsky S-58

Sikorsky built 1,821 examples of the S-58 between 1954–70, of which well over 1,300 were military versions for the US Army (CH-34 Choctaw), Navy (SH-34 Seabat) and Marine Corps (UH-34 Seahorse), and several foreign air arms. The first S-58 to fly, on March 8, 1954, was an XHSS-1 prototype for the US Navy, production deliveries of which began in August 1955. Main commercial versions were the 12-seat airline S-58C, certificated on August 2, 1956, and two passenger/cargo models, the S-58B and S-58D. Customers for the S-58C included Chicago Helicopter Airways, New York Airways and Belgium's Sabena.

Additional production was undertaken in France, where Sud-Aviation assembled 135 from US-built components and licence-built a further 166. In the UK the manufacturer was Westland, which built large numbers for domestic and various foreign air forces and navies. These aircraft had the name Wessex and were powered by gas-turbine engines, either a single Napier Gazelle or twin (coupled) Rolls-Royce Gnomes. Westland production included 15 examples of the Gnome-engined Wessex Mk 60, a 10-passenger version used extensively by Bristow Helicopters for the support of offshore oil and gas rigs in the North Sea.

Sikorsky also developed a twin-turboshaft model, the S-58T, marketing kits in the early 1970s for the conversion of existing piston-engined S-58s by installing the 1,800 shp Pratt & Whitney Aircraft of Canada PT6T Turbo Twin Pac.

One of the Westland-built S-58s: a Wessex Mk 60 (G-ATCA) used by Bristow Helicopters for offshore oil rig support in the North Sea

Sikorsky S-58T turbine-powered version

Vertol Model 44B, with US registration N74057, prior to delivery to Sabena of Belgium

Vertol Model 44

This single-engined tandem-rotor helicopter began life as the Piasecki PH-42, flying for the first time in the spring of 1956. Essentially it was a refined and civilianised version of the military H-21 (Models 42/43), which was built in large numbers during the first half of the 1950s for the US Army and Air Force as the Shawnee and Work Horse respectively. It was redesignated Model 44 when Piasecki Helicopter Corporation became Vertol Aircraft Corporation in 1956. Following CAB certification in April 1957 it was offered in three basic versions: the 19-passenger Model 44A, 15-passenger 44B and executive 44C. The 44A was however sold only in military form for troop/casualty/cargo transportation or anti-submarine patrol; the 44B differed in having oval (instead of circular) cabin windows.

Principal commercial operator was New York Airways, which acquired five Vertol 44Bs; others were operated by Sabena of Belgium and Spartan Air Service in Canada. The NYA Vertols were equipped for emergency operation from water, having watertight lower fuselages and inflatable flotation bags attached to the landing gear. A number of oil and construction companies bought Model 44s, but the advent of Vertol's newer, larger, turbine-powered Model 107 limited production of the Model 44 to relatively modest numbers. Two aircraft – a 44B and a 44C – were acquired by the USSR for undisclosed purposes.

The ultimate "Connie" stretch: an L-1649A Starliner (N7301C) in TWA markings

Air France Starliner F-BHBL *Rochambeau* **at Paris Orly**

Lockheed Starliner

As with the Constellation and Super Constellation, the prime mover in bringing about the L-1649A Starliner was TWA, which in the mid-1950s asked Lockheed to produce an even longer-range development of the L-1049 to meet the challenge of the Douglas DC-7Cs ordered by its competitors. Lockheed responded by adding another 2ft 7in to the fuselage and designing an entirely new thin-section wing with straight taper instead of the familiar curved trailing edge of the earlier Constellations. Of greater span than the original wing, it could accommodate much more fuel,

so providing the increase in range that was the principal requirement.

Given a new name to help promote the new image, the Starliner first flew on October 11, 1956, and entered service with TWA in June of the following year; other customers included Air France and Lufthansa. The spread of jet airliner services from 1958 onwards meant that the Starliner had arrived too late, however, and only 43 were produced.

A veteran of the post-war long-haul routes for a quarter of a century and more, the

"Connie" in its various guises was a familiar sight in all parts of the world, not least on the North Atlantic routes. By the mid-1970s, however, comparatively few remained in regular airline service, though several continued to serve in the cargo role. The Connie's elegant, serpentine shape is much missed: already, among the podded look-alikes of today's jet airliner scene, it seems to belong to a bygone age.

Prototype Boeing Vertol 107 in NYA markings, about to land at New York's downtown heliport

Boeing Vertol 107-II

Originated in 1956 by Vertol Aircraft Corporation (which became a part of Boeing four years later), the Model 107 prototype flew for the first time on April 22, 1958, powered by two 860 shp Lycoming T53 turboshaft engines. Initial US Army interest was transferred to the larger Model 114 (which became the Chinook), and one Army YCH-1A was refitted with 1,050 shp General Electric T58s to become a commercial prototype for the Model 107-II. Major US production of this tandem-rotor helicopter took the form of UH-46 and CH-46 Sea Knights for the US Navy and Marine Corps, or export equivalents for the air arms of Canada and Sweden. Boeing Vertol also built six civil Model 107-IIs for New York Airways, the first of which was flown on May 19, 1961. Powered by 1,250 shp CT58s, they entered service with NYA on July 1, 1962.

In June 1965 Boeing transferred manufacturing and marketing rights in the 107-II to Japan, where it continued in production with Kawasaki during 1982 as the KV-107IIA. Most of those built in Japan have also been military models, but other customers have included AirLift Inc of Japan (three), Pan Am/NYA (three), Columbia Helicopters, USA (six), Japan's Metropolitan Police Department (one), and the Saudi Arabian government (six). Several of these were to KV-107II standard; the IIA has uprated engines and increased fuel capacity; those for Saudi Arabia are equipped for fire-fighting (KV-107IIA-SM-1) or rescue/casevac duties (KV-107IIA-SM-2). The others are configured as airline passenger, VIP or cargo transports.

Lockheed L-188 Electra

In a curious reversal of fortunes America, which for so long has dominated the world of commercial jet transportation, failed in its only serious attempt at a turboprop airliner. That the aircraft itself is not to blame is evidenced strongly by the unqualified success of its military counterpart, the maritime P-3 Orion. The Electra's failure (it was contemporary with the Vickers Vanguard, Britain's attempt at a follow-up to the highly successful Viscount) was due chiefly to its timing, though no hint of this was evident when the prototype made its maiden flight on December 6, 1957. Orders for 144 Electras had then already been received, yet ultimately civil production totalled only 168, excluding prototypes.

The Electra was developed out of an earlier low-wing, four-Allison-engine design known as the CL-310 to meet initially the needs of American Airlines; this operator's order for 35 was followed immediately by a contract from Eastern for 40 L-188s. Eastern was the first, largest and most loyal operator of the Electra. After the initial L-188A version was certificated in August 1958, Eastern began to receive the type in October and put it into service on January 12, 1959. In the mid-1970s the Eastern fleet still included 10 Electras, though all had gone by the end of the decade. American Airlines' L-188As entered service 11 days after the Eastern aircraft. Other major customers included Braniff, Ansett/ANA (the first non-US operator) and KLM (the only European buyer). Several Electras were later converted for freight-carrying by the installation of a large side-loading door; Overseas National was among the operators of this version.

Production of the L-188A, which totalled 113 (excluding prototypes), was followed by 55 examples of the longer-range L-188C with more fuel, 74–99 passengers and higher operating weights. Initial orders for this version came from the US carriers Northwest and Western.

Cathay Pacific's VR-HFO was the fourth L-188A Electra built

Boeing Model 707
(domestic versions)

It is hard to believe it now, but the Boeing 707 — or, rather, its Model 367-80 prototype — appeared on the airline market at a bad time. In the mid-1950s many of the world's largest commercial operators had exhausted themselves financially in the race to score over each other with extra payload/range performance squeezed out of the stock piston-engined transports from Douglas and Lockheed, and the last thing they wanted was to be forced into buying jets. Fortunately for Boeing, there were large initial orders for the 367-80's military version, the KC-135. But then in October 1955 Pan American, with an initial order for six commercial 707s, gave the signal for the biggest spending spree the air transport world has ever seen.

Production of this first model, the 707-120, eventually amounted to 141, plus five of a "hot and high" version, the 707-220, for Braniff. Most KC-135 tooling could also be used for the 707, although the latter's fuselage was four inches wider and the 707-138s built for Qantas had a 10ft-shorter fuselage. From 1959 the fin height and area were increased, and some aircraft also incorporated a small underfin. First flight of a production 707-120 took place on December 20, 1957, and deliveries to Pan Am began in August 1958. Although intended for domestic routes the 707-120 was capable of trans-Atlantic range, and Pan Am's first jet services (started on October 26, 1958) were on this route, between New York and Paris. Domestic services (New York–Los Angeles) were begun on January 25, 1959, by 707-120s of American Airlines.

Most 707-120s, including three VC-137 VIP transports built for the US Air Force, were later converted to 707-120B standard by fitting JT3D-series turbofan engines and the wing improvements designed for the Boeing 720B.

October 26, 1958, and a worthwhile occasion for calling out the band: Pan American's first Boeing 707, N711PA *Clipper America*, is about to leave New York for Paris on the first jet service by a US airline

Qantas 707s had a shorter fuselage than other models and could carry a spare engine in a pod under the port wing centre-section

The rarely illustrated 707-220. Only five were built, all for Braniff

Engine pod for the JT3D-1, with which early 707s were converted to turbofan power as 707-120Bs

Beechcraft Models 65 and 80 Queen Air

Most Beech military aircraft for the US services have been examples of off-the-shelf commercial types, or developments of civil designs. The Queen Air reversed this trend, originating in 1958 as a civil conversion of the U-8F, an enlarged variant of the US Army's Seminole staff transport, which was itself developed from the Twin-Bonanza. Known as the Model 65 Queen Air, the prototype made its first flight on August 28, 1958. It was powered by two 340 hp Lycoming IGSO-480-A1B6 engines and could carry seven passengers. Certification was quickly achieved (February 1959), and deliveries began shortly afterwards.

Aimed at the executive transport market, the enlarged (six/nine-seat) Model 65-80 with 380 hp IGSO-540-A1A Lycomings and a sweptback vertical tail flew on June 22, 1961, receiving FAA type approval in the following February. A 5ft increase in wing span and an extended nose marked the Model A80 which replaced it in 1964; the B80 of 1965 was the slightly refined principal version.

Variants included the Model 70 (with Model 80 wings and Model 65 powerplant); the seven/nine-passenger Queen Airliner B80 commuter transport version; and the pressurised Queen Air 88 of the late 1960s. Manufacture of the Models 65/70 ended in 1971 with some 450 examples built. Production of the Model 80 series, which ended in 1977, totalled 956.

A British-registered Beechcraft Model B65 Queen Air, photographed in 1963

Late-production Queen Air B80s in the markings of Air Algérie

Gulfstream American (Grumman) Gulfstream I

Designed by Grumman as the Model G-159, the original Gulfstream prototype (N701G) made its first flight on August 14, 1958. Certification of this 10/12-seat (maximum 19) twin-Dart executive transport was obtained on May 21, 1959, and customer deliveries began in the following month. Certification for public transport use, authorising operation as a 24-passenger local-service airliner, was gained in 1962.

Production, which totalled 200, ended in February 1969, but ten years later Gulfstream American Corporation (which had meanwhile acquired all jigs and tooling) decided to reinstate the type in production as the G-159C Gulfstream I-C, a 32/38-seat commuter transport version with a 10ft 8in-longer fuselage. The prototype, a converted Gulfstream I (N5400C), flew for the first time on October 25, 1979, and received FAR Part 121 certification just over a year later. Among early customers for the Gulfstream I-C were Air North and Air US.

Corporate Gulfstream I (N798R), registered to R. J. Reynolds Industries in 1981

Eland Convair demonstration aircraft, photographed in 1957 in company with an Airspeed Ambassador (behind) and a Vickers Varsity (rearmost)

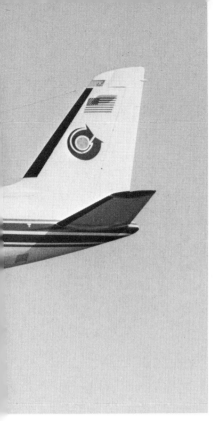

Convair Model 540

Seven Convair 340s were converted to turboprop-powered Model 540 standard, the first of these flying on February 9, 1955, with 3,060 ehp Napier Eland NEl.1s (the more powerful Eland 504A subsequently became standard). Major operator was Allegheny Airlines, which had six; these entered service from July 1959 but were withdrawn three years later when development of the Eland engine was terminated. The seventh, converted by Pacific Airmotive, was operated by Butler Air Transport in Australia.

Three other 540s were modified from Convair 440 airframes by Canadair, and two of these were delivered to Quebecair. Canadair then produced ten new aircraft to Convair 540 standard for the RCAF as the CL-66B. Known by that service as CC-109 Cosmopolitans, they were delivered from July 1960; eight were later re-sold on the civilian market and re-equipped to commercial 540 standard.

Convair 540 (N340EL), converted to Eland turboprops by Canadair

ZS-CKC *Cape Town*, a Boeing 707-320 of South African Airways,
showing the taller fin and small underfin fitted to many 707 models

Air-India's VT-DJI *Nandi Devi* was a 707-420 delivered with the
original short fin

Boeing Model 707
(intercontinental versions)

An 8ft 5in-longer fuselage typically seating 131–189 passengers, 11ft 7in more wing span and uprated JT4A-series turbojets characterised the Model 707-320 intercontinental version of the Boeing 707, which flew for the first time on January 11, 1959. Curiously, whereas the domestic model had begun its operating career on trans-Atlantic services, the first use of the intercontinental 707-320 (from August 1959) was on internal services across the United States. The operator in each case was Pan American, which started 707-320 services across the North Atlantic two months after the domestic inaugural. By that time a second intercontinental version had appeared in the form of the 707-420 ordered by BOAC. This designation covered not only a change of powerplant (to Rolls-Royce Conway turbofans), but also a 2ft 11in increase in fin height and the addition of a small underfin (later specified by several other airlines for their -120s and -320s). The 707-420 entered service in May 1960; other operators of this version included Air-India, El Al, Lufthansa and Varig. Production totalled 69 707-320s and 37 707-420s.

The first flight of the 707-320B, on January 31, 1962, introduced not only a change to JT3D-3 turbofan engines but also new low-drag wingtips which increased the overall span by 3ft 4in. In the following year Boeing announced a convertible passenger/cargo version, the 707-320C, with a large forward freight door on the port side and accommodation for 219 passengers or 9,115 cu ft of cargo space. In all-cargo configuration the payload volume was increased to 9,382 cu ft.

The 707-320C was the last commercial Boeing 707 variant to remain in production: 336 were built, including 28 for non-airline customers, before manufacture came to an end in 1980. Of all the 707 family, only the E-3A AWACS military development of the 707-320B was then still being built, for the USAF and NATO; output of -320Bs for commercial customers totalled 171. Orders for 707s totalled 962, of which 881 were for commercial operators, during the 24-year production run.

Boeing 707-320C (N322F *Pole Cat)* **used as a freighter by Flying Tiger Line**

DC-8 Series 30 (F-BIUY) operated by TAI of France

McDonnell Douglas DC-8

Coming about a year behind Boeing's Model 707, the DC-8 was Douglas's answer to the Seattle company's design. In the event, it achieved a far lower sales total than the 707, although orders were healthy enough to keep it in production for ten years. Go-ahead for the design, known originally as the Douglas Model 1881, was announced in June 1955, and Pan American ordered 25 of a US domestic model in the following October; by the end of the year an intercontinental model had also been projected.

The prototype DC-8 flew for the first time on May 30, 1958. Certification was granted on August 31, 1959, and the domestic Series 10 entered service, simultaneously with United and Delta, on September 18 that year. (Pan Am had meanwhile cancelled its original order, placed chiefly as an insurance in case the Boeing 707 programme foundered.) Twenty-eight DC-8 Series 10s, powered by 13,500lb st JT3C-6 turbojet engines, were built.

The Series 20 (first flight November 29, 1958), of which 34 were completed, had 15,800lb st JT4A-3s but was otherwise generally similar.

First of the three inter-continental models to appear was the DC-8 Series 30 (57 built). This made its maiden flight on February 21, 1959, and could be powered by 16,800lb st JT4A-9 or 17,500lb st JT4A-11 turbojets. Five months later, on July 23, 1959, came the initial flight of the first fan-engined version, the Series 40, with 17,500lb st Rolls-Royce Conway Mk 509s; 32 of this model were built. The most successful production model was the Series 50, first flown on December 20, 1960, with JT3D-1 or -3 turbofans; 89 of these were completed, and some earlier DC-8s were converted to Series 50 standard.

In April 1961 Douglas announced the DC-8F Jet Trader, an all-cargo or mixed passenger/cargo version based on the Series 50 and able to carry a maximum payload of 189 passengers or 95,282lb of freight. The first Jet Trader was flown on October 29, 1962, and 54 were produced in two versions: the Srs 54F basic model with JT3D-3 engines, and the Srs 55F with JT3D-3Bs.

Production of these standard-fuselage DC-8s thus totalled 294, ending in November 1968. Almost as many of the highly stretched Super Sixty models were built (see page 171).

The Lockheed 10A Electra in the foreground was one of TCA's first
aircraft. It was photographed in 1962 against this DC-8 Series 40 to
mark 25 years of passenger services by the Canadian airline

Registered to KLM as PH-DCP, this Series 50 DC-8 was leased to
Philippine Air Lines in 1962

Convair Model 580

The Convair 580, which entered airline service with Frontier in June 1964, was the most successful of the turboprop "transplants" based on the airframes of the piston-engined Convair-liners. The prototype, converted by PacAero from a Model 340, first flew on January 19, 1960, and the certification programme, aided by the use of the USAF's Allison-engined YC-131C, resulted in the award of an ATC for the 580 on April 21 of that year. Early deliveries were mainly to corporate owners, it being another four years before the type went into regular airline service.

The overall "production" total of 130 included 110 for airline customers, including Allegheny and Lake Central (which later, after amalgamation, had a fleet of 40). Substantial numbers were still in service in the mid-1970s, the major operator by that time being North Central Airlines. Frontier Airlines phased out its fleet of 15 Convair 580s in 1982.

Allison-engined Convair 580, another turboprop conversion of the Model 340

Convair Model 880

Produced in two versions, the Convair 880 was launched in the spring of 1956 with the announcement of simultaneous orders from Delta Air Lines (10) and TWA (30). At that time it was known as the Model 600 Skylark because of its design speed of 600 mph. Later this name was changed briefly to Golden Arrow before both the name and the model number were dropped in favour of the 880 designation (600 mph = 880ft per second). Faster but smaller than the 707 and DC-8, the domestic version (Convair 880 Model 22) made its first flight on January 27, 1959, and deliveries began a year later. Certification followed on May 1, 1960, and it entered service,

with Delta, in the same month. Seating, for a typical 88-110 passengers (maximum 124), was five-abreast.

The prototype meanwhile underwent modification before flying again on October 3, 1960, as the intercontinental 880-M Model 31 with uprated CJ805 engines, more fuel, leading-edge wing slats and a bigger fin. Certification was granted in July 1961, deliveries (to Civil Air Transport of Taiwan) having begun in the previous month. Seventeen 880-Ms were included in the total production of 65 Model 880s. Most had been withdrawn by the mid-1970s, at which time the major operator was Cathay Pacific of Hong Kong.

N8483H, a Convair 880 Model 22, was leased by Northeast Airlines from TWA in the early 1980s

United Air Lines was the launch customer for the Boeing 720

Boeing Model 720

With a fuselage shortened by 7ft 9in and seating 110–165 passengers, this "baby" version of the 707-120 was announced in July 1957 and received its definitive model number four months later when United Air Lines placed an order for 11. The first 720 was flown on November 23, 1959; certification followed on June 30, 1960, and on July 5 United put the aircraft into service. The other major difference from the 707-120 lay in the wing: although the span was the same, it had increased sweep inboard of the inner JT3C engines and the Krueger flaps ran the whole length of each leading edge. United eventually increased its order to 29, accounting for nearly half of the 65 Model 720s completed. Other US airline customers were American (ten), Braniff (five), Eastern (15) and Pacific Northern (two). One aircraft was delivered to the Federal Aviation Administration and there was one overseas customer, Aer Lingus, which ordered three.

The turbofan-engined 720B, with JT3D-1s, flew for the first time on October 6, 1960, was certificated in March 1961 and entered service in the same month. Possessing a range almost equal to that of the intercontinental 707-320/420, the 720B received domestic orders from American Airlines (the first operator, for 15), Continental (eight), Northwest (17), and Western (27). This version fared somewhat better in the export market than its predecessor, attracting orders from Avianca (three), El Al (two), Ethiopian (three), Lufthansa (eight), Pakistan International (four) and Saudia (two) to bring overall production of the 720B to 89.

Sikorsky S-61L/S-61N

The original S-61 was designed to meet a US Navy anti-submarine requirement, flying for the first time as the XHSS-2 prototype on March 11, 1959. Redesignated SH-3 three years later, it was still in production in developed naval/military versions in the early 1980s. The two commercial models, combining the same rotor and transmission system with a much enlarged fuselage, are the S-61L landplane and the fully amphibious S-61N. The latter has twin stabilising floats, into which the main wheels retract; the S-61L has non-retractable wheel gear. Both can seat 28–30 passengers.

The S-61L flew for the first time on December 6, 1960, and the S-61N on August 7, 1962. Certification of the L – the first awarded to a twin-turboshaft commercial helicopter – was received in November 1961, and both models were later cleared for all-weather operation. First operator was Los Angeles Airways, which began S-61L services in March 1962; New York Airways also operated the L model.

Of the two variants, the S-61N proved the more popular, being acquired by several airline and other operators, including All Nippon (Japan), Ansett-ANA (Australia), BEA/British Airways (UK), Bristow (UK), Court Line (South Africa), Greenlandair (Denmark), Helikopter Service (Norway), Japan Air Lines, KLM (Netherlands), Okanagan (Canada) and San Francisco & Oakland (USA). Commercial S-61 production by Sikorsky (13 Ls and 123 Ns) ended in June 1980, though Agusta is **offering a modified version in Italy.**

Sikorsky S-61N in Los Angeles Airways markings

The S-61N was operated by British European Airways on its Penzance—Isles of Scilly service, replacing obsolete Dragon Rapide biplanes

Convair Model 990A Coronado

This longer and faster development of the 880 (or Convair 600 as it then was), offering an extra 10ft of fuselage and an initial seating capacity for 104–131 passengers, was proposed in early 1958. Powerplant was four CJ805-23B turbofans, and other changes included an increased-area wing with area-ruled anti-shock fairings on the trailing edges in which additional fuel could be carried. Known as the 990 Model 30, it was certificated in December 1961, the maiden flight having been made on January 24 of that year by the first of 20 aircraft ordered in July 1958 by American Airlines. Deliveries to this operator, and to Swissair in Europe, began in January 1962. It was the latter that, in late February, became the first operator to put the Convair 990 into service and the first to adopt the name

"Coronado"; American followed some three weeks later.

Boeing and Douglas had however scooped the pool of early jetliner sales by this time. Convair sold the 990 to other prestigious airlines, including Garuda, SAS and Varig, but total sales amounted to only 37 aircraft. In 1962 they all underwent modification to 990A standard: the outer engine pylons were shortened, all four pylons were further streamlined, and Krueger flaps were added to the wing leading edges. The 990A received certification for overseas use in October 1962 and for domestic operation in January 1963. About two dozen Coronados were still in service in the mid-1970s, and by late 1981 the major fleet was that of the Spanish carrier Spantax, which still had 11.

Convair 990 (SE-DAY *Adils Viking***) of Scandinavian Airlines System**

Convair Model 990 (PP-VJE) of the Brazilian operator Varig

Nine-passenger Sabreliner 40A

Sabreliner 60, with extra cabin windows

Rockwell (North American) Sabreliner

The Sabreliner, first flown on September 16, 1958, was designed to meet a USAF requirement for an off-the-shelf utility and combat readiness trainer, and 210 were produced by North American Aviation Inc for both the Air Force and the Navy under T-39 designations. Certification to commercial standards, which was a condition of USAF acceptance, was obtained on March 23, 1962. It was followed in April 1963 by a type certificate for the first true commercial version, the seven/nine-passenger Sabreliner Series 40, of which some 125 examples were built.

The Sabreliner 60, certificated in April 1967, had a fuselage 3ft 2in longer and with two extra windows (making five in

all) on each side, and uprated (3,300lb st) JT12A-8/8A turbojets instead of the 3,000lb st JT12A-6As of the Series 40. In 1969–70 (first flight December 4, 1969) this received a facelift to become the Sabreliner 70 (changed to 75 in 1971), improvements including a deeper fuselage and square (instead of triangular) cabin windows.

Turbofan engines (4,315lb st CF700-2D-2s) were introduced on October 18, 1972, with the first flight of the Sabreliner 75A, offering much improved performance and fuel economy; delivery of a Model 75A in July 1977 marked the 500th Sabreliner to be built. Shortly before this, on June 29, Rockwell (which had

merged with North American in 1967) flew the first Sabreliner 65, which was still the standard current production model in 1981–82. This eight-passenger version combines a fuselage the same length as that of the Model 75A (but with triangular windows) with a new super-critical wing and Garrett TFE731 turbofans. The Model 60A, with aerodynamic improvements to the wings and tail, was introduced in 1978. Production of the Models 60A and 75A ended in the spring of 1979.

155

Howard 500

The Manufacturing Division of Howard Aero Inc was formed in 1955 to produce the Super Ventura, a version of the US Navy's PV-1 patrol aircraft modified as an executive transport. It first flew in May 1955 and production deliveries began three months later. The Howard 500, which made its initial flight in September 1959, differed in being a new-built aircraft with a pressurised fuselage and numerous other improvements.

The first production Howard 500 was flown on March 15, 1960, but certification was not received until February 1963. Meanwhile, Howard had produced two other, generally similar aircraft, the Models 250 and 350. The former (first flight April 3, 1961) was a smaller design based on the Lockheed Model 18 Lodestar and seating 10–12 passengers. The Howard 350, which first flew on April 1, 1962, was generally similar to the Model 500 but had shorter-span wings and reduced fuel capacity.

Howard 500, a Lockheed Ventura development with pressurised fuselage and other improvements

Transporting Airbus A300 components by Aeromaritime Super Guppy

Aero Spacelines Guppy/Super Guppy

Faced with the problem of reducing the time and expense involved in transporting large items of space hardware, including the Saturn launch vehicle, from the western United States to the space centre at Cape Canaveral, Aero Spacelines initiated one of the most unorthodox modifications yet devised for a transport aeroplane. A former Pan Am Stratocruiser had an extra 16ft 8in of fuselage from another Stratocruiser inserted aft of the wings, and upon this "chassis" was built a huge new upper lobe with a 20ft maximum internal height. This gave the fuselage room to contain Saturn rocket stages; loading and unloading was achieved by unbolting the entire rear portion of the aircraft. The nickname "Pregnant Guppy" was given official recognition when Boeing redesignated the conversion

Model 377-PG. Its first flight, on September 19, 1962, was followed by those of the 377-SG Super Guppy on August 31, 1965; the 377-MG Mini-Guppy on May 24, 1967; the Guppy-101 on March 17, 1970; and the Guppy-201 on August 24, 1970.

Each of these later models had individual differences. The Super Guppy had 7,000 ehp T34-P-7WA turboprop engines, increased span, length and fuselage volume, and a front-loading swing-nose. The Mini-Guppy had 3,500 hp R-4360-B6 piston engines, Super Guppy wings and a rear-loading swing-tail. The Guppy-101 had a swing-nose and 4,912 shp Allison 501-D22C turboprops but was otherwise similar to the Mini. Longest fuselage of all (143ft 10in) was built for the Guppy-201, which also had a taller, more angular vertical tail, a swing-nose and the same

powerplant as the 101.

In addition to their early work for the NASA space programme the Guppy series have carried a wide variety of outsize loads, including oil rig equipment, large components for DC-10s and TriStars, and even complete helicopters. Well known during the past decade have been the two Guppies operated under contract to Airbus Industrie for the airlifting of major sub-assemblies of the A300 wide-bodied transport to the final assembly centre at Toulouse. Airbus acquired production rights to the Super Guppy in 1980 and is having two more built for 1982/83 delivery to cater for the increasing A300/310 production rate.

Short-fuselage Boeing 727-100 (9Y-TCO) in British West Indian Airways livery

Boeing Model 727

Conceived a quarter of a century ago, the Boeing 727 was a logical follow-on to the 707/720 series and was intended to meet the needs of short or intermediate-range airline operations. Its rear-mounted tri-jet configuration was, and still is, unique among Boeing's many transport aircraft designs, and its sales record – more than 1,800 sold by January 1982 – is likely to remain unchallenged by any other competitor. The configuration was frozen in September 1960, and the first 727 (a production aircraft) made its maiden flight on February 9, 1963. Launch customers, each with an order for 40, were Eastern and United; following certification on Christmas Eve 1963, the 727 entered airline service with the former on February 1, 1964, and with the

latter four days later.

The initial version, seating up to 131 passengers, was designated Model 727-100 and ran to a total of 569 examples. It in fact improved on Boeing's estimate of range with full payload and made attractive the proposition of a shorter-range version with an increased payload. Accordingly, Boeing developed the 20ft-longer Model 727-200 with up to 189 seats. This flew for the first time on July 27, 1967, and entered service five months later with Northeast Airlines. Convertible passenger/cargo and corporate versions of both basic models have also been produced, and customers have a choice of variants of the JT8D engine.

By the end of 1970 the 727 had exceeded the sales total of the 707/720 series and went on

to become the world's best (and fastest) selling jet airliner ever. Deliveries passed 1,000 (a figure since achieved only by the DC-9 and Boeing 737 among other commercial transports) on January 4, 1974, and 1,500 in July 1979. The Advanced 727-200, introduced in 1971, has a more luxurious interior, increased fuel capacity, uprated engines with noise suppression, and higher operating weights. It is now the only version in production, and with the earlier 727-200 series accounts for more than 1,200 of the 727s sold so far. Whether the 727 will reach the magic figure of 2,000 seems doubtful, as Boeing expects orders to diminish once the new Models 757 and 767 become available.

The appropriately named *Mount Olympus* **(SX-CBA), a Boeing 727-200 of Olympic Airways of Greece**

The white, gold and black livery of Libyan Arab Airlines is among the more eye-catching of many
hundreds of airline colour schemes carried by Boeing 727s the world over

Rollout of the 1,500th Model 727 in the summer of 1979

Beechcraft King Air C90 (1979 model)

Beechcraft Models 90 and 100 King Air

After test-flying a Queen Air 65 with PT6A engines Beech decided to develop a turboprop production model with a pressurised cabin. The resulting King Air 90 prototype flew for the first time on January 20, 1964. Production aircraft, seating eight people (including one or two pilots), had 525 ehp PT6A-6 engines and began to be delivered soon after FAA certification on May 19 of the same year. The 1966 King Air A90 and the B90 of 1967 were slightly improved models with 527 ehp PT6A-20s. The C90, introduced in autumn 1970, offered cabin refinements and 550 ehp PT6A-21s.

Shorter-span wings, a 4ft 2in-longer fuselage and 680 ehp PT6A-28 turboprops character-ised the King Air 100, which could carry a two-man crew and six to eight passengers normally, or 13 in a commuter configuration. This was certifi-cated in July 1969 and was followed in 1971 by the King Air A100 with increased fuel capacity and higher operating weights. In 1972 Beech married the 100/A100 powerplant to the C90 airframe to produce the King Air E90, offering a much better performance than the earlier 90-series twins. Three years later came the B100, similar to the A100 but with a change of powerplant to Garrett TPE331s rated at 715 shp. Latest model,

introduced in mid-1979, is a hybrid known as the Super King Air F90. This has a C90 fuselage, B100 wings, the T tail of the Super King Air 200 and 750 shp PT6A-135 turboprops.

Production of the King Air 90 series by January 1982 totalled about 1,500, including more than 850 Model 90/A90/ B90/C90s, nearly 350 E90s, over 60 F90s, about 160 military U-21s and 61 US Navy T-44As, another hybrid combining features of the C90 and E90. By the same date over 360 King Air 100/A100/B100s had been built, including a few for the USAF (as U-21Fs) and ten for the Spanish Air Force.

1978 models of the King Air A100 (nearest camera) and B100

Gates Learjet Model 24D, showing airstair door to cabin

Gates Learjet

Since 1965 Learjets have been delivered at an average rate of more than one a week, and at a rate of two per week since 1977. The 500th Learjet was delivered in April 1975 and the 1,000th in March 1980, making the type the most numerous business jet in the world.

The design, by William P. Lear Sr, began life in Switzerland as the Swiss-American Aircraft Corporation SAAC-23, but in mid-1962 the programme was transferred to Wichita, USA, where it became the Learjet 23. The first of three prototypes flew on October 7, 1963, certification was gained on July 31, 1964, and production of the six-passenger Model 23 with CJ610-1 turbojet engines totalled 104. Then followed the Learjet 24 (first flown on February 24, 1966, and certificated in March), and the 4ft 2in-longer Learjet 25 (first flight August 12, 1966, certificated on October 10, 1967). Successively improved versions of these, resulting in model suffix letters through to 24F and 25F, differed mainly in variations of their CJ610 engines (-4, -6 and -8A), passenger capacities (generally six or eight), and fuel/range capabilities. Structural differences included disappearance of the early tailplane/fin bullet (from the 24D) and introduction (on the 25D) of a new "Century III" cambered wing leading edge to improve airfield characteristics. This latter feature has

Model 25 Learjet, with longer fuselage

Learjet 36, with turbofan engines and extended-span wings

been applied to all Learjets built since 1976.

A turbofan branch of the family was founded on January 4, 1973, with the first flight of the Learjet 26, a six-passenger Model 25 re-engined with Garrett TFE731s. On August 22 of that year it was joined by the Learjet 35 (eight passengers and less fuel), and both were certificated in mid-1974, the former becoming known as Learjet 36 in its production form. Learjets 35/36 also differ from the 25 in having extended wingtips and a longer fuselage with an extra cabin window in each side. With the Century III wing they are designated 35A

and 36A, and — in recent years at least — have outsold the 24/25 series by more than two to one.

In 1977 Gates introduced "Longhorn" versions of all four basic models, the CJ610-powered counterparts of the 24/25 being known as the Learjet 28 and 29, and those with TFE731s and a deeper, "stand-up" cabin as Learjet 55 and 56 Longhorns. The name Longhorn stems from the use of a modified Century III wing with a NASA-type winglet at each tip (to improve cruising efficiency) in place of the previously standard tip tank. First to fly, on August 24, 1977, was the Model 28 Longhorn with CJ610-8A

engines and seats for eight passengers; this was certificated on January 30, 1979. The Model 29 carries six passengers and extra fuel. The ten-passenger Model 55 Longhorn flew on April 19, 1979, and gained certification on March 18, 1981. The Model 56, with more fuel and range, carries up to eight passengers.

Prototype (N266GL) for the first Longhorn Learjets, the Models 28/29

First ''50-series'' Longhorn Learjet, the ten-passenger Model 55

Hamilton Westwind

Hamilton Westwind IV, a much modified Beechcraft Model 18

Hamilton's first variation on the Beechcraft Model 18 was the Little Liner, a nine-passenger refurbished D18S of the early 1960s with extended wingtips, new nosecone, cleaned-up engine cowlings, modified landing gear, airline-type seating, optional cargo door and other changes. The Westwind series have stretched fuselages accommodating up to 17 passengers or equivalent cargo. First to appear was the Westwind III, which made its initial flight in 1963 and was certificated in 1964. This carries eight passengers or a 4,000lb payload and has PT6A-20 turbo-prop engines as standard, with PT6A-27s, PT6A-28s and LTP 101s as options.

The Westwind II STD, which first flew in late 1973, is a 17-passenger commuter version with PT6A-34s and optional tricycle landing gear. The Westwind IV (no longer available) was similar to the Westwind III except for a 2ft 6in-longer fuselage with large cargo door, and a choice of six possible powerplants.

Aero Commander (ZS-CSN) of South West Airways

Rockwell Turbo Commander 690A, with turbocharged engines and pressurised cabin

Gulfstream American Commander series

Incredibly, the elegant Commanders have been with us for more than 30 years, with only the most subtle of external departures (except for the swept-back vertical tail, introduced in 1954) from the general appearance of Ted Smith's original L-3805 model, which made its first flight on April 23, 1948. Unable to interest his employer, Douglas, in his ideas for a business twin based on the military A-20 and A-26 attack aircraft, Smith and a handful of colleagues left in December 1944 to form the Aero Design and Engineering Company. Since then production of a succession of developed versions has continued unabated, initially as Aero Commanders, subsequently by North American (later acquired by Rockwell International) and currently by Gulfstream American. Douglas Aircraft Company executives must often wish they had listened to Ted Smith nearly 40 years ago!

The initial production model was the Aero Commander 520,

a seven-place aircraft with twin 240 hp Lycoming GO-435 engines. Certificated in 1952, it was followed by the Commander 560, 680, 500 (later named Shrike Commander), Grand Commander (later renamed Courser Commander), Commander 720 and Commander 685. All were produced with piston engines (mostly Lycomings) of various ratings. A swept tail was introduced on the Commander 560; most other differences concerned variations in accommodation, cabin length and comfort, including pressurised cabins on the 685 and some versions of the 680 and 720. The last piston-engined models built were the 685 and Shrike Commander, manufacture of which ended in 1977 and 1981 respectively.

Turboprop versions, all with variously rated Garrett TPE331s and pressurised cabins, began with the Turbo Commander 680T, a modified Grand Commander which first flew on December 31, 1964, and was certificated in September 1965.

Stretched (and otherwise improved) later basic models included the Turbo Commander 681, 681B and 690. None of these is now in production, but Rockwell developed three higher-powered Jetprop Commanders: the 840, 980 and 1000. Gulfstream American, which acquired these designs in February 1981, calls them Commander Jetprops; they have accommodation for a pilot and seven passengers normally, or 10/11 passengers maximum.

Texas International's N94226, a Dart-powered Convair 600

The slimness of the Dart nacelles is evident in this view of CF-PWS, a Pacific Western Convair 640

Convair Models 600 and 640

Taking the total number of turboprop-engined Convair-liner conversions past the 200 mark, the Dart-powered Convair 600 was based on the Model 240, the Convair 640 on the Models 340/440. Thirty-nine of the former and 28 of the latter were converted with kits marketed by Convair, and most were still in service in the early 1980s. The first Convair 600 flew on May 20, 1965, and went into service at the end of November with Central Airlines, which had ordered ten. In the following April it began operating in Europe with Martin's Air Charter in the Netherlands. Other operators included Texas International and Mandala (Indonesia).

The Convair 640, with 56 seats instead of 48, was launched by orders from Caribair and Hawaiian Airlines, entering service with the former in December 1965. Subsequent operators included Air Algérie, Pacific Western and Zantop.

DC-9 Series 10 (CF-TLC) of Air Canada

McDonnell Douglas DC-9

Early Douglas designs for a short/medium-haul jetliner were the Model 2000 of 1959 and Model 2086 of 1962, both using JTF10 turbofans. Neither attracted much airline interest and by April 1963, when the company decided to go ahead with what by then had become the DC-9, it still had no firm orders. However, a month later Delta decided to buy 15 (with another 15 on option) and Bonanza placed a small order soon afterwards. The first of two prototypes was flown on February 25, 1965, by which time further DC-9s had been ordered by Bonanza, Air Canada, Swissair and TWA. These orders were all for the 90-passenger Series 10, with JT8D turbofans,

and 137 of this version were eventually built (as the Model 11 with JT8D-5s and Model 15 with more powerful JT8D-1s). The Series 10 was certificated on November 22, 1965, and entered service with Delta seven days later.

After a slow start the DC-9 – the first US twin-jet airliner with rear-mounted engines – gathered momentum to become, in 1981, the second commercial transport aeroplane in history to exceed a sales total of one thousand. Sales picked up noticeably when the Series 30 was introduced. This stretched version has increased span and length, full-span leading-edge slats and JT8D-7, -9, -11, -15 or -17 engines, and carries up to

119 passengers. It first flew on August 1, 1966, and accounted for 275 of the first 375 DC-9s sold. SAS placed a special order for ten examples of the "hot and high" Series 20, which combined the Series 10 body, Series 30 wings and JT8D-9 engines; the first of these flew on September 18, 1968.

A further fuselage stretch, to seat a maximum of 132 passengers, produced the Series 40 (JT8D-9s, -15s or -17s), which first flew on November 28, 1967, and entered service (with SAS) in March 1968. Another 14ft 3in was added to result in the Series 50 (first flight December 17, 1974), with passenger capacity increased to 139; engine choice is between

the JT8D-15 and -17. All series have been made available in DC-9F (freighter), DC-9CF (convertible) and DC-9RC (mixed passenger/freight) versions. Production has included 21 C-9A Nightingale medevac transports for Military Airlift Command; 15 C-9B Skytrain II logistic support transports for the US Navy, plus two for the Kuwait Air Force; and three VC-9C special-purpose transports for the USAF. Including these 41, total DC-9 firm orders had reached 1,078 by January 1, 1982. This figure also includes sales of the latest (and probably ultimate) stretched version, the DC-9 Super 80 series (see page 171).

YU-AHN of JAT (Yugoslav Airlines), a DC-9 Series 30

Series 50 DC-9 (N991EA) in Eastern Air Lines insignia

N823E, a DC-8 Super 61 of Delta Air Lines

McDonnell Douglas DC-8/DC-9 Super 60/70/80 series

No company has interpreted the term "fuselage stretch" quite as literally as the Douglas Aircraft Company division of McDonnell Douglas. Its first step along this road was the announcement of the "Super Sixty" series of DC-8s in April 1965. Taking the DC-8-50 as a basis, the company offered three new models, beginning with the Super 61. This had a 36ft 8in-longer fuselage seating up to 259 passengers (with increased baggage/cargo space). It first flew on March 14, 1966, received FAA type approval on September 2 that year, and entered service in November with United Air Lines. The DC-8 Super 62 was stretched less (only 6ft 8in, to seat 189 passengers) but had new drag-reducing wingtips adding 6ft to the overall span, increased fuel tankage in the wings, and longer engine pods. The first DC-8-62 flew on August 29, 1966, and was certificated in April 1967; it entered service (with SAS) in the following month. Largest and heaviest of the trio was the Super 63 (first flight April 10, 1967), which combined the wings and other refinements of the 62 with the long fuselage of the 61 and (except on the prototype) JT3D-7 turbofan engines. In July 1967 this version entered service with KLM.

Super Sixty production totalled 262, comprising 88 Super 61s, 67 Super 62s and 107 Super 63s. These figures included ten DC-8-61F (freighter) or CF (convertible passenger/freight) Jet Traders, 16 DC-8-62F/CFs and 60 DC-8-63F/CFs. Orders for ten or more Super Sixties

were placed by Air Canada, Alitalia, Delta, Eastern, Flying Tiger, KLM, SAS, Seaboard World and United.

Under a re-engining programme launched in 1979 Super 61/62/63 aircraft can be refitted with General Electric/SNECMA CFM56 turbofans, resulting in the designations Super 71, 72 and 73. The first such conversion, a United Air Lines Super 71, made its new "first" flight on August 15, 1981, by which time well over a hundred orders and options for similar conversions had been placed.

The DC-9 has undergone similar development, resulting in three super-stretched models, of which two are based on the DC-9 Series 50: the Super 81, Super 82 and Super 80SF. The basic version, the Super 81, has increased-span wings of 28 per cent greater gross area, Pratt & Whitney JT8D-209 turbofan engines and a 14ft 3in-longer fuselage seating up to 172 (instead of 139) passengers. It flew for the first time on October 18, 1979, was certificated in August 1980 and entered service with Swissair in the following October. The Super 82 is generally similar, except for uprated JT8D-217 engines for hot-and-high operations. It made its initial flight on January 8, 1981, and was certificated on July 30 of that year, at which date total sales of these two models had reached 110. The Super 80SF, which in early 1982 had still to fly, is a proposed short-field version marrying the Super 80 wings and powerplant to a standard DC-9 Series 40 fuselage.

Iberia's EC-BSE, a DC-8 Super 63

McDonnell Douglas DC-9 Super 80, registered N1002W before delivery to Austrian Airlines

Fairchild FH-227 (N7804M) of Northeast Airlines

Fairchild Industries FH-227

The Dutch-designed Fokker Friendship, first flown on November 24, 1955, has been in continuous production for a quarter of a century and, with sales totalling 735 by August 1, 1981, is the world's best selling commercial turboprop aircraft by a handsome margin. Forming a substantial proportion of that total are the 205 aircraft, comprising 138 F-27s and 77 FH-227s, built in the USA by Fairchild Industries between 1958 and 1973. The F-27J and F-27M were US counterparts of existing Dutch models, respectively with 2,250 shp Dart Mk 532-7 and -7N engines. Fairchild Hiller (as it then was) developed the FH-227 (certificated on June 24, 1966) as a stretched F-27J. Powerplant was the same but the FH-227 had a 6ft-longer fuselage with increased cabin space for additional passengers and cargo, and a second cargo section to the rear.

Variants certificated in 1967 included the FH-227B (strengthened wings, larger-diameter propellers, redesigned windscreen and seats for 56 passengers instead of 52); FH-227C (227 airframe but with the propeller and performance improvements of the 227B); FH-227D (2,300 shp Dart Mk 532-7Ls, modified flap settings, improved braking); and the FH-227E (as 227C but incorporating the same improvements as the 227D). Principal airline customers for the FH-227 were Mohawk (23), Northeast (seven), Ozark (21) and Piedmont (ten).

Fairchild Swearingen Merlin IIIB twin-turboprop executive aircraft

Fairchild Swearingen Merlin and Metro

Swearingen produced an improved version of the Beechcraft Twin-Bonanza known as the Excalibur 800. This was followed on April 13, 1965, with the first flight of the prototype Merlin IIA, a business twin utilising Twin-Bonanza landing gear, the wings of the early Beechcraft Queen Air, a brand-new six/eight-passenger pressurised fuselage, and 578 shp PT6A-20 turboprop engines. Certification was gained in July 1966 and deliveries began in August 1966. In June 1968 came the similar Merlin IIB, with 665 shp Garrett TPE331-1-151Gs, and (from summer 1970) the uprated Merlin III with strengthened wings. Meanwhile, in 1968 Swearingen developed the 19-passenger Metro for the

commuter market. This made its first flight on August 26, 1969, and received FAA type approval on June 11, 1970. Features included a pressurised fuselage and weather radar. Commuter Airlines, Air Wisconsin and Mississippi Valley Airlines were among the early customers. The Merlin IV, flown on September 22, 1970, was a business transport version of the Metro which could seat 12 passengers.

Subsequent development has been carried out by Fairchild Industries, of which Swearingen became a subsidiary in 1971. Improved versions of the Merlin have included the IIIA and IIIB (extra cabin windows, internal refinements), and Merlin IVA (12/15-passenger version of the

Merlin IV, with the changes introduced on the Metro II). The Metro II introduced larger cabin windows and other improvements, and was also available without windows in an all-cargo version. It has been superseded by the 19/20-passenger Metro III, certificated under SFAR 41B for operation at higher all-up weights, and is expected to be joined in 1983 by a PT6A-engined Metro IIIA. Latest versions of the Merlin (in early 1982) were the IIIC (also certificated under SFAR 41B) and IVC (redesigned 11-passenger luxury interior). About 500 Merlins and Metros (all models) had been sold by spring 1982, of which approximately one-third were Metro variants.

Commuter version of the Merlin, the much stretched 19-passenger Metro II

Cessna 400 series

Cessna has produced eight basic models in its 400-series range of light twins, with passenger accommodation ranging from five to 11 seats. Six of these remained in production in 1982, four with piston engines (including two with pressurised cabins) and two pressurised turboprop-powered models. Model numbers (now dropped in some cases) are no guide to their order of appearance. First in the line was the Cessna 411, a six/eight-seater with twin 340 hp Continental GTSIO-520 engines, of which 301 were built. First flight was made on July 18, 1962, and production ended in 1968. The lower-powered Models 401 (no longer built) and 402, flown on August 26, 1965, and certificated on September 20, 1966, were essentially similar to each other, the latter having a convertible cabin. Current versions, designated 402C, are produced as the six/eight-seat Businessliner or nine/ten-seat Utililiner. Sales of the 401/402 have exceeded 1,850. Latest of the piston-engined unpressurised designs, which has more powerful

engines and offers a 30 per cent improvement in ton-miles per gallon over the 402, is the Titan, known originally as the Model 404. Over 370 have been sold in three basic versions: the eight/ten-seat Titan Ambassador, the ten-seat utility passenger/cargo Titan Courier, and the all-cargo Titan Freighter.

The first pressurised 400-series model was the Cessna 421, flown on October 14, 1965, and certificated on May 1, 1967. This embodied the basic Cessna 402 fuselage but introduced a 2ft increase in wing span and Continental engines more powerful than those of any of its predecessors. Nearly 1,900 examples of this aircraft have been sold, current models being the 421B (with tip tanks), 421C Golden Eagle (without tip tanks) and the ten-seat Executive Commuter. It was followed by the Cessna 414 (first flight November 1, 1968), combining the pressurised fuselage and tail of the 421 with the wings of the 402 and a pair of 310 hp TSIO-520 engines. The original 414 was superseded in 1978 by the 414A Chancellor, with

increased-span "wet" wings and extended nose/baggage compartment; combined sales of the 414/414A have exceeded 1,000.

In 1975 (first flight August 26) Cessna introduced the first turboprop member of the family, the Model 441 (now named Conquest). Powered by Garrett TPE331 engines, it has since sold over 300 examples. The latest turboprop pressurised design, with lower-powered PT6A engines, is the Model 425 Corsair. Based on the airframe of the Cessna 421, it flew for the first time on September 12, 1978 and was certificated in 1979. By early 1982 more than 100 had been sold.

The six/eight-seat Cessna 411, first of the 400 series to appear

Cessna 402 at Wellington Airport, New Zealand, in 1970 while
chartered as a transport for personnel of an offshore oil rig

1981 model of the eight/ten-seat Cessna Titan

The best-selling Model 421/Golden Eagle, first pressurised member of the 400 family

Features of the Chancellor include increased wing span and more baggage space

Cessna Conquest, with turboprops and pressurised cabin, in its 1979 version

N66863, a Piper Chieftain of Eastern Caribbean Airways

Piper PA-31 Navajo, Chieftain and Cheyenne

When in 1976 Piper became the second company in the world to deliver the staggering total of 100,000 aircraft, the subject of this distinction was a Cheyenne, one of a large family of executive/commuter twins which had sold to the extent of about 2,000 examples at that point. The range was launched on September 30, 1964, with the maiden flight of the PA-31-300 Navajo, a six/eight-place aircraft (including pilot) powered by 300 hp Avco Lycoming IO-540 engines. First production version was the Turbo Navajo, certificated in February 1966 with 310 hp TIO-540s; when the standard Navajo later became available with the latter engines, the Turbo was discontinued. The

1981 model of the Piper Cheyenne III

PA-31-325 Navajo C/R, with 325 hp "handed" TIO-540s, was added later, but the next new model was the PA-31P Pressurised Navajo, powered by 425 hp Lycoming TIGO-541s and first flown in March 1968. This was certificated in November 1969 and remained in production until 1978.

The PA-31-350, a stretched version seating up to ten people in a 2ft-longer fuselage, was introduced in 1973. This was known originally as the Navajo Chieftain and from 1978 simply as the Chieftain. It has 350 hp handed TIO-540 engines and since 1975 has been built also in Brazil as the EMBRAER EMB-820C.

A development of the Pressurised Navajo, and Piper's first turboprop-engined business aircraft, was the PA-31T Cheyenne, which flew on August 20, 1969, powered by 620 shp PT6A-28 engines and fitted with wingtip auxiliary fuel tanks. It received certification in May 1972 and in late 1977 became the Cheyenne II when Piper decided to add to the range a new, lower-cost Cheyenne I (with 500 shp PT6A-11s and the tip tanks as an option only) and a much improved Cheyenne III. More recently the company has added the PA-31T2 Cheyenne IIXL, with a 2ft-longer fuselage and 620 shp PT6A-135 turboprops. The Cheyenne III is sufficiently redesigned (longer fuselage, for up to 11 people; a T tail; 720 shp PT6A-41s located further out on the wings in redesigned nacelles which also provide space for additional baggage and/or fuel) to merit the new Piper model designation PA-42T. It flew for the first time on May 18, 1979, and deliveries began in June 1980. Well over 500 Cheyennes of all models have been built.

Gulfstream American (Grumman) Gulfstream II and III

Grumman developed the Gulfstream II from the twin-turboprop Gulfstream I (see page 142) by taking the same pressurised fuselage, stretching it some 2ft 2in, adding a sweptback wing and mounting on the rear fuselage a new powerplant consisting of two Rolls-Royce Spey turbofan engines. By the time that the first Gulfstream II (N801GA) made its maiden flight on October 2, 1966, more than 60 had been ordered. Certification was gained on October 19, 1967, and deliveries began shortly afterwards. Production, which ended in 1979, eventually totalled 256.

On December 2 of that year a converted Gulfstream II (N901G, c/n 249) made its first flight as the Gulfstream III, the most noticeable external difference being an extended-chord wing bearing a NASA-type winglet at each tip. Other changes included a lengthened fuselage, increased fuel capacity and greater fuel economy. The Gulfstream III received FAA certification on September 22, 1980, and by early 1982 about 30 of the 100 or so then on order had been delivered. In 1981 certification was received for the Gulfstream II-B, a retrofit of the existing Mk II with the wing of the Gulfstream III which had flown for the first time on March 17 of that year. Use of this wing enables the Gulfstream II-B to operate at higher weights, speeds and altitudes, and is expected to increase maximum range by more than 1,000 miles.

Generous flap area is a feature of the Gulfstream II corporate transport. This one (N117JJ) is registered to the Gavalin Corporation

Gulfstream III, with new wing, winglets and a longer fuselage

N73700, the Boeing 737-100 prototype

Boeing Model 737

Introduced as the ''baby'' member of the Boeing family of jet transports, the Model 737 has grown somewhat since its birth in February 1965 as an 80/115-passenger short-hauler. Retention of the Model 707/720/727 fuselage cross-section combined with a much reduced fuselage length to produce a rotund but not unattractive design with two close-mounted underwing turbofan engines. Initial model, first flown on April 9, 1967, and certificated on December 15 of that year, was the 737-100, for which Lufthansa (21 ordered) was the launch customer. Production of this version, which entered service in February 1968, totalled 29.

The inevitable stretched version, the 6ft 4in-longer 737-200, first flew on August 18,

1967, and entered service with United Air Lines (which ordered 40 initially and more later) on April 28 in the following year. Variants of the Series 200 included the 200C (convertible) and 200QC (quick-change) passenger/cargo models, and a longer-range corporate version known as the 737-200 Executive Jet.

Improved Advanced 737 versions, with enhanced short-field capability and (optionally) uprated JT8D-15 engines, were introduced in 1971 and were still in production 11 years later, along with longer-range, higher-weight counterparts of the 200 and 200C.

The latest version to be launched, in 1981, is the Model 737-300, with a further fuselage stretch of 8ft 8in (to seat up to 148 passengers) and 20,000lb st

CFM56-3 turbofans. Able to carry 20 more passengers over a 576-mile stage length than the Advanced 737-200, the Dash 300 is expected also to offer much improved fuel consumption and lower noise levels. Initial orders, for ten aircraft each, were placed in 1981 by USAir and Southwest Airlines. Total 737-series sales reached 1,000 on March 30, 1982, of which 849 (including 19 Dash 200s to the USAF as T-43A navigation trainers) had been delivered.

This 737-200 of Air Nauru (C2-RN6 *Nauru Chief*) is fitted with a "gravel kit" enabling it to operate from unpaved or gravel runways. External features of this kit are the nosewheel ski (to deflect gravel) and the small boom below each engine air intake (which blows compressed air through nozzles to prevent debris from entering the engine)

Boeing Advanced 737-200 (PP-CJN) of the Brazilian airline Cruzeiro do Sul

Beechcraft Model B99 (N99TH) in service with Allegheny Commuter

Bushmaster 2000, a 1960s attempt to modernise the Ford Tri-Motor

The twin-Dart Conroy Turbo Three conversion of the Douglas DC-3

Beechcraft Model 99 Airliner

Beech Aircraft Corporation produced 164 examples of the Model 99 series in various configurations between 1968 and 1974. Aimed chiefly at the commuter airline/air-taxi markets, it flew for the first time in July 1966 following trials with a stretched-fuselage Queen Air.

Deliveries began in 1968, the original Model 99 having 550 ehp PT6A-20 turboprops and the 99A a pair of 680 ehp PT6A-27s (derated to 550 ehp)

installed in nacelles developed originally for the Model 90 King Air. The B99 switched to similarly rated PT6A-28s and was built also as the B99 Executive with optional seating arrangements for six or more passengers and a choice of interior furnishing. Options on the Airliner versions included a double door at the rear to facilitate mixed passenger/cargo operation, and a 35.5 cu ft underfuselage baggage/cargo pannier.

Bushmaster 2000

After more than 35 years of operation several examples of the Ford Tri-Motor were still leading useful lives in the mid-1960s, causing William B. Stout – among others – to believe that a market might exist for a rejuvenated version. The outcome of this was the Bushmaster 2000, whose designation was probably meant to imply that it too would be good for 35 years of operation. The prototype, built by Aircraft Hydro-Forming Inc, was flown in 1966 and certification was obtained three years later. After a change

of ownership Bushmaster Aircraft Corporation was formed in August 1970 to put the aircraft into production, though this never in fact materialised.

Configured normally for a crew of two plus 15 passengers, the Bushmaster was cleared for single-pilot operation and could seat up to 23 passengers in a high-density layout. Major structural improvements compared with the original Ford "Tin Goose" included more powerful, lighter engines with three-blade constant-speed

propellers; trim tabs on all control surfaces; oleo-pneumatic shock-absorbers and disc brakes on the main landing gear; modernised cockpit instrumentation; multi-spar wings; lighter and stronger skin panels; a strengthened cabin floor; and a large cargo-loading door.

The Bushmaster was designed for utility operations, with the ability to fly from grass strips and unpaved runways, and had provision for wheel, ski or twin-float landing gear.

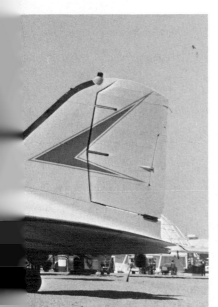

Conroy Turbo Three

Despite the apparent irreplaceability of the Douglas DC-3, several attempts to market versions re-engined with turboprops have met with a marked lack of success. A small number of ex-RAF Dakotas were flown in Britain in the late 1940s and early 1950s as Mamba and Dart engine testbeds (the latter on behalf of the Vickers Viscount), and were used briefly for cargo services by BEA.

A more serious attempt was

the Turbo Three, a twin-Dart-engined conversion by Conroy Aircraft Corporation of Santa Barbara, California, which first flew on May 13, 1969. Three years later this was still without a supplemental type certificate, and subsequently it was re-engined with three Canadian PT6A-45s and reflown as the Tri Turbo-3 on November 2, 1977. It failed once again to gain certification and the programme lapsed after the death of Jack M.

Conroy, Tri Turbo Corporation's president, in December 1979. The general consensus of opinion seems to be that the proposed conversion – which also included four-blade propellers, increased fuel tankage in the outer wings, and improved payload/"hot and high" airfield capability – was too extensive to have much chance of being covered by a **supplemental type certificate from the FAA**

Boeing Model 747

Twenty years ago forecasts of airline passenger and freight traffic growth indicated that by the mid-1970s operators would need either enormous fleets of "standard" aircraft, or smaller fleets equipped with aircraft of very much greater carrying capacity. Douglas chose to meet this challenge initially with its ultra-long Super Sixty versions of the DC-8, and Boeing's preliminary studies also covered enlarged versions of the 707/720 series. Increasingly, however, the Seattle company's market research indicated the design of a new, outsize aircraft as the more attractive solution. This became a firm decision in March 1966 with announcement of the Model 747, whose elephantine proportions quickly earned it the nickname "Jumbo jet".

Embodying design work done for Boeing's unsuccessful contender in the USAF's heavy-lift transport competition (won by the Lockheed C-5A Galaxy), the Model 747 was technologically unremarkable except for its sheer size. In this area, however, it outstripped everything that had gone before it in the field of commercial air transportation, boasting a 185ft-long, 20ft-wide passenger cabin with up to 8ft 4in of headroom and spacious enough for comfortable eight-abreast seating, or ten-abreast in a high-density layout. Its weight, unprecedented for a civil aeroplane, was supported by a twin-wheel nose unit and 16-wheel, four-bogie main landing gear.

Manufacturing go-ahead, on the strength of a conditional order from Pan American for 25 of the new aircraft, was given in

Pan Am's *Clipper Victor*, **a 747-100, reveals the complex 18-wheel landing gear of the "Jumbo"**

A Boeing 747-200B in British Airways colours

July 1966 and the first Boeing 747 made its initial flight on February 9, 1969. Certification followed on December 30 of that year and the 747 went into service on January 22, 1970, on Pan Am's New York–London route. Within little more than a year the order book had reached 200, and by January 1, 1982, it stood at 586, of which 540 had been delivered. These totals include 167 examples of the original 747-100, which was superseded in 1978 by the current -100B with wings, fuselage and landing gear strengthened for operation at higher all-up weights.

Major version, with 262 sold by January 1, 1982 (including 62 Combis), is the 747-200B, first flown on October 11, 1970, and delivered from January 1971. The greatest weight at which any aeroplane has ever taken off (although this is not officially recognised as a record) is the 850,920lb — nearly 425½ US tons (386 tonnes metric) — scaled by a 747-200B in May 1979. The 200C and 200F are, respectively, convertible passenger/cargo and all-freight variants of the basic 747-200; the 747SR is a short-range **version of the -100B modified for more frequent take-offs and** landings.

A more radical departure from the standard 747 airframe is the "Special Performance" 747SP. Boeing has sold over 40 examples of this model, which is instantly recognisable by its much shorter fuselage, reducing overall length by 47ft 1in. Seating capacity is reduced from 452 to 331 (standard) or from 516 to 440 (high-density), in each case with 32 passengers on the upper deck. Boeing's latest redesign of the standard 747 includes an extension of this upper-deck section rearwards by 23ft 4in to increase its capacity to 69 passengers in standard economy-class six-abreast seating. Deliveries of SUD (Stretched Upper Deck) 747s are due to begin in 1983, and the stretch will be offered on all models except the 200C, 200F and SP. Initial customers are Swissair and South African Airways.

All versions of the 747 are available with a choice of Pratt & Whitney JT9D-7, General Electric CF6 or Rolls-Royce RB.211-524 engines, each in a variety of models and power ratings. The weight and performance data given in the table at the end of this book are typical for the versions quoted.

Air France's F-BPVS is a -200C Combi version of the 747

Seaboard World Airlines, one of the major international freight
carriers, naturally chose the 747-200F

The much-shortened fuselage of the 747SP is immediately evident
in this photograph of Braniff's N603BN

Retouched photograph showing how the stretched-upper-deck 747 will look when it enters service in mid-1983

Evangel 4500-300

A rugged and not unattractive utility twin, the Evangel 4500-300 was the vicitim of a market that disappeared just when the type's career seemed all set to take off. Designed in 1962 by Evangel Aircraft Corporation of Orange City, Iowa, it flew for the first time in June 1964, exhibiting a long, boxy fuselage with a 3ft 8in-square cabin cross-section. Four and a half years later, in January 1969, the first production Evangel was flown, and FAA certification followed on July 21, 1970. One production aircraft (N4505L, designated 4500-300-II) was flown with Rajay turbocharged engines, receiving a supplemental type certificate in March 1973. By the beginning of the following year Evangel had built seven production aircraft and was planning an output of three per month before the end of the year in response to a healthy demand. This was not to be, however, and in late 1974 or early 1975 production was brought to an end.

Early production Evangel 4500-300 Stol utility transport

Bell Models 212 Twin Two-Twelve, 214 and 412

The Twin Two-Twelve is an outgrowth of the highly successful single-turboshaft Bell 204/205/Iroquois family and came into being when the Canadian Armed Forces ordered a twin-engined version with a PT6T-3 Turbo Twin Pac coupled engine in 1968. More than 360 were built for the CAF (CUH-1N), the US Air Force/ Navy/Marine Corps (UH-1N), and export customers. The commercial version was certificated in October 1970 and obtained a Category A transport certificate in the following June.

Since then it has been made available with the improved PT6T-3B engine and has qualified for IFR as well as VFR operation. The Model 212 has a two-blade main rotor; in early August 1979 Bell flew the first Model 412, which has a four-blade rotor, improving performance and reducing noise and vibration, but is otherwise similar. Versions of both designs are licence-built in Italy by Agusta.

The Bell 214, an unrelated design, has a single Lycoming turboshaft driving a two-blade

main rotor with swept tips. The 214A was a military model for Iran; the standard 214B (certificated in January 1976) and 214B-1 BigLifter are available in 14-passenger, cargo, agricultural and firefighting versions; the twin-engined multi-purpose 214ST can seat up to 18 passengers and is licence-built in Japan by Mitsubishi.

Bell 212 of the Asahi Helicopter Co (JA9510) on offshore oil rig support work in the Japan Sea

Boeing 2707-300 in the configuration envisaged at the time of its cancellation in 1971 (artist's impression)

Boeing Model 2707-300

By the second half of the 1960s the prolonged selection of an American supersonic transport aircraft – initiated in 1963 by President Kennedy – had narrowed down to a two-horse race. Lockheed had proposed the L-2000, a double-delta fixed-wing 273-seater with Pratt & Whitney JTF17A turbofans and a cruising speed of Mach 2.7. Boeing's much more advanced proposal (then provisionally allocated the model number 2707) was announced as the chosen design at the beginning of 1967. Powered by four rear-mounted General Electric GE4/J5P turbojet engines, it had variable-geometry wings and maximum seating for 350 passengers, and was also designed to cruise at Mach 2.7. Range with a maximum 75,000lb payload was given as more than 4,000 miles.

It soon became apparent that the technology needed to surmount the double hurdle of VG and supersonic passenger transport was too complex and too costly, and this configuration was abandoned in October 1968. In its place Boeing announced the much different Model 2707-300 with ogival-delta "gull" wings, underwing GE4 engines and seating capacity for 250-321 passengers. The first of two prototypes ordered in September 1969 was scheduled to fly in late 1972 or early 1973, with deliveries to begin in 1978. Initial orders were placed by Pan American (two), TWA (two) and Alitalia (one), and by March 24, 1971, delivery positions for 122

aircraft had been reserved by no fewer than 26 airlines. On that date, however, the US Senate voted – by the narrow majority of five – to discontinue funding construction and development of the prototypes. Boeing, GE and their subcontractors could not finance the programme without large-scale government support, and it was officially terminated on the following day.

McDonnell Douglas DC-10

Like Lockheed's TriStar, the DC-10 started out as a twin-turbofan design and acquired a third, tail-mounted engine later. It too was devised to meet the 1966 requirements of American Airlines, and in 1968 it was launched on the strength of orders from American (25) and United (30). Five development aircraft were built, the first of them flying on August 10, 1970. Type approval and initial deliveries followed in July 1971 and services began in August. For these the operators used the basic US domestic short/medium-haul Series 10. In 1972 the first examples of the long-range intercontinental DC-10 Series 40 (on February 28) and Series 30 (June 21) were flown; both were certificated by the end of the year. Seating capacity remained unchanged but the Series 40 (known originally as the Srs 20) and Series 30 introduced a 10ft increase in wing span, extra fuel, additional landing wheels and a choice between uprated General Electric CF6-50 turbofans in the Srs 30 and Pratt & Whitney JT9Ds in the Srs 40.

Convertible passenger/freight versions became available as the Srs 10CF and 30CF, following the first flight by a DC-10-30CF on February 28, 1973. Maximum passenger capacity in the CF models is 380; alternatively, they can carry a cargo payload of 155,700lb loaded through a large port-side door forward of the wing. In December 1977 the USAF selected the Srs 30CF in preference to the Boeing 747 to meet its ATCA (Advanced Tanker/Cargo Aircraft) requirement. It is being procured as the KC-10A Extender in yearly batches during the course of the 1980s, having first flown on July 12, 1980; deliveries began in March 1981.

Other recent variants of the DC-10 have included the Series 15, a "hot and high" version of the Series 10 ordered initially by Aeromexico (two) and Mexicana (five). First flown on January 8, 1981, the Srs 15 is basically the same aircraft as the Srs 10 but has more powerful CF6-50C2 engines. Deliveries began in 1981. A development of the Series 30 with an additional fuel tank in the rear of the cargo hold is designated Series 30ER (for Extended Range). It was first ordered, by Swissair, in mid-1980 and is available as a new-built aircraft or by conversion of existing Srs 30 airframes.

By January 1982 McDonnell

Douglas had delivered 358 DC-10s out of 367 then on order. Dwindling commercial sales had earlier made it uncertain whether the DC-10 could be kept in production beyond the end of 1982, but the USAF now plans to acquire 60 KC-10s (instead of 36), and new commercial versions are being evaluated.

The ubiquitous Pan American has operated all three US wide-bodied transports: N69NA *Clipper Star Light* **is a DC-10 Series 10**

DC-10 Series 30 (G-BEBM *Robert Burns*) **of British Caledonian Airways**

A DC-10-30 of Air New Zealand (ZK-NZP) about to touch down

Cessna Citation

The first of two prototypes of this small executive twin-jet, known originally as the Fanjet 500, made its initial flight on September 15, 1969. The second prototype, and production Model 500 Citations, introduced a dihedral tailplane, larger fin and rudder, longer fuselage and a more rearward location of the JT15D-1 turbofan engines. Deliveries began soon after the receipt of FAA type approval on September 9, 1971, and 349 had been built (with gradually increasing operating weights) by the end of 1976. Production then switched to the Model 501 Citation I with 7ft 3in more wing span and uprated JT15D-1A engines.

On January 31, 1977, Cessna flew the prototype Citation II with further uprated engines (2,500lb st JT15D-4s), further increased wing span, a lengthened fuselage (seating two more passengers) and much more range. This version received FAA certification in March 1978. Both models were still in production in early 1982, when sales had reached a total of 1,000: 642 Citation Is and 358 Citation IIs.

Despite its name the Citation III is virtually an entirely new aeroplane. It is significantly larger and has sweptback supercritical-section wings, 3,650lb st Garrett TFE731 engines, a 13-passenger cabin and gross weight of 20,000lb. It first flew on May 30, 1979, and certification and initial deliveries were scheduled for the autumn of 1982.

Cessna Citation I twin-turbofan executive transport

The stretched and more powerful Citation II

Citation III, with supercritical sweptback wings, T tail and other improvements

Lockheed L-1011 TriStar

Although aesthetically more attractive than its two US rivals, the TriStar failed to translate that appeal into orders as effectively as the Boeing 747 and McDonnell Douglas DC-10. This was no doubt a legacy of the early difficulties with the RB.211 engine, which led to the bankruptcy of Rolls-Royce in 1971 and brought Lockheed to the brink of a similar fate. American Airlines, whose 1966 requirement for a 300-seat airbus on its Chicago–Los Angeles route inspired the TriStar's design, eventually bought the DC-10 instead. Nevertheless, in early 1982 a dozen major world operators were obtaining excellent results with over 200 of the 250 or so TriStars then on order.

Conceived originally as a twin-turbofan design, the TriStar soon became a three-engined aircraft and was named accordingly. The first metal was cut in March 1969 and the L-1011 prototype, one of five development aircraft built, made its maiden flight on November 16, 1970. Provisional certification, for route-proving and demonstration flights, was gained on December 22, 1971, followed by a full ATC on April 17, 1972. The initial production version, the L-1011-1, began regular scheduled services with Eastern 12 days later and with TWA shortly afterwards. This and the extended-range L-1011-100 are both powered by 42,000lb st RB.211-22Bs (though the -1 originally had -22Cs), but the latter, which entered service in 1975, can carry an extra 18,000lb of fuel in additional centre-section tanks. A similar long-range model is the L-1011-200 with 48,000lb-thrust RB.211-524s and improved take-off and climb performance, especially from "hot and high" airfields. Range with maximum payload is increased some 27–28 per cent compared with the L-1011-1; with maximum fuel the increase is about 10–12 per cent.

A more dramatic increase in range is evident in the L-1011-500, which first flew in October 1978: over 80 per cent with maximum payload, over 40 per cent with maximum fuel. Also evident in the Dash 500 is the first major external change, a 13ft 6in-shorter fuselage seating up to 330 passengers compared with 400 in the other in-service models; the engines are 50,000lb-thrust RB.211-524Bs or B4s. The L-1011-500 entered service in May 1979, with British Airways, and has been ordered by eight other airlines in the USA, Canada, the Caribbean, South America, the Far East and Europe. However, it is expected that TriStar production will be phased out during 1983.

More than a decade after its first flight, the original TriStar prototype is still flying, now known by Lockheed as the Advanced TriStar and incorporating numerous aerodynamic and avionics improvements aimed at increased safety and fuel economy. Among these features are automatic brakes and a new digital autopilot, which are also fitted to Pan American's TriStar-500s, and extended wingtips (an extra 4ft 6in on each wing) incorporating automatically actuated ailerons, which have already been shown to result in fuel savings of up to three per cent. The latter modifications are specified for the Dash 500 TriStars of Air Canada, Delta, LTU, Pan Am and TAP/Air Portugal. Looking further ahead, Lockheed has studied the possible use of a TriStar testbed burning liquid hydrogen as an alternative future fuel.

L-1011-100 TriStar (N10112) of Pacific Southwest, "America's largest commuter airline"

"Hot and high" TriStar 200 of Saudi Arabian Airlines (HZ-AHE) taking off from Jeddah

Short-fuselage L-1011-500 in British Airways livery

Beechcraft Super King Air 200 (PK-TRB) of Indonesia Air Transport

Beechcraft Super King Air 200

Beech's top-of-the-range business twin/general-purpose transport was first flown on October 27, 1972, as the Model 101, a development of the King Air 100 line with greater overall dimensions, higher-powered engines, increased fuel tankage and (the immediately obvious difference) a T tail. A second prototype flew on December 15, 1972, and FAA type approval was issued a year later. Deliveries started in early 1974 and had totalled about 1,200 by April 1982.

Increased cabin pressure differential compared with the King Air, and the location of the powerplant farther away from the fuselage, combine in the Super to offer a quieter passenger environment; slower-turning propellers also help to reduce the cabin noise level. Fuselage basic cross-section (4ft 9in × 4ft 6in) is identical to that of the low-tailed King Airs, and wingtip auxiliary fuel tanks are available optionally. One version equipped with these is the Model 200T, a specially fitted high-altitude photographic/meteorological version of which two were built for the French Institut Géographique National. Other specialised models have been developed for Egypt (mineralogical research), Taiwan (navaid calibration), the US Customs Service (border patrol), and Japan and Uruguay (Maritime Patrol 200T). Military Super King Airs for the US Army (C-12A, C and D, and RU-21J), Navy (UC-12B) and Air Force (C-12A) amounted to 201 **examples by 1982. The C-12D is** fitted with a large cargo-loading door; this became optional on the civil models in 1979.

In April 1981 Beech introduced a "B" version — with PT6A-42 engines (giving better cruise and altitude performance than the -41) and a further slight increase in pressure differential — to replace the earlier models. Current Super King Airs are thus designated B200 (standard civil version), B200C (with 4ft 4in-square cargo door), B200T (with tip tanks) and B200CT (with cargo door and tip tanks).

Bell Model 222 and Sikorsky S-76

The rapid growth of offshore oil exploration in the 1970s led to a boom in the sales of medium-sized helicopters, which rapidly established themselves as ideal for ferrying workers and equipment between the rigs and the mainland. Among the newer generation of designs aimed at this lucrative market are the Bell 222 and the Sikorsky S-76, announced in April 1974 and January 1975 respectively. They flew for the first time on August 13, 1976 (222), and March 13, 1977 (S-76), entering service in February 1979 (S-76) and January 1980 (222).

The Bell design accommodates eight (optionally ten) people, including one or two pilots, and is powered by twin LTS 101 turboshaft engines. The Allison-engined S-76 can seat two pilots and up to 12 passengers. Total sales of the two types were well in excess of 600 by early 1982, the S-76 accounting for about two-thirds of these, of which about half were for offshore duties. Both types are fully certificated for VFR and IFR operation.

Bell 222 operated by Helikopter Service AS of Oslo

G-BMAL, a Sikorsky S-76 of Management Aviation subsidiary North Scottish Helicopters, landing on a North Sea oil platform

Boeing Vertol Model 234 Commercial Chinook

The military Chinook was a Vertol design which won a 1959 US Army competition for a standard medium-lift helicopter. Production, by Boeing and overseas licensees, had reached close on a thousand CH-47s when, in mid-1978, a commercial passenger/cargo/ utility version was announced. Based on the CH-47D, the Model 234 features a redesigned nose with weather radar, glass-fibre rotor blades and modified landing gear. The long-range version, first ordered by British Airways (six, mainly for North Sea oil rig support), has large fuel tanks in long, continuous fuselage-side fairings, and made its initial flight on August 19, 1980.

A shorter-range utility version has internally mounted tanks and lacks the external fairings. Conversion from long-range to utility configuration can be accomplished by four workers in about eight hours. A typical mixed-traffic combination is 18 passengers seated four abreast and 16,000lb of internal cargo. Alternatively, up to 28,000lb can be carried externally on the Chinook's underfuselage cargo hooks.

Long-range version of the Commercial Chinook (G-BJAC for British Airways)

Beechcraft Commuter C99

The Commuter C99 is essentially a modernised version of the Beechcraft 99 Airliner, and its prototype was converted from a 1969-built Model 99. It was first flown on June 20, 1980, powered by two 750 shp Pratt & Whitney Aircraft of Canada PT6A-34 turboprops. More economical PT6A-36s of 715 shp are installed in the production version, deliveries of which began in July 1981. Apart from the better performance offered by the new engines, the principal changes comprise the installation of improved avionics and airline-standard seating.

Delivery of a Beechcraft Commuter C99 to Sunbird Airlines, one of the first recipients of this upgraded version

Ahrens AR 404

Design of this boxy, robust passenger/cargo transport began in January 1975 and Ahrens Aircraft Corporation started building the prototype seven months later. It flew for the first time on December 1, 1976, followed by a longer-fuselage version on October 26, 1979. By the beginning of the following year about two dozen delivery positions had been confirmed. Most of these were for operators in the Caribbean area (the AR 404 is built in Puerto Rico); others were for mainland US and Canadian airlines. The first aircraft to full production standard was flown on September 23, 1981, and deliveries were due to begin in 1982, following certification to FAR Part 25. Target initial production rate was one per month, rising eventually to four.

Ahrens AR 404 prototype, with non-retractable main wheels and six cabin windows each side. A modified version flew for the first time on September 23, 1981

Prototype Boeing 767 during its maiden flight in September 1981

Boeing Models 757 and 767

Wide-bodies or narrow-bodies for the 1980s? We have yet to see. Meanwhile Boeing, which has a larger crystal ball than most airline planemakers, is hedging its bets with one of each, both announced in early 1978: the slim-line 757 and the shorter, tubbier, longer-range 767. The real name of the game, however, is the fuel efficiency of present-day aero-engines, and once again potential customers have a choice: P & W JT9Ds or General Electric CF6-80As on the Model 767 (with the Rolls-Royce RB.211-524 as a possible later option) and newer-technology RB.211-535Cs or PW2037s on the Boeing 757.

Launch customer for the 767 (which, on September 26, 1981, was the first of the two designs to fly) was United Air Lines, whose huge order for 39 aircraft helped to decide the final configuration. The Boeing 757, which made its maiden flight on February 19, 1982, was launched by firm orders from Eastern Air Lines (21) and British Airways (19), with options totalling 42 more. Both operators specified RB.211-535C engines, making the 757 the first Boeing airliner ever to be launched with a non-American engine. Worldwide firm orders by April 1, 1982, totalled 173 for the 767 and 136 for the 757, which were scheduled to enter service in August 1982 and January 1983 respectively.

Two Boeing 767s for United Air Lines (N601UA, nearest camera, and N602UA) flank the prototype (N767BA) on the Boeing flight line in December 1981

The Boeing 757 prototype (N757BA), which flew for the first time on February 19, 1982

Data

Type	Powerplant	Dimensions	Weights	Performance	Accommodation
Benoist	One 75 hp Roberts or 70 hp Sturtevant	Wing span: 45ft 0in Length: 26ft 0in Wing area: approx 416 sq ft	Empty: 1,190lb AUW: approx 1,500lb	Max speed: 64 mph	Crew: 1 Passengers: 1
Aeromarine 75	Two 420 hp Liberty 12A	Wing span: 103ft 9¼in Length: 49ft 3¾in Height: 18ft 9¼in Wing area: 1,397 sq ft	Empty: 8,456lb AUW: 12,823lb	Max speed: 85 mph Range: 340 miles	Crew: 2 Passengers: 10
Dayton-Wright KT Cabin Cruiser	One 420 hp Liberty 12	Wing span: 43ft 7½in Length: 30ft 19/16in Height: 11ft 2½in Wing area: 441.09 sq ft	Empty: 2,686lb AUW: 4,128lb	Max speed: 120 mph Endurance: 6hr	Crew: 1 Passengers: 3
Curtiss Eagle I	Three 150 hp Curtiss K-6 or 160 hp Curtiss C-6	Wing span: 61ft 4in Length: 36ft 9in Height: 12ft 4in Wing area: 900 sq ft	Empty: 5,130lb AUW: 7,450lb	Max speed: 107 mph Range: 475 miles	Crew: 2 Passengers: 6
Martin GMP/ Mail Plane	Two 420 hp Liberty 12	Wing span: 71ft 5in Length: 46ft 0in Height: 14ft 0in Wing area: 1,070 sq ft	Empty: 6,500lb AUW: 10,300lb	Max speed: 115 mph Range: 550 miles	Crew: 2 Payload: 1,500lb of mail/cargo
Davis-Douglas/ Ryan Cloudster	One 420 hp Liberty 12	Wing span: 55ft 11in Length: 36ft 9in Height: 12ft 0in Wing area: 800 sq ft	Empty: 4,500lb AUW: 9,600lb	Max speed: 110 mph Cruising speed: 90 mph Normal range: 550 miles	Crew: 2 Passengers: 4–10
Jacuzzi Monoplane	One 210 hp Hall-Scott L-6	Wing span: 52ft 0in Length: 29ft 0in Height: 10ft 6in Wing area: 400 sq ft	Empty: 1,800lb AUW: 3,400lb	Max speed: 105 mph Range: 900 miles (estimated)	Crew: 1 Passengers: 6
Friesley Falcon	Two 350 hp Liberty 12	Wing span: 65ft 3in Length: 40ft 0in Height: 15ft 0in Wing area: 897 sq ft	Empty: 5,600lb AUW: 8,600lb	Max speed: 110 mph	Crew: 1 Passengers: 12
Remington-Burnelli RB-1	Two 420 hp Liberty 12	Wing span: 74ft 0in Length: 41ft 2in Height: 18ft 0in Wing area: 1,323 sq ft	Empty: 8,121lb AUW: 14,621lb	Max speed: 105 mph Range: 760 miles	Crew: 2 Passengers: 25
Dayton-Wright FP2	Two 420 hp Liberty 12	Wing span: 51ft 5in Length: 36ft 10¼in Height: 14ft 2in Wing area: 668 sq ft	Empty: 5,726lb AUW: 7,588lb	Max speed: 120 mph Normal range: 325 miles	Crew: 4 Passengers: None
Barnhart Model 15 Wampus Kat	Two 90 hp Curtiss OX-5	Wing span: 50ft 0in Length: 30ft 10in Height: 11ft 0in Wing area: 485 sq ft	Empty: 2,611lb AUW: 4,015lb	Max speed: 85 mph Cruising speed: 43 mph	Crew: 1 Passengers: 3
Stout Air Pullman	One 420 hp Liberty 12	Wing span: 58ft 4in Length: 45ft 8in Height: 11ft 10in Wing area: 600 sq ft	Empty: 3,638lb AUW: 6,017lb	Max speed: 116 mph Endurance: 4hr	Crew: 1–2 Passengers: 6–7
Douglas M-4	One 420 hp Liberty 12	Wing span: 44ft 6in Length: 28ft 11in Height: 10ft 1in Wing area: 465 sq ft	Empty: 3,405lb AUW: 4,900lb	Max speed: 140 mph at S/L Cruising speed: 110 mph Range: 700 miles	Crew: 1 Payload: 1,000lb (or 1 passenger)
Fokker Universal	One 220 hp Wright J5 Whirlwind	Wing span: 47ft 9in Length: 33ft 3in Height: 8ft 0in Wing area: 341 sq ft	Empty: 2,192lb AUW: 4,000lb	Max speed: 118 mph Cruising speed: 105 mph Max endurance: 7hr	Crew: 1–2 Passengers: 4

Type	Powerplant	Dimensions	Weights	Performance	Accommodation
Boeing Model 40B-4	One 525 hp Pratt & Whitney R-1690 Hornet A	Wing span: 44ft 2¼in Length: 33ft 2¼in Height: 12ft 3⅛in Wing area: 547 sq ft	Empty: 3,722lb AUW: 6,075lb	Max speed: 137 mph Cruising speed: 125 mph Range: 535 miles	Crew: 1 Passengers: 4 + 500lb of mail
Fairchild FC-2W2 (floatplane)	One 410 hp Pratt & Whitney R-1340 Wasp B	Wing span: 50ft 0in Length: 33ft 2in Height: 9ft 6in Wing area: 310 sq ft	Empty: 3,072lb AUW: 5,500lb	Max speed: 127 mph Cruising speed: 104 mph Range: 700 miles	Crew: 1 Passengers: 4
Buhl CA-6 Airsedan	One 300 hp Wright J6 Whirlwind	Wing span: 40ft 0in Length: 29ft 8in Height: 8ft 7in Wing area: 315 sq ft	Empty: 2,478lb AUW: 4,200lb	Max speed: 140 mph Cruising speed: 120 mph	Crew: 1–2 Passengers: 4–5
Stinson SM-1 Detroiter	One 220 hp Wright J5C Whirlwind	Wing span: 45ft 10in Length: 32ft 0in Height: 8ft 3in Wing area: 292 sq ft	Empty: 1,970lb AUW: 3,485lb	Max speed: 122 mph Cruising speed: 105 mph Range: 700 miles	Crew: 1 Passengers: 5
Ryan B-5 Brougham	One 300 hp Wright J6 Whirlwind	Wing span: 42ft 4in Length: 28ft 4in Height: 8ft 10in Wing area: 280 sq ft	Empty: 2,251lb AUW: 4,000lb	Max speed: 140 mph Cruising speed: 120 mph Range: 720 miles	Crew: 1 Passengers: 5
Lockheed Model 5B Vega	One 450 hp Pratt & Whitney R-1340 Wasp	Wing span: 41ft 0in Length: 27ft 6in Height: 8ft 6in Wing area: 275 sq ft	Empty: 2,490lb AUW: 4,265lb	Max speed: 180 mph Cruising speed: 155 mph Range (max fuel): 690 miles	Crew: 1 Passengers: 6
Fokker Super Universal	One 420 hp Pratt & Whitney R-1340 Wasp	Wing span: 50ft 7¾in Length: 36ft 7in Height: 8ft 11in Wing area: 370 sq ft	Empty: 3,000lb AUW: 5,150lb	Max speed: 138 mph Cruising speed: 118 mph Range: 675 miles	Crew: 1–2 Passengers: 6–7
Fokker F-10A	Three 420 or 450 hp Pratt & Whitney R-1340 Wasp	Wing span: 79ft 2in Length: 50ft 7in Height: 12ft 9in Wing area: 850 sq ft	Empty: 7,780lb AUW: 13,100lb	Max speed: 145 mph Cruising speed: 123 mph Range: 765 miles	Crew: 2 Passengers: 14
Sikorsky S-38B	Two 425 hp Pratt & Whitney R-1340 Wasp	Wing span: 71ft 8in Length: 40ft 3in Height (on land): 13ft 10in Wing area: 720 sq ft	Empty: 6,550lb AUW: 10,480lb	Max speed: 125 mph Cruising speed: 110 mph Range: 750 miles	Crew: 1 Passengers: 10
Cessna AW	One 110 hp Warner Scarab	Wing span: 40ft 2in Length: 24ft 8½in Height: 7ft 5½in Wing area: 224 sq ft	Empty: 1,225lb AUW: 2,260lb	Max speed: 130 mph Cruising speed: 110 mph Normal range: 650 miles	Crew: 1 Passengers: 3
Loening C2C Air Yacht	One 525 hp Wright R-1750 Cyclone	Wing span: 46ft 8in Length: 34ft 8in Height (wheels down): 13ft 2in Wing area: 517 sq ft	Empty: 3,894lb AUW: 5,900lb	Max speed: 124 mph Cruising speed: 102 mph Range: 550 miles	Crew: 1 Passengers: 6
Hamilton H-45 Metalplane (increased span version)	One 410/450 hp Pratt & Whitney R-1340 Wasp	Wing span: 54ft 5in Length: 34ft 8in Height: 9ft 3in Wing area: 387 sq ft	Empty: 3,342lb AUW: 5,750lb	Max speed: 138 mph Cruising speed: 115 mph Range: 675 miles	Crew: 1 Passengers: 7
Ford 4-AT-B	Three 220 hp Wright J5 Whirlwind	Wing span: 74ft 0in Length: 49ft 10in Height: 12ft 8in Wing area: 785 sq ft	Empty: 6,169lb AUW: 10,130lb	Max speed: 114 mph Cruising speed: 95 mph Range: 520 miles	Crew: 2 Passengers: 12
Ford 5-AT-C	Three 420/450 hp Pratt & Whitney R-1340 Wasp	Wing span: 77ft 10in Length: 50ft 3in Height: 12ft 8in Wing area: 835 sq ft	Empty: 7,500lb AUW: 13,500lb	Max speed: 164 mph Cruising speed: 140 mph Range: 630 miles	Crew: 2 Passengers: 15
Fairchild Model 71 (landplane)	One 420 hp Pratt & Whitney R-1340 Wasp	Wing span: 50ft 2in Length: 33ft 0in Height: 9ft 4in Wing area: 332 sq ft	Empty: 2,930lb AUW: 5,500lb	Max speed: 135 mph Cruising speed: 110 mph Range: over 650 miles	Crew: 1 Passengers: 6

Type	Powerplant	Dimensions	Weights	Performance	Accommodation
Commercial Aircraft C-1 Sunbeam	One 300 hp Wright J6 Whirlwind	Wing span: 34ft 6in	AUW: 3,910lb	Max speed: 125 mph	Crew: 2 Passengers: 4
Lockheed Air Express	One 450 hp Pratt & Whitney R-1340 Wasp	Wing span: 41ft 0in Length: 27ft 6in Height: 9ft 6in Wing area: 275 sq ft	Empty: 2,533lb AUW: 4,375lb	Max speed: 167 mph Cruising speed: 135 mph Normal range: 725 miles	Crew: 1 Passengers: 4
Bach Model 3-CT-6 Air Yacht	One 525 hp Pratt & Whitney R-1690 Hornet A and two 130 hp Comet	Wing span: 58ft 5in Length: 36ft 10in Height: 9ft 9in Wing area: 512 sq ft	Empty: 4,739lb AUW: 8,000lb	Max speed: 154 mph Cruising speed: 126 mph Range: 600 miles	Crew: 2 Passengers: 8
Bellanca Pacemaker Model E	One 420 hp Wright R-975-E2 Whirlwind	Wing span: 47ft 6in Length: 27ft 10in Height: 8ft 4in Wing area: 291 sq ft	Empty: 2,706lb AUW: 4,657lb	Max speed: 150 mph Max cruising speed: 125 mph Normal range: 700 miles	Crew: 1 Passengers: 5
Kreutzer K-5 Air Coach	Three 100 hp Kinner K5	Wing span: 48ft 10in Length: 33ft 6in Height: 9ft 6in Wing area: 315 sq ft	Empty: 2,745lb AUW: 4,443lb	Max speed: 130 mph Cruising speed: 110 mph Normal range: 520 miles	Crew: 1 Passengers: 5
Cunningham-Hall PT-6F	One 365 hp Wright R-975E-1 Whirlwind	Wing span: 41ft 8in Length: 30ft 0in Height: 9ft 7in Wing area: 370 sq ft	Empty: 2,875lb AUW: 4,550lb	Max speed: 150 mph Cruising speed: 130 mph Normal range: 700 miles	Crew: 1 Passengers: 5 (PT-6) or 1,128lb of cargo (PT-6F)
Metal Aircraft G-2-W Flamingo	One 450 hp Pratt & Whitney R-1340 Wasp	Wing span: 50ft 0in Length: 32ft 8in Height: 9ft 6in Wing area: 365 sq ft	Empty: 3,370lb AUW: 5,800lb	Max speed: 135 mph Cruising speed: 115 mph Normal range: 745 miles	Crew: 2 Passengers: 6
Cessna DC-6A	One 300 hp Wright J6 Whirlwind	Wing span: 40ft 8½in Length: 27ft 11½in Height: 7ft 8in Wing area: 268 sq ft	Empty: 1,932 lb AUW: 3,180 lb	Max speed: 161 mph Cruising speed: 130 mph Normal range: 650 miles	Crew: 1 Passengers: 3
Boeing Model 80A	Three 525 hp Pratt & Whitney R-1860 Hornet B	Wing span: 80ft 0in Length: 56ft 6in Height: 15ft 3in Wing area: 1,220 sq ft	Empty: 10,582lb AUW: 17,500lb	Max speed: 138 mph Cruising speed: 125 mph Range: 460 miles	Crew: 2–3 Passengers: 18 + 898lb of mail/cargo
Keystone K-78D Patrician	Three 525 hp Wright R-1750 Cyclone	Wing span: 86ft 6in Length: 61ft 7in Height: 13ft 0in Wing area: 930 sq ft	Empty: 10,224lb AUW: 16,600lb	Max speed: 144 mph Cruising speed: 120 mph Typical range: 480 miles Max range: 550 miles	Crew: 2 Passengers: 18
Consolidated Model 16 Commodore	Two 575 hp Pratt & Whitney R-1860 Hornet B	Wing span: 100ft 0in Length: 61ft 8in Height (above waterline): 13ft 8in Wing area: 1,110 sq ft	Empty: 10,550lb AUW: 17,600lb	Max speed: 128 mph Cruising speed: 108 mph Normal range: 1,000 miles	Crew: 3 Passengers: 18–30
Fokker F-32	Four 575 hp Pratt & Whitney R-1860 Hornet B	Wing span: 99ft 0in Length: 73ft 0in Height: 16ft 6in Wing area: 1,350 sq ft	Empty: 14,910lb AUW: 24,250lb	Max speed: 157 mph Max cruising speed: 123 mph Range (day): 480 miles Range (night): 850 miles	Crew: 4 Passengers: 32 (day) or 16 (night)
Consolidated Model 17 Fleetster	One 575 hp Pratt & Whitney R-1860 Hornet B	Wing span: 45ft 0in Length: 31ft 9in Height: 9ft 2in Wing area: 313.5 sq ft	Empty: 3,150lb AUW: 5,570lb	Max speed: 172 mph Cruising speed: 145 mph Range: 600 miles	Crew: 2 Passengers: 6
Bellanca CH-400 Skyrocket	One 420 hp Pratt & Whitney R-1340-C1 Wasp	Wing span: 46ft 4in Length: 27ft 10in Height: 8ft 4in Wing area: 273 sq ft	Empty: 2,592lb AUW: 4,600lb	Max speed: 155 mph Cruising speed: 134 mph Normal range: 670 miles	Crew: 1 Passengers: 5
Boeing Model 200 Monomail	One 575 hp Pratt & Whitney R-1860 Hornet B	Wing span: 59ft 1½in Length: 41ft 2½in Height: 16ft 0in Wing area: 535 sq ft	Empty: 4,758lb AUW: 8,000lb	Max speed: 158 mph Cruising speed (60% power): 135 mph Range: 530 miles	Crew: 1 Passengers: None (200), 6 (221) or 8 (221A)

Type	Powerplant	Dimensions	Weights	Performance	Accommodation
Ogden Osprey Model PC	Three 90 hp ACE Cirrus	Wing span: 50ft 0in Length: 34ft 6in Height: 9ft 3in Wing area: 312 sq ft	Empty: 2,898lb AUW: 4,548lb	Max speed: 128 mph Cruising speed: 102 mph Normal range: 450 miles	Crew: 1–2 Passengers: 4–5
Stinson SM-6000-B1	Three 215 hp Lycoming R-680	Wing span: 60ft 0in Length: 42ft 10in Height: 12ft 0in Wing area: 490 sq ft	Empty: 5,670lb AUW: 8,600lb	Max speed: 146 mph Cruising speed: 122 mph Normal range: 350 miles	Crew: 1–2 Passengers: 10
Solar MS-1	One 420 hp Pratt & Whitney R-1340 Wasp C	Wing span: 56ft 6in Length: 35 ft 11 in Height: 10ft 2in Wing area: 496·5 sq ft	Empty: 3,665lb AUW: 5,650lb	Max speed: 130 mph Cruising speed: 115 mph	Crew: 2 Passengers: 6
Curtiss-Wright Travel Air Sedan 6-B	One 300 hp Wright J6 Whirlwind	Wing span: 48ft 7in Length: 31ft 5in Height: 9ft 3in Wing area: 282 sq ft	Empty: 2,707lb AUW: 4,420lb	Max speed: 135 mph Cruising speed: 115 mph Normal range: 575 miles	Crew: 2 Passengers: 4
Bellanca P-200 Airbus	One 575 hp Wright R-1820-E Cyclone	Wing span: 65ft 0in Length: 42ft 9in Height: 10ft 4in Wing area: 652 sq ft	Empty: 5,155lb AUW: 9,590lb	Max speed: 143 mph Cruising speed: 122 mph Normal range: 720 miles	Crew: 1 Passengers: 12
Northrop Alpha 4	One 450 hp Pratt & Whitney Wasp SC1	Wing span: 43ft 10in Length: 28ft 5in Height: 9ft 0in Wing area: 312 sq ft	Empty: 2,800lb AUW: 4,700lb	Max speed: 177 mph Cruising speed: 155 mph Normal range: 650 miles	Crew: 1 Passengers: 6 max
Sikorsky S-41A	Two 575 hp Pratt & Whitney R-1860 Hornet B	Wing span: 78ft 9in Length: 45ft 2in Height: 15ft 3in Wing area: 729 sq ft	Empty: 8,100lb AUW: 13,800lb	Max speed: 133 mph Cruising speed: 115 mph Range (max payload): 575 miles Range (max fuel): 920 miles	Crew: 2 Passengers: 14
Lockheed Model 9 Orion	One 450 hp Pratt & Whitney R-1340 Wasp SC	Wing span: 42ft 9¼in Length: 27ft 6in Height: 9ft 3in Wing area: 294·1 sq ft	Empty: 3,250lb AUW: 5,200lb	Max speed: 210 mph at 6,000ft Cruising speed: 180 mph Range (max payload): 650 miles Range (max fuel): 800 miles	Crew: 1 Passengers: 6
Pilgrim Model 100-A	One 575 hp Pratt & Whitney R-1860 Hornet B	Wing span: 57ft 0in Length: 38ft 1in Height: 12ft 3in Wing area: 459 sq ft	Empty: 4,362lb AUW: 7,750lb	Max speed: 136 mph Cruising speed: 118 mph Normal range: 510 miles	Crew: 1 Passengers: 9
Sikorsky S-40	Four 575 hp Pratt & Whitney R-1860 Hornet B	Wing span: 114ft 0in Length: 76ft 8in Height: 23ft 10in Wing area: 1,868 sq ft	Empty: 24,748lb AUW: 34,000lb	Max speed: 134 mph Cruising speed: 115 mph Range (40 passengers): 500 miles Range (24 passengers): 950 miles	Crew: 4 Passengers: 40 max
Beechcraft Model D17S	One 450 hp Pratt & Whitney R-985-SB Wasp Junior	Wing span: 32ft 0in Length: 25ft 11in Height: 8ft 0in Wing area: 296·4 sq ft	Empty: 2,570lb AUW: 4,250lb	Max speed: 212 mph Max cruising speed: 202 mph at 9,700ft Range (75% power): 800 miles	Crew: 1 Passengers: 4
Boeing Model 247	Two 550 hp Pratt & Whitney R-1340-S1D1 Wasp	Wing span: 74ft 0in Length: 51ft 4in Height: 15ft 5in Wing area: 836·13 sq ft	Empty: 8,400lb AUW: 12,650lb	Max speed: 182 mph Cruising speed: 155 mph Range: 485 miles	Crew: 2 Passengers: 10
Curtiss AT-32-B Condor	Two 720 hp Wright SGR-1820-F2 Cyclone	Wing span: 82ft 0in Length: 48ft 7in Height: 16ft 4in Wing area: 1,208 sq ft	Empty: 12,235lb AUW: 17,500lb	Max speed: 190 mph Cruising speed: 167 mph at 8,000ft Max range: 716 miles	Crew: 2 Passengers: 12
Pitcairn PA-19	One 420 hp Wright R-975-E2 Whirlwind	Rotor dia: 50ft 8in Length: 25ft 9in Height: 13ft 0in Disc area: 2,085 sq ft	Empty: 2,681lb AUW: 4,041lb	Max speed: 120 mph Cruising speed: 100 mph Normal range: 350 miles	Crew: 1 Passengers: 3–4
Stinson SR-8B Reliant	One 245 hp Lycoming R-680-B6	Wing span: 41ft 7in Length: 27ft 2in Height: 8ft 5in Wing area: 256·5 sq ft	Empty: 2,347lb AUW: 3,750lb	Max speed: 147 mph at S/L Max cruising speed: 138 mph at 3,000ft Normal range: 645 miles	Crew: 1 Passengers: 4
Douglas DC-1	Two 710 hp Wright SGR-1820-F3 Cyclone	Wing span: 85ft 0in Length: 60ft 0in Height: 16ft 0in Wing area: 942 sq ft	Empty: 11,780lb AUW: 17,500lb	Max speed: 210 mph Cruising speed: 200 mph at 14,000ft Normal range: 1,000 miles	Crew: 2 Passengers: 12

Type	Powerplant	Dimensions	Weights	Performance	Accommodation
General Aviation GA-43A	One 715 hp Wright GR-1820-F1 Cyclone	Wing span: 53ft 0in Length: 43ft 1in Height: 12ft 6in Wing area: 464 sq ft	Empty: 5,283lb AUW: 8,750lb	Max speed: 195 mph Cruising speed: 170 mph at 5,000ft Normal range: 425 miles Max range: 850 miles	Crew: 1–2 Passengers: 10–11
Douglas DC-2	Two 760 hp Wright SGR-1820-F52 Cyclone	Wing span: 85ft 0in Length: 61ft 11¾in Height: 16ft 3¾in Wing area: 939 sq ft	Empty: 12,408lb AUW: 18,560lb	Max speed: 210 mph at 8,000ft Cruising speed: 190 mph at 8,000ft Normal range: 1,000 miles	Crew: 2 Passengers: 14
Sikorsky S-42A	Four 800 hp Pratt & Whitney Hornet S1E-G	Wing span: 118ft 2in Length: 68ft 0in Height: 21ft 5in Wing area: 1,340 sq ft	Empty: 23,200lb AUW: 40,000lb	Max speed: 188 mph at 7,000ft Cruising speed: 163 mph at 7,000ft Normal range: 1,200 miles	Crew: 5 Passengers: 32 (day) or 14 (night)
Vultee V-1A	One 735 hp Wright SR-1820-F2 Cyclone	Wing span: 50ft 0in Length: 37ft 0in Height: 10ft 2in Wing area: 384 sq ft	Empty: 5,382lb AUW: 8,500lb	Max speed: 240 mph at 12,000ft Cruising speed: 217 mph Normal range: 950 miles	Crew: 2 Passengers: 8
Lockheed Model 10A Electra	Two 450 hp Pratt & Whitney R-985-SB2 Wasp Junior	Wing span: 55ft 0in Length: 38ft 7in Height: 10ft 1in Wing area: 458 sq ft	Empty: 6,325lb AUW: 10,100lb	Max speed: 210 mph at 5,000ft Cruising speed: 195 mph at 9,600ft Range (max payload): 550 miles Range (max fuel): 750 miles	Crew: 2 Passengers: 10
Northrop Delta 1D	One 735 hp Wright SR-1820-F2 Cyclone	Wing span: 47ft 9in Length: 33ft 1in Height: 10ft 1in Wing area: 363 sq ft	Empty: 4,540lb AUW: 7,350lb	Max speed: 219 mph at 6,300ft Cruising speed: 200 mph at 8,000ft Range (max payload): 1,100 miles Range (max fuel): 1,500 miles	Crew: 2 Passengers: 8
Stinson Model A	Three 260 hp Lycoming R-680-5	Wing span: 60ft 0in Length: 36ft 10in Height: 14ft 2in Wing area: 500 sq ft	Empty: 7,200lb AUW: 10,200lb	Max speed: 180 mph at S/L Cruising speed: 163 mph at 5,000ft Range: 490 miles	Crew: 1–2 Passengers: 8
Burnelli UB-14A	Two 680 hp Pratt & Whitney R-1535 Twin Wasp Junior	Wing span: 71ft 2in Length: 44ft 0in Height: 10ft 4in Lifting area: 686 sq ft	Empty: 8,200lb AUW: 14,200lb	Max speed: 225 mph at 10,000ft Cruising speed: 185 mph at S/L Normal range: 600 miles	Crew: 2 Passengers: 12
Burnelli (Cancargo) CBY-3 Loadmaster	Two 1,200 hp Pratt & Whitney R-1830 Twin Wasp	Wing span: 86ft 0in Length: 54ft 6¾in Height: 13ft 4in Lifting area: 1,234 sq ft	Empty: 16,800lb AUW: 27,000lb	Max speed: 223 mph at 7,500ft Cruising speed: 193 mph at 10,000ft Normal range: 1,200 miles	Crew: 2 Passengers: 38 max or 22 plus 2,875lb of cargo
Bellanca 66-75 Aircruiser	One 730 hp Wright SGR-1820-F53 Cyclone	Wing span: 65ft 0in Length: 43ft 4in Height: 11ft 9in Wing area: 465·7 sq ft	Empty: 6,115lb AUW: 11,400lb	Max speed: 165 mph at 6,900ft Max cruising speed: 155 mph at 12,000ft Range (max cruising speed): 700 miles	Crew: 1–2 Passengers: 15 or 3,625lb of cargo
Cessna C-34	One 145 hp Warner Super Scarab	Wing span: 34ft 2in Length: 24ft 8in Height: 7ft 0in Wing area: 181 sq ft	Empty: 1,380lb AUW: 2,350lb	Max speed: 162 mph at S/L Cruising speed: 143 mph at S/L Normal range: 550 miles	Crew: 1 Passengers: 3
Martin M-130	Four 800 hp Pratt & Whitney R-1830-S2A5G Twin Wasp	Wing span: 130ft 0in Length: 90ft 10½in Height: 24ft 7¾in Wing area (incl sponsons): 2,315 sq ft	Empty: 25,363lb AUW: 52,252lb	Max speed: 181 mph at 7,000ft Max cruising speed: 163 mph at 1,200ft Range (12 passengers): 3,200 miles Range (mail only): 4,000 miles	Crew: 7 Passengers: 36–43 (day) or 18 (night)
Sikorsky S-43	Two 800 hp Pratt & Whitney Hornet S1E-G	Wing span: 86ft 0in Length: 51ft 2in Height: 17ft 8in Wing area: 780·6 sq ft	Empty: 12,750lb AUW: 19,500lb	Max speed: 194 mph at 7,000ft Max cruising speed: 181 mph at 8,000ft Normal range: 775 miles	Crew: 3 Passengers: 16 (22 max)
Douglas DC-3A	Two 1,200 hp Pratt & Whitney Twin Wasp S1C3G	Wing span: 95ft 0in Length: 64ft 5½in Height: 16ft 11⅛in Wing area: 987 sq ft	Empty: 16,865lb AUW: 25,200lb	Max speed: 230 mph at 8,500ft Cruising speed: 207 mph Normal range: 2,125 miles	Crew: 3 Passengers: 21–28 (32 max)
Lockheed Model 12A Electra	Two 450 hp Pratt & Whitney R-985-SB2 Wasp Junior	Wing span: 49ft 6in Length: 36ft 4in Height: 9ft 9in Wing area: 352 sq ft	Empty: 5,960lb AUW: 8,650lb	Max speed: 225 mph at 5,000ft Cruising speed: 213 mph at 9,600ft Range (max payload): 750 miles Range (max fuel): 950 miles	Crew: 2 Passengers: 6
Cessna C-37	One 145 hp Warner Super Scarab	Wing span: 34ft 2in Length: 24ft 8in Height: 7ft 0in Wing area: 181 sq ft	Empty: 1,380lb AUW: 2,350lb	Max speed: 162 mph at S/L Cruising speed: 143 mph at S/L Normal range: 525 miles	Crew: 1 Passengers: 3

Type	Powerplant	Dimensions	Weights	Performance	Accommodation
Beechcraft Model H18S	Two 450 hp Pratt & Whitney R-985AN-14B Wasp Junior	Wing span: 49ft 8in Length: 35ft 2½in Height: 9ft 4in Wing area: 360·7 sq ft	Empty: 5,845lb AUW: 9,900lb	Max speed: 236 mph at 4,500ft Max cruising speed: 220 mph at 10,000ft Econ cruising speed: 185 mph at 10,000ft Max range: 1,530 miles	Crew: 2 Passengers: 7–9
Volpar Turboliner	Two 705 ehp Garrett TPE331-1-101B	Wing span: 46ft 0in Length: 44ft 2½in Height: 9ft 7in Wing area: 374 sq ft	Empty: 6,600lb AUW: 11,500lb	Max cruising speed: 280 mph at 10,000ft Econ cruising speed: 256 mph at 10,000ft Range (max payload): 346 miles Range (max fuel): 2,076 miles	Crew: 2 Passengers: 15
Alcor C-6-1	Two 250 hp Menasco C-6-S Super Buccaneer	Wing span: 49ft 0in Length: 31ft 8in Height: 9ft 0in Wing area: 318 sq ft	Empty: 4,141lb AUW: 6,200lb	Max speed: 211 mph at 5,500ft Max cruising speed: 190 mph at 5,500ft Normal range: 738 miles	Crew: 2 Passengers: 6
Grumman G-21A Goose	Two 450 hp Pratt & Whitney R-985-SB2 Wasp Junior	Wing span: 49ft 0in Length: 38ft 4in Height: 12ft 2in Wing area: 375 sq ft	Empty: 5,450lb AUW: 8,000lb	Max speed: 201 mph at 5,000ft Max cruising speed: 190 mph at 9,600ft Range (max fuel): 900 miles	Crew: 1 Passengers: 7
McKinnon Turbo-Goose	Two 680 shp Pratt & Whitney (Canada) PT6A-27	Wing span: 50ft 10in Length: 39ft 7in Height: 15ft 0in Wing area: 377·64 sq ft	Empty: 6,700lb AUW: 12,500lb	Max operating speed: 243 mph Range (max fuel): 1,600 miles	Crew: 1 Passengers: 11
Barkley-Grow T8P-1	Two 400 hp Pratt & Whitney R-985-SB Wasp Junior	Wing span: 50ft 8¾in Length: 36ft 2in Height: 9ft 7¾in Wing area: 354 sq ft	Empty: 5,750lb AUW: 8,250lb	Max speed: 224 mph at 5,000ft Cruising speed: 216 mph at 9,600ft Cruising range: 810 miles	Crew: 2 Passengers: 6–8
Lockheed Model 14-F62 Super Electra	Two 900 hp Wright SGR-1820-F62 Cyclone	Wing span: 65ft 6in Length: 44ft 4in Height: 11ft 5in Wing area: 551 sq ft	Empty: 10,750lb AUW: 17,500lb	Max speed: 250 mph at 5,800ft Max cruising speed: 228 mph at 13,000ft Range (max payload): 850 miles Range (max fuel): 1,590 miles	Crew: 3–4 Passengers: 10–11
Kinner Invader	Two 370 hp Kinner C-7	Wing span: 50ft 0in Length: 33ft 9½in Height: 10ft 6¾in Wing area: 396·6 sq ft	Empty: 5,320lb AUW: 8,500lb	Max speed: 210 mph at 5,000ft Cruising speed: 190 mph at 5,000ft Range (5 passengers): 900 miles	Crew: 2 Passengers: 7
Cessna C-145 Airmaster	One 145 hp Warner Super Scarab	Wing span: 34ft 2in Length: 24ft 8in Height: 7ft 0in Wing area: 181 sq ft	Empty: 1,380lb AUW: 2,350lb	Max speed: 162 mph at S/L Cruising speed: 151 mph at S/L Normal range: 525 miles	Crew: 1 Passengers: 3
Kellett KD-1B	One 225 hp Jacobs L-4MA	Rotor dia: 40ft 0in Length: 28ft 10in Height: 10ft 3in Disc area: 1,257 sq ft	Empty: 1,625lb AUW: 2,250lb	Max speed: 120 mph Cruising speed: 102 mph Normal range: 200 miles	Crew: 1 Passengers: 1
Boeing Model 314	Four 1,500 hp Wright GR-2600 Double Cyclone	Wing span: 152ft 0in Length: 106ft 0in Height: 27ft 7in Wing area: 2,867 sq ft	Empty: 50,268lb AUW: 82,500lb	Max speed: 193 mph at 10,000ft Cruising speed: 183 mph Range: 3,500 miles	Crew: 10 max Passengers: 74 (day) or 40 (night)
Douglas DC-5	Two 1,100 hp Wright R-1820-G102A Cyclone	Wing span: 78ft 0in Length: 62ft 2in Height: 19ft 10in Wing area: 824 sq ft	Empty: 13,674lb AUW: 20,000lb	Max speed: 230 mph at 7,700ft Cruising speed: 202 mph Max range: 1,600 miles	Crew: 3 Passengers: 22 max
Douglas DC-4E	Four 1,450 hp Pratt & Whitney R-2180-S1A1-G Twin Hornet	Wing span: 138ft 3in Length: 97ft 7in Height: 24ft 6½in Wing area: 2,155 sq ft	Empty: 42,564lb AUW: 66,500lb	Max speed: 245 mph at 7,000ft Cruising speed: 200 mph at 10,000ft Normal range: 2,200 miles	Crew: 3 Passengers: 30 (night) or 52 (day)
Lockheed Model 18-56 Lodestar	Two 1,200 hp Wright GR-1820-G205A Cyclone	Wing span: 65ft 6in Length: 49ft 9¾in Height: 11ft 10½in Wing area: 551 sq ft	Empty: 11,790lb AUW: 18,500lb	Max speed: 272 mph Econ cruising speed: 251 mph Range (max fuel): 1,890 miles	Crew: 2 Passengers: 14
Boeing Model 307 Stratoliner	Four 900 hp Wright GR-1820-102A/105A Cyclone	Wing span: 107ft 3in Length: 74ft 4in Height: 20ft 9in Wing area: 1,486 sq ft	Empty: 30,310lb AUW: 42,000lb	Max speed: 246 mph at 17,300ft Cruising speed: 220 mph at 15,700ft Range: 2,390 miles	Crew: 5 Passengers: 33 (day) or 16 sleeping berths + 9 seated
Grumman G-44A Widgeon	Two 200 hp Ranger L-440C-5	Wing span: 40ft 0in Length: 31ft 1in Height: 11ft 5in Wing area: 245 sq ft	Empty: 3,240lb AUW: 4,525lb	Max speed: 160 mph Typical cruising speed: 130 mph Range (max fuel): 800 miles	Crew: 1–2 Passengers: 4–5

Type	Powerplant	Dimensions	Weights	Performance	Accommodation
Consolidated PBY-5A Catalina	Two 1,200 hp Pratt & Whitney R-1830-92 Twin Wasp	Wing span: 104ft 0in Length: 63ft 10in Height: 18ft 10in Wing area: 1,400 sq ft	Empty: approx 17,000lb AUW: 35,100lb	Max speed: 160 mph at 7,500ft Typical cruising speed: 130 mph at 6,000ft Range (max payload): 650 miles Range (max fuel): 4,650 miles	Crew: 6 Payload: 1,000lb (3 passengers + mail)
Consolidated Model 32-3 Liberator II (LB-30)	Four 1,200 hp Pratt & Whitney R-1830-S3C4-G Twin Wasp	Wing span: 110ft 0in Length: 67ft 1in Height: 17ft 11in Wing area: 1,048 sq ft	Empty: 37,000lb AUW: 60,000lb	Max speed: 275 mph Normal range: 2,290 miles	Crew: 3 Passengers: 30 max
Curtiss CW-20	Two 1,700 hp Wright R-2600-17A Cyclone	Wing span: 108ft 1in Length: 76ft 4in Height: 21ft 9in Wing area: 1,360 sq ft	Empty: 27,600lb AUW: 40,000lb	Max speed: 254 mph at 7,000ft Cruising speed: 222 mph at 10,000ft Range: 1,500 miles	Crew: 4 Passengers: 36
Curtiss C-46A	Two 2,000 hp Pratt & Whitney R-2800-51 Double Wasp	Wing span: 108ft 0in Length: 76ft 4in Height: 21ft 9in Wing area: 1,360 sq ft	Empty: 30,000lb AUW: 45,000lb	Max speed: 270 mph at 15,000ft Cruising speed: 173 mph at 10,000ft Range at 237 mph: 1,000 miles Range at 173 mph: 3,150 miles	Crew: 2 Passengers: 52 (typical)
Vought-Sikorsky VS-44A	Four 1,200 hp Pratt & Whitney R-1830-S1C3-G Twin Wasp	Wing span: 124ft 0in Length: 79ft 3in Height: 27ft 7¼in Wing area: 1,670 sq ft	Empty: 30,200lb AUW: 59,534lb	Max speed: 211 mph Cruising speed: 160 mph at 10,000ft Max range (40 passengers): 3,600 miles	Crew: 6–11 Passengers: 40 (day) or 16 (night)
Budd Conestoga	Two 1,050 hp Pratt & Whitney R-1830-92 Twin Wasp	Wing span: 100ft 0in Length: 68ft 0in Height: 31ft 9in Wing area: 1,400 sq ft	Empty: 20,115lb AUW: 33,850lb	Max speed: 197 mph at 7,000ft Econ cruising speed: 155 mph at 7,500ft Normal range: 600 miles Max range (standard fuel): 1,800 miles	Crew: 2 Passengers: 24 or 9,520lb of cargo
Lockheed L-749A Constellation	Four 2,500 hp Wright R-3350-18BD 1 Cyclone	Wing span: 123ft 0in Length: 95ft 2in Height: 22ft 5in Wing area: 1,650 sq ft	Empty: 69,000lb AUW: 107,000lb	Max cruising speed: 275 mph at 18,000ft Range (max payload): 2,600 miles Range (max fuel): 4,150 miles	Crew: 3 Passengers: 69
Douglas DC-4 (C-54D)	Four 1,350 hp Pratt & Whitney R-2000-11 Twin Wasp	Wing span: 117 ft 6in Length: 93ft 10in Height: 27ft 6in Wing area: 1,460 sq ft	Empty: 38,000lb AUW: 73,000lb	Max speed: 275 mph at 20,000ft Cruising speed: 203 mph at 10,000ft Range (14,000lb payload): 3,100 miles	Crew: 4 Passengers: 44 standard (86 max)
Bell Model 47G	One 200 hp Franklin 6V4-200-C32	Rotor dia: 35ft 1½in Length: 27ft 4in Height: 9ft 3¾in Disc area: 969 sq ft	Empty: 1,435lb AUW: 2,350lb	Max speed: 86 mph at S/L Cruising speed: 70 mph Normal range: 212 miles	Crew: 1 Passengers: 2
Sikorsky S-51	One 450 hp Pratt & Whitney R-985 Wasp Junior	Rotor dia: 49ft 0in Length: 41ft 1¾in Height: 12ft 11in Disc area: 1,810 sq ft	Empty: 3,805lb AUW: 5,500lb	Max speed: 103 mph at S/L Cruising speed: 85 mph at 1,000ft Normal range: 260 miles	Crew: 1 Passengers: 3
Northrop N-23 Pioneer	Three 800 hp Wright 744C7BA1 Cyclone	Wing span: 85ft 0in Length: 60ft 7in Height: 17ft 10in Wing area: 1,100 sq ft	Empty: 14,400lb AUW: 25,500lb	Max cruising speed: 193 mph at 10,000ft Cruising speed (60% power): 150 mph Max range: 1,750 miles	Crew: 2 Payload: 5,600lb of cargo or 30–40 passengers
Boeing B-17G Flying Fortress (bomber)	Four 1,200 hp Wright R-1820-97 Cyclone	Wing span: 103ft 9in Length: 74ft 4in Height: 19ft 1in Wing area: 1,420 sq ft	Empty: 36,135lb AUW: 65,500lb	Max speed: 287 mph at 25,000ft Max cruising speed: 220 mph Econ cruising speed: 162 mph Range (max cr speed): 1,100 miles	Crew: 10 Max bomb load: 17,600lb
Beechcraft Model V35B Bonanza	One 285 hp Continental IO-520-BB	Wing span: 33ft 6in Length: 26ft 5in Height: 7ft 7in Wing area: 181 sq ft	Empty: 2,117lb AUW: 3,400lb	Max speed: 209 mph at S/L Max cruising speed: 198 mph at 6,000ft Econ cruising speed: 157 mph at 8,000 ft Max range: 1,023 miles	Crew: 1 Passengers: 3–4
Beechcraft Model F33A Bonanza	One 285 hp Continental IO-520-BB	Wing span: 33ft 6in Length: 26ft 8in Height: 8ft 3in Wing area: 181 sq ft	Empty: 2,132lb AUW: 3,400lb	Max speed: 209 mph at S/L Max cruising speed: 198 mph at 6,000 ft Econ cruising speed: 157 mph at 8,000 ft Max range: 1,023 miles	Crew: 1 Passengers: 3–4
Douglas DC-6B	Four 2,500 hp Pratt & Whitney R-2800-CB17 Double Wasp	Wing span: 117ft 6in Length: 106ft 8in Height: 28ft 8in Wing area: 1,463 sq ft	Empty: 64,000lb AUW: 106,000lb	Max cruising speed: 311 mph at 22,500ft Econ cruising speed: 270 mph at 20,000ft Range (max payload): 3,050 miles	Crew: 4 Passengers: 107 max
Martin Model 2-0-2	Two 2,400 hp Pratt & Whitney R-2800-CA18 Double Wasp	Wing span: 93ft 3⅜in Length: 71ft 4in Height: 28ft 5⅜in Wing area: 864 sq ft	Empty: 24,649lb AUW: 39,900lb	Max speed: 306 mph at 14,500ft Max cruising speed: 277 mph at 10,000ft Econ cruising speed: 248 mph at 10,000ft Max range: 1,560 miles	Crew: 3 Passengers: 40 max (36 standard)

Type	Powerplant	Dimensions	Weights	Performance	Accommodation
Grumman G-73 Mallard	Two 600 hp Pratt & Whitney R-1340-S3H1 Wasp	Wing span: 66ft 8in Length: 48ft 4in Height: 18ft 9in Wing area: 444 sq ft	Empty: 9,350lb AUW: 12,750lb	Max speed: 215 mph at 6,000ft Econ cruising speed: 180 mph at 8,000ft Range (max payload): 730 miles Range (max fuel): 1,380 miles	Crew: 2 Passengers: 10–12
Convair Model 240	Two 2,400 hp Pratt & Whitney R-2800-CA18 Double Wasp	Wing span: 91ft 9in Length: 74ft 8in Height: 26ft 11in Wing area: 817 sq ft	Empty: 29,526lb AUW: 42,500lb	Max cruising speed: 270 mph Econ cruising speed: 245 mph Range (max payload): 400 miles Range (max fuel): 1,030 miles	Crew: 2 Passengers: 40
Boeing Model 377 Stratocruiser	Four 3,500 hp Pratt & Whitney R-4360 Wasp Major	Wing span: 141ft 3in Length: 110ft 4in Height: 38ft 3in Wing area: 1,720 sq ft	Empty: 78,920lb AUW: 135,000lb	Max speed: 375 mph Cruising speed: 340 mph at 25,000ft Range (max fuel): 4,200 miles	Crew: 5 Passengers: 100 max
Martin Model 4-0-4	Two 2,400 hp Pratt & Whitney R-2800-CB16 Double Wasp	Wing span: 93ft 3⅜in Length: 74ft 7in Height: 28ft 5⅜in Wing area: 864 sq ft	Empty: 29,126lb AUW: 44,900lb	Max speed: 312 mph at 14,500ft Normal cruising speed: 280 mph at 18,000ft Normal range: 1,080 miles	Crew: 3 Passengers: 40
Lockheed L-1049G Super Constellation	Four 3,400 hp Wright R-3350-EA3 Turbo Compound	Wing span: 123ft 0in Length: 113ft 7in Height: 24ft 9in Wing area: 1,650 sq ft	Empty: 79,237lb AUW: 137,500lb	Typical cruising speed: 305 mph at 20,000ft Range (max payload): 3,070 miles Range (max fuel): 4,020 miles	Crew: 4–5 Passengers: 106 max
Sikorsky S-55A	One 600 hp Pratt & Whitney R-1340-S1H2 Wasp	Rotor dia: 53ft 0in Length: 42ft 2in Height: 13ft 4in Disc area: 2,206 sq ft	Empty: 4,785lb AUW: 6,835lb	Max speed: 105 mph at S/L Cruising speed: 90 mph at 1,000ft Normal range: 440 miles	Crew: 2 Passengers: 8–10
Convair Model 340	Two 2,400 hp Pratt & Whitney R-2800-CB17 Double Wasp	Wing span: 105ft 4in Length: 79ft 2in Height: 28ft 2in Wing area: 920 sq ft	Empty: 31,609lb AUW: 47,000lb	Max speed: 314 mph at 16,000ft Normal cruising speed: 284 mph at 18,000ft Range (max payload): 100 miles Range (max fuel): 1,930 miles	Crew: 2 Passengers: 44
Douglas DC-7C	Four 3,400 hp Wright R-3350-EA-4 Turbo Compound	Wing span: 127ft 6in Length: 112ft 3in Height: 31ft 8in Wing area: 1,637 sq ft	Empty: 80,000lb AUW: 143,000lb	Typical cruising speed: 360 mph at 23,500ft Range (max payload): 3,610 miles Range (max fuel): 5,642 miles	Crew: 3 Passengers: 105 max
Boeing Model 367-80	Four 9,500lb st Pratt & Whitney JT3P	Wing span: 129ft 8in Length: 127ft 10in Height: 38ft 0in Wing area: 2,400 sq ft	Empty: 92,120lb AUW: 190,000lb	Max speed: 582 mph at 25,000ft Cruising speed: 550 mph Range: 3,530 miles	Crew: 3 Passengers: 0
Convair Model 440 Metropolitan	Two 2,500 hp Pratt & Whitney R-2800-CB17 Double Wasp	Wing span: 105ft 4in Length: 81ft 6in Height: 28ft 2in Wing area: 920 sq ft	Empty: 33,314lb AUW: 49,700lb	Max cruising speed: 300 mph at 13,000ft Econ cruising speed: 289 mph at 20,000ft Range (max payload): 285 miles Range (max fuel): 1,930 miles	Crew: 2 Passengers: 52
Sikorsky S-58C	One 1,525 hp Wright R-1820-84 Cyclone	Rotor dia: 56ft 0in Length: 46ft 9in Height: 15ft 11in Disc area: 2,460 sq ft	Empty: 7,675lb AUW: 13,000lb	Max speed: 123 mph at S/L Cruising speed: 101 mph Max range: 280 miles	Crew: 2 Passengers: 12–18
Vertol Model 44B	One 1,425 hp Wright 977C9-HD1 Cyclone	Rotor dia: 44ft 0in Length: 52ft 6in Height: 15ft 5in Disc area: 3,041 sq ft	Empty: 8,990lb AUW: 14,350lb	Max speed: 127 mph at S/L Cruising speed: 101 mph Normal range: 280 miles	Crew: 2 Passengers: 14–15
Lockheed L-1649A Starliner	Four 3,400 hp Wright R-3350-EA2 Turbo Compound	Wing span: 150ft 0in Length: 116ft 2in Height: 24ft 9in Wing area: 1,850 sq ft	Empty: 94,500lb AUW: 160,000lb	Max cruising speed: 290 mph at 22,000ft Range (max payload): 4,940 miles Range (max fuel): 6,180 miles	Crew: 4–5 Passengers: 81
Boeing Vertol Model 107-II	Two 1,250 shp General Electric CT58-110-1	Rotor dia: 50ft 0in Length: 44ft 7in Height: 16ft 8½in Disc area: 3,925 sq ft	Empty: 10,732lb AUW: 19,000lb	Max speed: 168 mph Typical cruising speed: 155 mph Range (6,600lb payload): 115 miles	Crew: 2 Passengers: 25
Lockheed L-188 Electra	Four 3,750 ehp Allison 501-D13A	Wing span: 99ft 0in Length: 104ft 6½in Height: 32ft 10in Wing area: 1,300 sq ft	Empty: 61,500lb AUW: 116,000lb	Max cruising speed: 405 mph at 22,000ft Econ cruising speed: 374 mph Range (max payload): 2,200 miles Range (L-188C, max fuel): 3,020 miles	Crew: 2–3 Passengers: 99 max
Beechcraft Model B80 Queen Air	Two 380 hp Avco Lycoming IGSO-540-A1D	Wing span: 50ft 3in Length: 35ft 6in Height: 14ft 2½in Wing area: 293·9 sq ft	Empty: 5,277lb AUW: 8,800lb	Max speed: 225 mph at 15,000ft Econ cruising speed: 183 mph at 15,000ft Max range (max cr speed): 1,102 miles Max range (econ cr speed): 1,517 miles	Crew: 1–2 Passengers: 4–9

Type	Powerplant	Dimensions	Weights	Performance	Accommodation
Grumman G-159 Gulfstream I	Two 2,210 ehp Rolls-Royce Dart Mk 529-8X or -8E	Wing span: 78ft 6in Length: 63ft 9in Height: 22ft 9in Wing area: 610·3 sq ft	Empty: 21,900lb AUW: 35,100lb	Max cruising speed: 348 mph at 25,000ft Econ cruising speed: 288 mph at 25,000ft Range (max fuel, with reserves): 2,540 miles	Crew: 2 Passengers: 14 (exec) or 24 (airline)
Gulfstream American G-159C Gulfstream I-C	Two 1,990 ehp Rolls-Royce Dart Mk 529-8X	Wing span: 78ft 4in Length: 75ft 4in Height: 23ft 0in Wing area: 610·3 sq ft	AUW: 36,000lb	Max cruising speed: 345 mph Range (max payload): 500 miles Range (max fuel): 2,500 miles	Crew: 2 Passengers: 38
Convair Model 540	Two 3,500 ehp Napier Eland 504A	Wing span: 105ft 4in Length: 81ft 6in Height: 28ft 2in Wing area: 920 sq ft	Empty: 34,500lb AUW: 53,200lb	Max cruising speed: 314 mph at 20,000ft Range (max payload): 975 miles Range (max fuel): 2,415 miles	Crew: 2 Passengers: 44
Boeing Model 707-320C	Four 19,000lb st Pratt & Whitney JT3D-7	Wing span: 145ft 9in Length: 152ft 11in Height: 42ft 5in Wing area: 3,050 sq ft	Empty: 146,400lb AUW: 333,600lb	Max speed: 627 mph Max cruising speed: 605 mph at 25,000ft Econ cruising speed: 550 mph Max range: 5,755 miles	Crew: 3–5 Passengers: 219 max
McDonnell Douglas DC-8 Series 50	Four 18,000lb st Pratt & Whitney JT3D-3	Wing span: 142ft 5in Length: 150ft 6in Height: 42ft 4in Wing area: 2,868 sq ft	Empty: 132,325lb AUW: 325,000lb	Max cruising speed: 580 mph at 30,000ft Range (max payload): 5,720 miles Range (max fuel): 7,000 miles	Crew: 3–5 Passengers: 179 max
Convair Model 580	Two 3,750 ehp Allison 501-D13H	Wing span: 105ft 4in Length: 81ft 6in Height: 28ft 2in Wing area: 920 sq ft	AUW: 58,140lb	Cruising speed: 342 mph Range (max payload): 645 miles Range (max fuel): 2,866 miles	Crew: 2 Passengers: 52
Convair Model 880-M	Four 11,650lb st General Electric CJ805-3B	Wing span: 120ft 0in Length: 129ft 4in Height: 36ft 4in Wing area: 2,000 sq ft	Empty: 94,600lb AUW: 193,000lb	Max cruising speed: 587 mph Econ cruising speed: 541 mph Range (max payload): 2,880 miles Range (max fuel): 3,385 miles	Crew: 3 Passengers: 110
Boeing Model 720	Four 12,000lb st Pratt & Whitney JT3C-7/12	Wing span: 130ft 10in Length: 136ft 2in Height: 37ft 11in Wing area: 2,433 sq ft	Empty: 110,800lb AUW: 229,000lb	Max speed: 627 mph Cruising speed: 601 mph at 25,000ft Range: 5,240 miles	Crew: 4 Passengers: 165
Sikorsky S-61N Mk II	Two 1,500 shp General Electric CT58-140 1/2	Rotor dia: 62ft 0in Length (incl rotors): 72ft 10in Height: 18ft 5½in Disc area: 3,019 sq ft	Empty: 12,510lb AUW: 20,500lb	Max cruising speed: 150 mph Typical cruising speed: 138 mph Max range (std fuel): 282 miles Max range (aux fuel): 495 miles	Crew: 3 Passengers: 30
Convair Model 990A Coronado	Four 16,050lb st General Electric CJ805-23B	Wing span: 120ft 0in Length: 139ft 2½in Height: 39ft 6in Wing area: 2,250 sq ft	Empty: 120,900lb AUW: 253,000lb	Max speed: 625 mph at 21,000ft Econ cruising speed: 556 mph at 35,000ft Range (max payload): 3,800 miles Range (max fuel): 5,446 miles	Crew: 3–4 Passengers: 106
Rockwell Sabreliner 65	Two 3,700lb st Garrett TFE731-3-1D	Wing span: 50ft 5⅛in Length: 46ft 11in Height: 16ft 0in Wing area: 380 sq ft	Empty: 14,154lb AUW: 24,000lb	Max operating speed: Mach 0·83 (IAS) High-speed cruise: Mach 0·81 Long-range cruising speed: Mach 0·73 Range (max fuel): 3,222 miles	Crew: 2 Passengers: 8
Howard 500	Two 2,500 hp Pratt & Whitney R-2800-CB17 Double Wasp	Wing span: 70ft 4in Length: 58ft 5½in Height: 13ft 7in Wing area: 592·2 sq ft	Empty: 23,000lb AUW: 35,000lb	Max speed: 410 mph at S/L Econ cruising speed: 350 mph at 21,000ft Range (max fuel): 2,600 miles	Crew: 2 Passengers: 10–14
Aero Spacelines Guppy-201	Four 4,912 shp Allison 501-D22C	Wing span: 156ft 3in Length: 143ft 10in Height: 48ft 6in Wing area: 1,965 sq ft	Empty: 100,000lb AUW: 170,000lb	Max cruising speed: 288 mph at 20,000ft Econ cruising speed: 253 mph at 20,000ft Range (max payload): 505 miles Range (max fuel): 2,920 miles	Crew: 4 Max payload: 54,000lb
Boeing Advanced Model 727-200	Three 14,500lb st Pratt & Whitney JT8D-9A	Wing span: 108ft 0in Length: 153ft 2in Height: 34ft 0in Wing area: 1,700 sq ft	Empty: 102,900lb AUW: 209,500lb	Max speed: 621 mph at 20,500ft Max cruising speed: 599 mph at 24,700ft Econ cruising speed: 570 mph at 30,000ft Max range: 2,729 miles	Crew: 3 Passengers: 189 max
Beechcraft Model C90 King Air	Two 550 ehp Pratt & Whitney (Canada) PT6A-21	Wing span: 50ft 3in Length: 35ft 6in Height: 14ft 3in Wing area: 293·94 sq ft	Empty: 5,765lb AUW: 9,650lb	Max cruising speed: 256 mph at 12,000ft Max range (max cr speed): 1,384 miles Max range (econ cr speed): 1,474 miles	Crew: 1–2 Passengers: 4–9
Gates Learjet 24F	Two 2,950lb st General Electric CJ610-8A	Wing span: 35ft 7in Length: 43ft 3in Height: 12ft 3in Wing area: 231·77 sq ft	Empty: 7,064lb AUW: 13,500lb	Max operating speed: 547 mph at 25,000ft Max cruising speed: 519 mph at 47,000ft Econ cruising speed: 493 mph at 47,000ft Max range (4 passengers): 1,697 miles	Crew: 2 Passengers: 6

Type	Powerplant	Dimensions	Weights	Performance	Accommodation
Gates Learjet 28 Longhorn	Two 2,950lb st General Electric CJ610-8A	Wing span: 43 ft 9½in Length: 47ft 7·6in Height: 12ft 3·1in Wing area: 264·5 sq ft	Empty: 8,268lb AUW: 15,000lb	Max speed: 549 mph at 25,000ft Max cruising speed: 520 mph at 47,000ft Econ cruising speed: 470 mph at 51,000ft Max range (4 passengers): 1,309 miles	Crew: 2 Passengers: 10
Gates Learjet 35A	Two 3,500lb st Garrett TFE731-2-2B	Wing span: 39ft 6in Length: 48ft 8in Height: 12ft 3in Wing area: 253·3 sq ft	Empty: 9,571lb AUW: 17,000lb	Max speed: 542 mph at 25,000ft Max cruising speed: 529 mph at 41,000ft Econ cruising speed: 481 mph at 45,000ft Max range (4 passengers): 2,636 miles	Crew: 2 Passengers: 8
Gates Learjet 55 Longhorn	Two 3,650lb st Garrett TFE731-3A-2B	Wing span: 43ft 9½in Length: 55ft 1¼in Height: 14ft 8¼in Wing area: 264·5 sq ft	Empty: 12,130lb AUW: 19,500lb	Max speed: 541 mph at 30,000ft Max cruising speed: 506 mph at 45,000ft Econ cruising speed: 462 mph at 49,000ft Max range (4 passengers): 2,492 miles	Crew: 2 Passengers: 10
Hamilton Westwind III	Two 579 ehp Pratt & Whitney (Canada) PT6A-20	Wing span: 46ft 0in Length: 35ft 7¼in Wing area: 326·4 sq ft	Empty: 5,500lb AUW: 11,230lb	Max speed: 270 mph at 12,000ft Max cruising speed: 250 mph at 12,000ft Econ cruising speed: 235 mph at 10,000ft Range (max payload): 933 miles	Crew: 2 Passengers: 8
Rockwell Shrike Commander 500S	Two 290 hp Avco Lycoming IO-540-E1B5	Wing span: 49ft 0½in Length: 36ft 9¾in Height: 14ft 6in Wing area: 255 sq ft	Empty: 4,635lb AUW: 6,750lb	Max cruising speed: 215 mph at S/L, 203 mph at 9,000ft Range (standard fuel): 797 miles Max range: 1,190 miles	Crew: 1 Passengers: 3–7
Aero Commander Turbo Commander 680T	Two 605 shp Garrett TPE331-43	Wing span: 44ft 0in Length: 41ft 3¼in Height: 14ft 6in Wing area: 242·5 sq ft	Empty: 5,450lb AUW: 8,950 lb	Max cruising speed: 285 mph at 15,000ft Range (max fuel): 1,000 miles	Crew: 1 Passengers: 4–10
Gulfstream Commander Jetprop 980	Two 980 shp Garrett TPE331-10-501K	Wing span: 52ft 1½in Length: 42ft 11¾in Height: 14ft 11½in Wing area: 279·37 sq ft	Empty: 6,727lb AUW: 10,325lb	Max cruising speed: 356 mph at 22,000ft Econ cruising speed: 287 mph at 31,000ft Range (max payload): 1,175 miles Range (max fuel): 2,349 miles	Crew: 1 Passengers: 7–10
Convair Model 640	Two 3,025 ehp Rolls-Royce Dart Mk 542-4	Wing span: 105ft 4in Length: 81ft 6in Height: 28ft 2in Wing area: 920 sq ft	Empty: 30,275lb AUW: 57,000lb	Max and econ cruising speed: 300 mph Range (max payload): 1,230 miles Range (max fuel): 1,950 miles	Crew: 2 Passengers: 56
McDonnell Douglas DC-9 Series 30	Two 14,000lb st Pratt & Whitney JT8D-7	Wing span: 93ft 5in Length: 119ft 3½in Height: 27ft 6in Wing area: 1,000·7 sq ft	Empty: 57,190lb AUW: 121,000lb	Max speed: 575 mph Max cruising speed: 564 mph at 25,000ft Econ cruising speed: 510 mph at 35,000ft Typical range (80 passengers): 1,923 miles	Crew: 2 Passengers: 119 max
McDonnell Douglas DC-8 Super 63	Four 19,000lb st Pratt & Whitney JT3D-7	Wing span: 148ft 5in Length: 187ft 5in Height: 42ft 5in Wing area: 2,927 sq ft	Empty: 153,749lb AUW: 350,000lb	Max speed: 600 mph at 30,000ft Range (max payload): 4,500 miles Range (max fuel, no payload): 7,700 miles	Crew: 3 Passengers: 259 max
McDonnell Douglas DC-9 Super 81	Two 18,500lb st Pratt & Whitney JT8D-209	Wing span: 107ft 10in Length: 147ft 10in Height: 29ft 8in Wing area: 1,270 sq ft	Empty: 79,757lb AUW: 140,000lb	Max speed: 575 mph Max cruising speed: Mach 0·80 Normal cruising speed: Mach 0·76 Range (max fuel): 3,060 miles	Crew: 2 Passengers: 172 max
Fairchild FH-227E	Two 2,300 shp Rolls-Royce Dart RDa.7 Mk 532-7L	Wing span: 95ft 2in Length: 83ft 8in Height: 27ft 7in Wing area: 754 sq ft	Empty: 22,923lb AUW: 43,500lb	Max cruising speed: 294 mph at 15,000ft Econ cruising speed: 270 mph at 25,000ft Range (max payload): 656 miles Range (max fuel): 1,655 miles	Crew: 2 Passengers: 52
Fairchild Swearingen Merlin IIIC	Two 900 shp Garrett TPE331-10U-503G	Wing span: 46ft 3in Length: 42ft 2in Height: 16ft 10in Wing area: 277·5 sq ft	Empty: 8,150lb AUW: 13,230lb	Max cruising speed: 345 mph at 10,000ft Range (4 passengers): 2,231 miles Range (6 passengers): 1,964 miles	Crew: 2 Passengers: 6–9
Fairchild Swearingen Metro III	Two 1,000/1,100 shp Garrett TPE331-11U-601G	Wing span: 57ft 0in Length: 59ft 4¼in Height: 16ft 8in Wing area: 309 sq ft	Empty: 8,737lb AUW: 14,000lb	Max operating speed: 285 mph (CAS) Max cruising speed: 312 mph at 15,000ft Range (19 passengers and max fuel): 714 miles	Crew: 2 Passengers: 20
Cessna Model 402C Utililiner	Two 325 hp Continental TSIO-520-VB	Wing span: 44ft 1½in Length: 36ft 4½in Height: 11ft 5½in Wing area: 225·8 sq ft	Empty: 4,098lb AUW: 6,850lb	Max speed: 266 mph at 16,000ft Max cruising speed: 245 mph at 20,000ft Econ cruising speed: 191 mph at 20,000ft Max range: 1,466 miles	Crew: 1–2 Passengers: 8–9
Cessna Titan Ambassador	Two 375 hp Continental GTSIO-520-M	Wing span: 46ft 4in Length: 39ft 6¼in Height: 13ft 3in Wing area: 242 sq ft	Empty: 4,834lb AUW: 8,400lb	Max speed: 267 mph at 16,000ft Max cruising speed: 250 mph at 20,000ft Econ cruising speed: 161 mph at 10,000ft Max range: 2,115 miles	Crew: 2 Passengers: 6–8

Type	Powerplant	Dimensions	Weights	Performance	Accommodation
Cessna Conquest	Two 635·5 shp Garrett TPE331-8-401S/402S	Wing span: 49ft 4in Length: 39ft 0¼in Height: 13ft 1¾in Wing area: 253·6 sq ft	Empty: 5,706lb AUW: 9,850lb	Max speed: 340 mph at 16,000ft Max cruising speed: 337 mph at 24,000ft Max range: 2,638 miles	Crew: 1 Passengers: 4–10
Cessna Model 414A Chancellor	Two 310 hp Continental TSIO-520-NB	Wing span: 44ft 1½in Length: 36ft 4½in Height: 11ft 5½in Wing area: 225·8 sq ft	Empty: 4,356lb AUW: 6,750lb	Max speed: 271 mph at 20,000ft Max cruising speed: 258 mph at 24,500ft Econ cruising speed: 165 mph at 10,000ft Max range: 1,528 miles	Crew: 1–2 Passengers: 4–7
Cessna Model 421C Golden Eagle	Two 375 hp Continental GTSIO-520-N	Wing span: 41ft 1½in Length: 36ft 4½in Height: 11ft 5½in Wing area: 215 sq ft	Empty: 4,640lb AUW: 7,450lb	Max speed: 297 mph at 20,000ft Max cruising speed: 278 mph at 25,000ft Econ cruising speed: 176 mph at 10,000ft Max range: 1,710 miles	Crew: 1–2 Passengers: 4–7
Cessna Model 425 Corsair	Two 450 shp Pratt & Whitney Aircraft (Canada) PT6A-112	Wing span: 44ft 1½in Length: 35ft 10¼in Height: 12ft 7¼in Wing area: 224·98 sq ft	Empty: 4,870lb AUW: 8,200lb	Max cruising speed: 304 mph at 17,700ft Max range: 1,854 miles	Crew: 1–2 Passengers: 4–6
Piper PA-31 Navajo	Two 310 hp Avco Lycoming TIO-540-A2C	Wing span: 40ft 8in Length: 32ft 7½in Height: 13ft 0in Wing area: 229 sq ft	Empty: 4,003lb AUW: 6,500lb	Max speed: 261 mph Max cruising speed: 248 mph at 22,000ft Econ cruising speed: 197 mph at 12,000ft Max range: 1,226 miles	Crew: 1 Passengers: 5–7
Piper PA-31-350 Chieftain	Two 350 hp Avco Lycoming TIO/LTIO-540-J2BD	Wing span: 40ft 8in Length: 34ft 7½in Height: 13ft 0in Wing area: 229 sq ft	Empty: 4,221lb AUW: 7,000lb	Max speed: 266 mph Max cruising speed: 254 mph at 20,000ft Econ cruising speed: 199 mph at 12,000ft Max range (standard fuel): 1,094 miles	Crew: 1–2 Passengers: 5–9
Piper PA-42 Cheyenne III	Two 720 shp Pratt & Whitney (Canada) PT6A-41	Wing span: 47ft 8⅛in Length: 43ft 4¾in Height: 14ft 9in Wing area: 293 sq ft	Empty: 6,389lb AUW: 11,200lb	Max speed: 341 mph Max cruising speed: 333 mph at 21,000ft Max range (max cr speed): 2,050 miles Max range (econ cr speed): 2,533 miles	Crew: 1–2 Passengers: 5–10
Gulfstream American Gulfstream II	Two 11,400lb st Rolls-Royce Spey Mk 511-8	Wing span: 68ft 10in Length: 79ft 11in Height: 24ft 6in Wing area: 809·6 sq ft	Empty: 30,938lb AUW: 65,500lb	Max cruising speed: 581 mph at 25,000ft Econ cruising speed: 483 mph at 43,000ft Range (IFR): 3,662 miles Range (VFR): 4,123 miles	Crew: 2–3 Passengers: 19
Gulfstream American Gulfstream III	Two 11,400lb st Rolls-Royce Spey Mk 511-8	Wing span: 77ft 10in Length: 83ft 1in Height: 24ft 4½in Wing area: 934·6 sq ft	Empty: 38,300lb AUW: 68,200lb	Max cruising speed: Mach 0·85 Long-range cruising speed: Mach 0·775 Range (1,600lb payload): 4,200 miles Max range (VFR): 4,842 miles	Crew: 2–3 Passengers: 19
Boeing Advanced Model 737-200	Two 14,500lb st Pratt & Whitney JT8D-9A	Wing span: 93ft 0in Length: 100ft 2in Height: 37ft 0in Wing area: 980 sq ft	Empty: 61,050lb AUW: 115,500lb	Max speed: 586 mph at 23,500ft Max cruising speed: 576 mph at 22,600ft Econ cruising speed: 480 mph at 30,000ft Typical range: 2,648 miles	Crew: 2 Passengers: 130 max
Beechcraft Model B99 Airliner	Two 680 ehp Pratt & Whitney (Canada) PT6A-28	Wing span: 45ft 10½in Length: 44ft 6¾in Height: 14ft 4¼in Wing area: 279·7 sq ft	Empty: 5,777lb AUW: 10,900lb	Max cruising speed: 285 mph at 12,000ft Max range (max cr speed): 1,035 miles Max range (econ cr speed): 1,173 miles	Crew: 2 Passengers: 15
Bushmaster 2000	Three 450 hp Pratt & Whitney R-985-AN-1 or -14B Wasp Junior	Wing span: 77ft 11in Length: 50ft 8in Height: 13ft 5in Wing area: 851·7 sq ft	Empty: 7,500lb AUW: 12,500lb	Max speed: 128 mph (IAS) Max range: 700 miles	Crew: 1–2 Passengers: 15–23
Conroy Turbo Three	Two 1,350/1,600 shp Rolls-Royce Dart Mk 510	Wing span: 95ft 0in Length: 64ft 5½in Height: 16ft 11⅛in Wing area: 987 sq ft	AUW: 26,900lb	Max speed: 215 mph Max cruising speed: 215 mph Range (standard fuel): 940 miles Range (max optional fuel): 2,250 miles	Crew/Passengers: similar to Douglas DC-3
Boeing Model 747-200B	Four 52,500lb st General Electric CF6-50E1 (typical)	Wing span: 195ft 8in Length: 231ft 10in Height: 63ft 5in Wing area: 5,500 sq ft	Empty: 386,000lb AUW: 833,000lb	Max speed: 602 mph at 30,000ft Max range: 6,563 miles	Crew: 3 Passengers: 516 max
Boeing Model 747SP	Four 50,000lb st Pratt & Whitney JT9D-7J	Wing span: 195ft 8in Length: 184ft 9in Height: 65ft 5in Wing area: 5,500 sq ft	Empty: 326,000lb AUW: 700,000lb	Max speed: 609 mph at 30,000ft Max range: 6,736 miles	Crew: 3 Passengers: 440 max
Evangel 4500-300	Two 300 hp Avco Lycoming IO-540-K1B5	Wing span: 41ft 3in Length: 31ft 6in Height: 9ft 6in Wing area: 251 sq ft	Empty: 3,455lb AUW: 5,500lb	Max cruising speed: 182 mph at 6,000ft Econ cruising speed: 175 mph at 10,000ft Max range (75% power): 637 miles Max range (55% power): 750 miles	Crew: 1 Passengers: 8

Type	Powerplant	Dimensions	Weights	Performance	Accommodation
Bell Model 212 Twin Two-Twelve	One 1,290 shp Pratt & Whitney (Canada) PT6T-3B Turbo Twin Pac	Rotor dia: 48ft 2¼in Length: 42ft 4¾in Height: 14ft 10¼in Disc area: 1,809 sq ft	Empty: 6,143lb AUW: 11,200lb	Max cruising speed: 142 mph at S/L Max range: 261 miles	Crew: 1 Passengers: 14
Bell Model 412	One 1,308 shp Pratt & Whitney (Canada) PT6T-3B Turbo Twin Pac	Rotor dia: 46ft 0in Length: 42ft 4¾in Height: 14ft 2¼in Disc area: 1,662 sq ft	Empty: 6,223lb AUW: 11,600lb	Max cruising speed: 143 mph at S/L Max range: 261 miles	Crew: 1 Passengers: 14
Bell Model 214ST	Two 1,625 shp General Electric CT7-2A	Rotor dia: 52ft 0in Length: 50ft 0in Height: 15ft 10½in Disc area: 2,123·7 sq ft	AUW: 17,200lb	Normal cruising speed: 159 mph at S/L Max cruising speed: 155 mph at 4,000ft Range (standard fuel): 406 miles Max range (aux fuel, no payload): 633 miles	Crew: 2 Passengers: 18 max
Boeing Model 2707-300	Four 68,600lb st General Electric GE4/J5P	Wing span: 141ft 8in Length: 286ft 8in Height: 50ft 1in Wing area: 8,497 sq ft	AUW: 635,000lb (prototypes, max ramp weight)	Max speed: 1,780 mph Range: approx 4,000 miles	Crew: 3 Passengers: 250–321
McDonnell Douglas DC-10 Series 30	Three 51,000lb st General Electric CF6-50C	Wing span: 165ft 4·4in Length: 182ft 1in Height: 58ft 1in Wing area: 3,958 sq ft	Empty: 267,197lb AUW: 572,000lb	Max speed: 610 mph at 25,000ft Max cruising speed: 564 mph at 30,000ft Normal cruising speed: Mach 0·82 Range (max payload): 4,606 miles	Crew: 3–5 Passengers: 380 max
Cessna Citation I	Two 2,200lb st Pratt & Whitney (Canada) JT15D-1A	Wing span: 47ft 1in Length: 43ft 6in Height: 14ft 4in Wing area: 278·5 sq ft	Empty: 6,557lb AUW: 11,850lb	Typical cruising speed: 405 mph Range (6 passengers): 1,525 miles	Crew: 2 Passengers: 5–7
Lockheed L-1011-500 TriStar	Three 50,000lb st Rolls-Royce RB. 211-524B/B4	Wing span: 155ft 4in Length: 164ft 2½in Height: 55ft 4in Wing area: 3,456 sq ft	Empty: 240,963lb AUW: 496,000lb	Max cruising speed: 605 mph at 30,000ft Econ cruising speed: 558 mph at 35,000ft Range (max passengers): 5,998 miles Range (max fuel): 7,082 miles	Crew: 5 Passengers: 246 typical, 330 max
Beechcraft Model 200 Super King Air	Two 850 shp Pratt & Whitney (Canada) PT6A-41	Wing span: 54ft 6in Length: 43ft 9in Height: 15ft 0in Wing area: 303 sq ft	Empty: 7,543lb AUW: 12,500lb	Max cruising speed: 320 mph at 25,000ft Econ cruising speed: 313 mph at 25,000ft Max range (max cr speed): 2,022 miles Max range (econ cr speed): 2,172 miles	Crew: 1–2 Passengers: 7–14
Sikorsky S-76	Two 650 shp Allison 250-C30	Rotor dia: 44ft 0in Length: 43ft 4½in Height: 14ft 5¾in Disc area: 1,257 sq ft	Empty: 5,600lb AUW: 10,000lb	Max cruising speed: 167 mph Econ cruising speed: 144 mph Max range (std fuel): 465 miles Max range (aux fuel): 691 miles	Crew: 2 Passengers: 12
Bell Model 222	Two 675 shp Avco Lycoming LTS 101-650C-2	Rotor dia: 39ft 9in Length: 36ft 0¼in Height: 11ft 6in Disc area: 1,241 sq ft	Empty: 4,860lb AUW: 7,850lb	Max cruising speed: 155 mph Max range: 325 miles	Crew: 1 Passengers: 7–9
Boeing Vertol Model 234 Commercial Chinook	Two 4,075 shp Avco Lycoming AL 5512	Rotor dia: 60ft 0in Length: 52ft 1in Height: 18ft 7·8in Disc area: 5,655 sq ft	Empty: 25,500lb AUW: 47,000lb	Max cruising speed: 167 mph Econ cruising speed: 157 mph Max range: 852 miles	Crew: 2 Passengers: 44
Beechcraft Commuter C99	Two 715 shp Pratt & Whitney (Canada) PT6A-36	Wing span: 45ft 10½in Length: 44ft 6¾in Height: 14ft 4¼in Wing area: 279·7 sq ft	Empty: 6,494lb AUW: 11,300lb	Max speed: 308 mph at 8,000ft Max cruising speed: 287 mph at 8,000ft Range (max fuel): 1,048 miles	Crew: 2 Passengers: 15
Ahrens AR 404	Four 420 shp Allison 250-B17C	Wing span: 66ft 0in Length: 60ft 0½in Height: 19ft 0in Wing area: 422 sq ft	Empty: 9,980lb AUW: 18,500lb	Max speed: 219 mph at 5,000ft Max cruising speed: 201 mph at 8,000ft Normal range: 978 miles Max range: 1,380 miles	Crew: 2 Passengers: 30 (or max payload of 4,325lb)
Boeing Model 767-200 (basic)	Two 48,000lb st Pratt & Whitney JT9D-7R4D	Wing span: 156ft 1in Length: 159ft 2in Height: 52ft 0in Wing area: 3,050 sq ft	Empty: 164,352lb AUW: 300,000lb	Normal cruising speed: Mach 0·80 Typical range: 3,201 miles	Crew: 2–3 Passengers: 211 basic, 289 max
Boeing Model 757-200 (basic)	Two 37,400lb st Rolls-Royce RB.211-535C	Wing span: 124ft 6in Length: 155ft 3in Height: 44ft 6in Wing area: 1,951 sq ft	Empty: 131,020lb AUW: 240,000lb	Cruising speed: Mach 0·80 Max range: 2,476 miles	Crew: 2–3 Passengers: 178 typical, 224 max

Photograph Credits

AB Aerotransport: Page 112
Ahrens: Page 206(B)
Air Canada: Page 169(T)
Air France: Page 135
American Airlines: Page 75(B)
Aviation Traders: Page 107(T)
BEA: Pages 77(T); 152
Beech Aircraft Corporation: Pages 84(T); 114; 115; 141(B);
    161; 162; 186(T); 202; 206(T)
Bell: Pages 194; 203
BOAC: Pages 105; 107(B); 120(B); 127(B)
Warren M. Bodie: Page 53(B)
Boeing: Pages 41(T); 47(B); 92(T); 96(T); 113; 128; 129;
    136; 138(T,B); 140; 144(B); 150; 158; 160(T,B); 184;
    185(B); 190; 191; 193(T); 195; 207; 208(T,B)
Boeing Vertol: Page 205
Braniff International: Pages 127(T); 192
Austin J. Brown: Page 180
Bushmaster: Page 186(M)
Canadian Pacific: Page 116(T)
Central Press Photos: Page 24(T)
Cessna: Pages 29(T); 72(T); 83; 90; 177(T); 178(T,B);
    179(T,B); 198; 199(T,B)
Chicago and Southern: Pages 104
Civil Air Transport of Taiwan: Page 116(B)
A. Cole: Page 143
Delta Air Lines: Pages 46(T); 69; 76; 106(B); 170(B); 174
DETA: Page 89
Douglas: Pages 21(T); 93; 94
Eastern Air Lines: Page 91
Evangel: Page 193(B)
Fairchild Swearingen: Pages 175; 176
Fairey Aviation Company: Page 109(T)
Flight International: Page 65(B)
Flying Tiger Line: Pages 103; 145
Fokker: Pages 21(B); 27(T); 44(T)
Ford Motor Company: Page 32(B)
Frontier Airlines: Page 125
Gates Learjet: Pages 163(T,B); 164; 165
Gibraltar Airways: Page 79(T)
Gulfstream American: Page 183
Hamilton: Page 166(T)
Hawker Siddeley Aviation: Page 157
KLM: Page 147(B)
Howard Levy: Page 23(B)
Lockheed: Pages 26(T); 35(B); 53(T); 82; 88; 137; 200
Los Angeles Airways: Page 123
Macrobertson-Miller Airlines: Page 80(B)
Glenn L. Martin Company: Page 117
Harold G. Martin: Pages 86; 118; 142(T); 182; 196

A. McDonald: Page 141(T)
McDonnell Douglas: Page 169(B); 170(T); 172; 173; 197(T)
Mount Cook Airlines: Page 81
D. Napier & Sons: Page 142(B)
North Central Airlines: Page 124
Northeast Airlines: Pages 48(B); 67(B); 101; 149
Northrop: Page 111
Okanagan Helicopters: Page 109(B)
Olympic: Page 159
Pacific Western: Page 168(B)
Pakistan International Airlines: Page 80(T)
Pan American: Pages 65(T); 68(T); 73; 92(B); 126; 138
Stephen P. Peltz: Pages 46(B); 97; 102(B)
Piedmont Airlines: Page 121
Stephen Piercey: Pages 77(B); 98; 122(B)
Piper: Page 181
RAE Bedford: Page 197(B)
Rockwell International: Pages 154; 155; 167
Rolls-Royce: Pages 189; 201(T,B)
Sabena: Pages 132; 134(T)
SAS: Pages 79(B); 131; 153(T)
Scottish Aviation: Page 100(T)
Brian M. Service: Pages 99; 186(B); 188
Sikorsky: Pages 56(T); 74(T); 102(T); 110; 133(B); 151;
    204
Smithsonian Institution: Pages 11; 12; 13(T,B); 14;
    16(T,B); 17; 18; 19(T,B); 23(T); 26(B); 27(B); 28; 29(B);
    30(T); 31; 32(T); 33; 34; 35(T); 36(T,B); 37; 38(T,B); 39;
    40; 42; 43; 45; 48(T); 49; 50; 51; 52(B); 54; 55; 56(B);
    57; 58(B); 59; 60; 62; 66; 68(B); 70; 71; 72(B); 74(B);
    85(T,B); 87; 89(B); 95; 96(B)
Smithsonian Institution/Boeing: Page 47(T)
Smithsonian Institution/Ryan: Page 15
South African Airways: Page 144(T)
South African Railways: Page 106(T)
South West Airways: Page 166(B)
Sperry Gyroscope Company: Page 61
Swissair: Pages 64(B); 130
TAI: Page 146
Norman E. Taylor: Page 168(T)
Teledyne Ryan Aeronautical: Page 24(B)
Trans-Canada Air Lines: Page 122(T); 147(T)
Trans-Texas Airways: Page 78
TWA: Pages 25; 52(T); 134(B)
United Air Lines: Page 41(B)
Varig: Page 153(B)
Wellington Airport: Pages 84(B); 177(B); 185(T)
Western Air Lines: Pages 20; 22; 30(B); 44(B); 58(T); 63;
    64(T); 75(T); 119
Westland: Page 133(T)

Index